LETTERS OF
HERBERT HENSLEY HENSON

"DEAR ME, DEAR ME, DEAR ME!"

[Frontispiece

LETTERS OF HERBERT HENSLEY HENSON

Chosen and Edited
with an Introduction

by

EVELYN FOLEY BRALEY

Canon of Worcester Cathedral

LONDON

S · P · C · K

1950

First published in 1950 by S.P.C.K.
Northumberland Avenue, London, W.C.2

Printed in Great Britain by
Richard Clay and Company, Ltd., Bungay, Suffolk

CONTENTS

viii CONTENTS

LIST OF ILLUSTRATIONS

INTRODUCTION

At the end of an obituary notice in *The Times* of 29 September 1947 the writer states of Bishop Hensley Henson: "He did himself grave injustice in his autobiography, the two volumes of which were published in 1941 and 1943. It reveals him as little more than a lover of controversy, assured that he was perfectly consistent and that his critics were invariably in the wrong. Yet the controversialist was but one aspect of Henson's character; there were others very different and vastly more attractive."

In frequent conversations with him about his *Retrospect* I insisted that there were aspects of his character which were not obvious to readers of his autobiography who did not know him intimately and I suggested that he should supplement it by a volume of letters. In answer to a letter of mine of 8 May 1944, he said that "it confirmed what indeed I know to be true, that I have no fondness for controversy, though a certain temperamental dislike of unreality, which has led me into many conflicts, and perhaps inevitably created the impression that controversy for its own sake is dear to me. Only this morning I received from no less a person than the Lord Chancellor, whom I have known ever since we made acquaintance in All Souls some fifty years ago, a letter in which he says 'I have been reading your Vol. two with real interest. Your tombstone should describe you as a "good man who enjoyed controversy".' I am sure the Lord Chancellor is mistaken, though I cannot dispute that he has plausible grounds for his mistake. In any case tombstone inscriptions have no great value as records of fact." In answer to the suggestion that he should put together a selection of his letters, Hensley Henson actually did choose from his books of letters about 250, which were written between 1928 and 1942. After his death, Mrs Hensley Henson asked me to edit a volume of her husband's letters and sent me copies of the letters he had himself selected, together with seven books of letters he had copied in his own hand. I felt, however, that these would not serve the purpose which I had in mind, for they were largely personal letters dealing with topics he had already discussed in his *Retrospect*. I therefore inserted a letter in *The Times* and the Church newspapers, asking for letters from

Hensley Henson, however trivial in character the subjects might be. To my surprise I received no fewer than 1,450 letters from all parts of the world. It appears that all Hensley Henson's correspondents had carefully preserved his letters: from several people I received more than fifty letters, some of them bound in book form; other collections were numbered and indexed; many people had also kept copies of their own letters to which his letters were the replies. It is from this source that the following collection of letters is mainly compiled.

In addition to sending letters, many of his correspondents sent verbatim accounts of conversations with him, stories which he told, excerpts from his speeches which they had heard, and various accounts of incidents in his life.

I shall have succeeded in my purpose if I have been able to place Hensley Henson in his right perspective, and have been able to provide the material for an authoritative judgement of his character—which must form an important contribution to the religious history of the 20th century. The letters appear in chronological order and relate the various phases of his career, first at Barking and St Mary's Hospital, Ilford, then at Westminster and St Margaret's, the Deanery of Durham, Hereford, Auckland Castle and Hyntle Place. I have carefully avoided including many letters I have received which deal with topics he himself dealt with fully in his *Retrospect*, except perhaps where they throw additional light on the subjects in question, but I have selected mainly those which in my judgement serve as a revelation of his character, for his comments on persons throw not a little light on the man himself. The freshness of their first-hand and unreflecting character gives most of them their interest. It will be observed that a substantial part of this volume deals with Hensley Henson's activities in his own diocese. As one of his clergy, I perceived an undercurrent of censure, or at least of disappointment, that his *Retrospect* had not included more reference to his colleagues and contemporaries in the diocese of Durham. And since the *Retrospect* did not contain any reference to his life in retirement at Hyntle Place or to his second appointment to the Canonry at Westminster, I have included many letters which deal with that period of his life, and they might not inaptly be described as " The impressions and reflections of an octogenarian Bishop ".

In editing his letters I have tried first of all to show what he could be to his friends, men, women and children who loved and honoured him, and tried to enter into his real character, for they clearly reveal the man in his charm.   To his friends he disclosed the more " human " side of his nature, and it is literally true to say that they *did enjoy* his friendship.

And in the second place my editing has been determined by the pleasure the letters themselves may give to the general public, not only as masterpieces of the epistolary art—" the stainless steel of perfect English prose " as Dr Alington wrote in his poem to *The Times*—but also as the revelation of the character and personality of the writer, disclosed in the spontaneity and unguarded intimacy of his private correspondence.   For this second reason the publishing of some of these letters is a delicate matter.   On the one hand it may hurt the susceptibilities of, and even be thought to cast some reflection upon, certain persons; but on the other, the withholding of it may deny some understanding of the character of the writer.   This is particularly the case in regard to Hensley Henson, for even in his published writings and public utterances he revealed an incisive and accurate mind, a tremendous sense of humour, and a devastatingly sharp tongue, and was fearlessly outspoken.   It must, therefore, be expected that in his private letters he would be even less restrained. But a careful reading of the letters will show that whenever he criticized anybody, he followed up his criticism by saying something pleasant about the person.   " I knew that your affection would not misunderstand, and your literary sense not fail to appreciate the alliteration ", he wrote to a distinguished man who mildly rebuked him for something in his *Retrospect*.   " Besides, everybody knows, who knows me, how highly I appreciate and how greatly I admire your gifts, industry and person."

But there is something else to be borne in mind.   In the first place, no personal reference in these letters is set out as having any objective significance.   Hensley Henson would be the first to admit that there was in almost every case another side to the criticism, which the immediate and intimate utterance of a private letter does not take into consideration.   " One knows little and far too little to justify judgement: and if I express myself freely, it is because I hold such freedom the privilege of friendship."   Secondly, Hensley Henson was a " great " man, and those whom he criticized were generally " great " men, whose reputations could not be seriously affected by the unguarded positiveness of a private letter.

I have decided, therefore, to sacrifice caution to candour, and although I have as far as possible submitted the letters to the persons named in them and obtained their consent for publishing them, if any of them should feel " flicked in the raw " by any personal reference, I would ask them to sacrifice their feelings to the aim and purpose of revealing as intimately as possible the working of a scintillating, if not always perhaps wisely controlled, intellect, and of a heart whose hatred of unreality sometimes provoked its owner to unguarded criticism. And after all, Hensley Henson's criticisms were, though sometimes severe, only what would be easily tolerated in a review of a book. Dr Williams, the Bishop of Durham, said in his speech to his Diocesan Conference on 4 October 1947 : " If anything is certain, it is that Dr Henson was extraordinarily unlike anyone else." That we recognize to be the case. In a letter to his friend, Dr Cranage, Hensley Henson said that there was only one person who knew him inside and out and that was Professor Grey Turner (the distinguished surgeon who performed an abdominal operation on him !).

Some of his correspondents in reading through their letters in this volume will observe that certain deletions have been made. When he came upon an amusing incident, or invented a particularly good phrase, Hensley Henson would share it with different friends—sometimes repeating whole paragraphs. In order to cancel the repetitive phrases a certain amount of omission has been necessary.

The recipients of Hensley Henson's letters will know that underlining was a characteristic of his correspondence. He himself gives the reason for it in the letter addressed to a Churchwarden (No. 79). This will explain the underlining printed in this volume.

In conclusion, I wish to thank all who have made the compilation of this book possible. They are too numerous to enumerate, and I know they would not wish to be named. There are, however, two friends of the Bishop who must be specifically thanked, viz. Mr David Rolt, who at the age of 16 made the caricature of Hensley Henson which appears as a Frontispiece, and the Reverend James Nankivell, whose picture of Hensley Henson in his study at Auckland Castle is to be seen opposite page 232.

I am personally very much indebted to the Reverend Selby Johnson, Rector of Hooton Roberts, Rotherham, for undertaking the preparation of the Index.

E. F. BRALEY

1. *Letter to a godson.*

St Mary's Hospital, Ilford,
January 7th, 1898.

My dear Alfred,

I am very pleased to hear that you are having a good time by the sea, and seeing as much as you can of the island. You must try to make an expedition to Ebbsfleet, which is a little inland from Pegwell Bay, and see the granite cross which marks the place, (or what is thought to be the place) [at] which St Augustine and his 40 monks landed, more than 1300 years ago. You know the history, unless you have forgotten all I told you about it last spring. There is a very pretty Roman Catholic Church dedicated to St Augustine in Ramsgate, which is well worth looking at on a wet afternoon, when long expeditions are out of the question.

Tommie got up in good time for the 7 o'clock service yesterday. It was his birthday. Epiphany is a splendid day to be born on; for one thing, you are always likely to have the opportunity of receiving the Holy Communion on that day, if you wish to do so; and all good Christians ought to wish to do so on such an occasion. I was very pleased to hear of your intention to get up, and go to St George's, and hope the good intention was successfully carried out.

Your friends the Japs are really getting a little alarmed at the progress of events in China; and I see there is some talk of our making an alliance with them against the other pirates; but somehow I don't quite like joining hands with these yellow-skinned pagans against white Christian peoples. They are so horribly cruel in victory, and so pitifully abject in defeat.

Messrs Elliott & Fry want to have another shot at me; but I don't think I shall have the pluck to stand up to the guns, I mean the camera, without you to take care of me. . . .

Now my paper is run out—so goodbye; don't do too much, but get as much good sea air into you as possible and come back to us bright and strong for duty.

Your v. affectionate godfather,
H. Hensley Henson.

B   I

From other letters, written when Hensley Henson was 80, *we learn how this friendship began :*

" I recall our first meeting, when you came—a fair-haired boy with wide blue eyes and a great smile—to be tried for the Choir; and then your baptism and confirmation."

" Do you remember when I came to see you after you had broken something—an arm or a collar-bone? As I leant over you in your bed, you put an arm round my neck, and kissed me; and, as—in spite of Lord Birkenhead—the world is largely governed by sentiment— I took you to my heart from that moment. But time and distance are mighty estrangers; and we don't often get into touch now. We were both younger then, and love springs quickly in young hearts."

" And that fair-haired boy, who stumbled into my friendship half a century ago, is a grandfather. It is hard to picture him in that character; but it cannot but mean that his voyage through life has been lightened and enriched by the best blessing which belongs to temporal life—a full and happy home. And therefore, in these later days of strain and anxiety, you will still be able to keep the boy's winning smile, and in the sanctuary of your heart sing the old familiar hymn, *Te Deum*."

" Age dims much, and destroys much, but it cannot dim the picture of what was good, nor destroy one's delight in looking at it."

2. *A parochial Mission at South Shields.*

Holy Trinity Vicarage, South Shields,
January 30th, 1898.

My dear boy,
     . . . The Mission is going along; and, I hope, fairly well. The wind is blowing so violently that we daren't carry our torches in procession. I was Cross-bearer through the streets tonight; and there was a great crowd in church.

My boys had best receive the Sacrament next Sunday; you will perhaps tell them particularly from me to prepare themselves honestly, and to pray for God's blessing on this Mission. I hope we shall all come to Communion on Ash Wednesday, and so make a good start on Lent.

The Mission has kept me very busy; we begin at 8 a.m. with Holy Communion, then at 10 a.m. with intercessions, when I give an address to the Church workers. At 12.35 there is an address, limited to 20 minutes, to men. About 50 or 60 come, just as they are, " with their war-paint on ", black faces and working clothes. Between these services I go round some ship-building yard or other place of work. Yesterday, I saw a glass-making factory. The whole thing was on view from the raw material to the packed-up table glass. I actually blew out some molten glass myself to a globe nearly as big as you are. Then from 2.15 to 3, I am in church on duty to see anybody who wants to see me.

. . . At 6.45 we start on procession through the streets. I lead the way carrying the Cross, and two lads with lanterns walk along with me. At 7.30 we are back at church for the Mission Service. I take all the preaching every night, a sermon at least 3/4 hour. The people flock in great numbers; every night the church has been full, and it holds more than 1,000 people. And now we have got to the critical point when people begin to take resolution cards, which is a very anxious business for us. I am getting very tired, but I like these stern reticent, north-country folk; and I think they are beginning to like me. At least, I nearly had my hand pulled off, in shaking hands last night, and that seems friendly. We go on till Monday night, and return to London by the night train.

Peg away like a Briton at that Latin. Some day we'll take a Mission together, and then let them look out, that's all!

Your affectionate godfather,

H. Hensley Henson.

3.   THE GUARDIAN.

All Souls College, Oxford,
February 26th, 1900.

*To The Rev. W. Hobhouse.**

My dear Hobhouse,

I was very glad to get your letter, and to know that you are happily started on your editorial career. I wish you success with all my heart: the Church cannot afford to lose the *Guardian*, or, what is the same thing, to have the *Guardian* dwarfed and distorted into the service of a faction. I regret the necessity of Lathbury's retirement, but I have no doubt at all as to the necessity; and as to Lord Halifax's utterances they have the same fanatical colour as that which has distinguished his attitude for some years.

I do not know that my opinion counts for anything, but there are just 3 points which, as I judge, an ideal Editor of the *Guardian* will insist on as the pilot stars of his course.

1. He will back the Bishops against the priests; it is the issue of the Catholic Church against Congregationalism.

2. He will back the New Criticism against the mediævalists. It is the issue of intellectual self-respect against traditionalism.

3. He will uniformly discourage associations within the Church. The course of the E.C.U. is suggestive enough. I see Dr Cobb and others are moving heaven and earth to repeat the blunder which has cost us so dear. These associations are incompatible with episcopal government on the one hand, and personal liberty on the other.

I shall hope to see you sometimes.

Yours ever,
H. Hensley Henson.

* Editor of *The Guardian*; more recently Chancellor of Birmingham Cathedral and afterwards Canon of Gloucester.

4. *The prospect of Westminster.*

St Mary's Hospital, Ilford,
November 27th, 1900.

To The Rev. W. Hobhouse.

Dear Hobhouse,

Thank you much. This has been the most complete surprise.*
I never thought myself farther from preferment. I will try to do my
duty at Westminster, and I ask my friends to pray for me. It is no
small comfort to be helped along by such a volume of goodwill.
Yrs is the 112th letter acknowledged in the last 3 days, all most kind
and generous.

Yrs aff.,
H. Hensley Henson.

5. *A reply to a letter of congratulation upon his engagement to be married.*

17 Dean's Yard, Westminster Abbey, S.W.,
July 28th, 1902.

To The Rev. A. D. Tupper Carey.

Dear Tupper,

Thank you much. I hope it's all right. What do you want
me to recant? My objection to improvident clerical matrimony?
or to a diaconate of spooning? or my dislike of the conventional
clergyman's wife? But these heresies flourish rankly in me still,
although I pour out libations to Hymen. However you may so far
triumph, if you will, that I also have to confess myself too craven for
the unaccompanied journey. I hope you will like the lady.

Affectionately yrs,
H. Hensley Henson.

* Offer of Canonry of Westminster with Rectory of St Margaret's.

6.   *Family Ties.*

Yarrells, Lytchett, Poole,
September 25th, 1902.

*To The Rev. C. A. Alington.**

My dear Alington,

     .   .   .   .

    Yes, yes, "family ties" are, in my deliberate conviction, the sacredest things on earth; but I nearly lost my faith this afternoon when I accidentally lighted on John Sarum in a 2nd class carriage with his women and children—disgustingly domestic.   The violation of good taste in the service of a legitimate interest was pushed to such excessive length, that the interest itself became doubtful.

    I prefer the Cranmerian black-box method.   But this confession of undying prejudice must be made *sub sigillo.*

    On Saturday I go to Cardiff, where I am pledged to preach 3 sermons.   Then I return (on Tuesday) to Westminster, paying a visit to Robertson in the New Forest on the way.   So the last days of my independence are slipping away; and my neck goes into the collar of convention on October 20th.

Yours always affectionately,
H. Hensley Henson.

7.   *To one of his old boys at Ilford.*

17 Dean's Yard,
December 17th, 1903.

     .   .   .   .

    Yes; you may certainly tell anybody who repeats such silly tattle about your godfather that it is nought but the malicious moonshine of idle, and worse than idle gossip; and as to —— you may tell him from me that I look to my old boys to have something better to do than dishonour their old chief behind his back.   You may also take authority in advance to deny the following, which might proceed from the same sources of information.

* A master at Eton; now Dean of Durham.

1. I have not robbed the Bank of England.
2. I have no dynamite in my possession.
3. I did not poison my father.
4. I have not strangled the Dean.
5. I do not contemplate either wife-murder, coining, or arson.

.   .   .   .

8. *In reply to an invitation to preach in a non-Anglican church.*

17 Dean's Yard,
December 21st, 1903.

To The Rev. Dr John Hunter,★ D.D.

Dear Doctor Hunter,

.   .   .   .

Frankly, my first disposition of mind was to return a prompt acceptance, and if, on reflection, I must decide to send you a very reluctant refusal, I shall ask you to believe that my decision is determined by no personal unwillingness to do what you have been good enough to ask, and by no doubt as to my own legal right so to do, but simply by considerations of expediency. I fear that just now, when, as seems not improbable, I shall have to stand the brunt of a very sharp conflict with prevailing Anglican sentiment on the matter raised by Bishop Gore, my coming to you might have the effect of weakening my hands, and of putting weapons into the hands of my opponents. I shall trespass so far on the good feeling which you have expressed towards me, as to ask you to renew your invitation presently, when circumstances may be more kindly, and the legitimate effect of my public association with you, on terms of frank ministerial equality, might not run the risk of being prejudiced in the Anglican mind.

.   .   .   .

I am,
Most sincerely yours,
H. Hensley Henson.

★ Minister of King's Weigh House Church, Duke Street, London.

9.   Bishop Winnington-Ingram.

17 Dean's Yard,
November 18th, 1907.

*To Miss Violet Markham.**

Dear Miss Markham,

I am much obliged to you for sending me Dr Symonds's two sermons, with the main intention and argument of which, it hardly needs saying, I am in cordial agreement.   What you say of the effect of the Bishop of London's visit to Canada is equally melancholy and interesting.   It is, however, in no respect surprising.   As much might be said of his Lordship's influence on the religious life of his own diocese, and of the country.   He is attempting to govern a Church in the spirit of an enthusiastic High Church curate in the fervour and confidence of his first curacy.   None can question his absolute sincerity : few can resist his charm of manner and person : all must admire his ardour and devotion.   But he is the apostle of obscurantism, and the mainstay of the ecclesiastical self-assertion, which he honestly thinks that he abhors.   And he is Bishop of London : really the 2nd person in the hierarchy, with all but the succession to Lambeth in his hands !   Only the student of English Church History can know what a calamity to the National Church is involved in the absence from this great Chair of the strong wisdom of moderate churchmanship which in the main has been its tradition.   The Bishop of London now speaks no longer with the authority of his predecessors, nor does his Chair count for more in the higher politics of the Church—the politics which determine the courses of religious thought—than the Bishop of Lebombo.   It is certainly the case that the prestige of the diocese, and therein of the National Church (in which the London diocese has since the Reformation had the part of the brain) has fallen, and is falling.   I had been turning over in my mind a visit to Canada next year in response to many invitations, but I have given up the notion.   I could do no good, even if Canadian hospitality would give me a hearing, now that every element of obscurantism can contradict me in the name of the English Episcopate.

* Now Mrs James Carruthers, C.H.

I have let my pen run on unduly: but you must take the consequences of moving me to write!

>Believe me,
>Sincerely yours,
>H. Hensley Henson.

10. To a young student at a Theological College.

>17 Dean's Yard,
>June 4th, 1910.

To H. W. R. Elsley,* Esq.

Dear Sir,

It is, as you will readily understand, very difficult to offer any serviceable advice to anyone of whom one has no personal knowledge. Perhaps, indeed, the attempt is futile and had best not be made. Yet I am loth to leave such a letter as yours altogether unanswered.

Evidently you are passing through a difficult experience. The distinctive aspects of religious parties are most sharply presented in Theological Colleges, which mostly have their *raison d'être* in the desire to emphasize such aspects. Moreover the narrowest versions of partisan theories are commonly presented by the young, who have recently accepted them. And the atmosphere of training colleges is likely to be more fervid than charitable, more aggressively dogmatic than broadly Christian. The moral is two-fold. (1) You must not be surprised and need not be distressed at a partisan narrowness, which in the circumstances is probably inevitable. (2) You must give yourself to the proper work of a training college, viz. the acquisition of knowledge, and the forming of the habits of a disciplined Christian life.

The bigotry which troubles you may be a valuable element in your spiritual training; warning you against the risks of premature dogmatising, and showing you the sinfulness of the fanatical temper.

My own views of religion as it affects an English clergyman have been set forth in a series of books and in many sermons. Perhaps the

* Now Vicar of Tokyngton, Wembley, Middlesex.

three volumes published by Macmillan & Co. best hang together. They are titled respectively

The Value of the Bible
The National Church
The Liberty of Prophesying.

I have a few copies left of another book, and send you one, which you may be interested in reading.*

Meanwhile, you must look inward, and look upward, inward in self-questioning, upward in self-oblation. It doesn't really much matter whether the atmosphere of your training college be pleasant or unpalatable, so long as your time is being consecrated to God in a humble effort to learn His will, and be taught of His Spirit. Hold all partisanship at arm's length, and be content to learn and pray.

With all good wishes,
I am,
Yours sincerely,
H. Hensley Henson.

11. *Appointment to the Deanery of Durham.*

21 Kirkland Street, Cambridge, Mass.,
To Miss Mary Scott.   November 6th, 1912.

My dearest Mary,

More than once I have started a letter to you, and given up the attempt in despair. It seems quite impossible to say with even a tolerable measure of truth what exactly I feel about leaving West-minster. Everything has been settled with such terrific rapidity, that there has been no time to realize what the change means.

. . . .

I hope you think I did rightly in accepting the Deanery. There is a limit to one's freedom of action in these matters; I mean, one can hardly separate one's self altogether from the notion of subordination to one's superiors, who have a responsibility in deciding where one

* *Moral Discipline in the Christian Church.*

ought to work. The abominable crudity of the composition reveals the difficulty which I find in expressing my meaning. You always understand me better than everybody else, and therefore I shall not hesitate to confess that one factor in making me feel that it was my duty to accept this position was the fact that the offer came to me in circumstances which absolutely prevented me from having any hand in it. I had not so much as heard that Dean Kitchin had died until the day before I received a cable asking whether, if I were offered the Deanery of Durham, I would accept it. You know how genuinely I hate wire-pulling and log-rolling, especially in connexion with ecclesiastical office. It seems to me to empty the appointment of every trace of Divine Vocation if one has had a finger in securing it. My appointment to Westminster came to me as an absolute surprize; and so now does this to Durham. Then, Mary, you know that for some while past I have felt that I ought to leave Westminster; and indeed, I had settled it with myself that I would accept the first suitable offer that came to me. And I could hardly deny that the Deanery of Durham was so to be described; and so, with a sigh, but not I think with any real hesitation, I cabled an acceptance to the Prime Minister. I am really sorry to leave the Southern Province, where I am known and needed; and to go into the Northern Province where I am neither known nor needed. And I don't at all like the change of Archbishops; or the distance from London; or the severer climate of the North; or the colliery districts; or, in short, a large number of things, none of which seem to bear on anything more considerable than my preferences. My duty is independent of them all. It is, of course, horribly inconvenient being held in America until the end of the month. I told the P.M. that I desired to carry out my intention of preaching in St Margaret's until the end of the year; and the arrangement of the houses could hardly be managed sooner. Who will be my successor? I hope not Masterman, who has just gone to Bow Church; Gamble would be pleasant, and would be infinitely more successful than I have been. . . .

Affectionately always,
H. Hensley Henson.

12.   *Delight in W. R. Inge's writing and preaching.*

Deanery, Durham,
May 26th, 1914.

To The Dean of St Paul's.★

My dear Ralph,

Your leader in the *Church Family Newspaper* is excellent, and must be very serviceable to the cause of common sense and common justice.   Your χάρισμα of pointed and lucid speech in union with a fine brain and a bold heart is as precious as it is within our Church just now unparalleled.   But I must not indulge myself in compliments.   Denny's leader in the *British Weekly* is good, though he might have said more; but, of course, he was handicapped by Robertson Nicol.   Lacey in the *Church Times* plays the sophist deftly; but his tacit assumption that the difficulty is with the " fact ", and not also with the documentary evidence for it, ought not to escape the notice of any reader of sense— if indeed there be such in the *clientèle* of the *C.T.*

The most mischievous pronouncement on the subject is Wace's in the *Record.*

I returned yesterday from Scotland, where I visited the General Assemblies, and preached in Glasgow Cathedral.   If you are asked to preach in Edinburgh, accept the invitation.   Your presence would do good, and I want these relatively rude Northerners to hear what Anglican preaching can be.

Are your lectures on Plotinus accessible?   If so, tell me where I can get them.   The snippets in the *Times* could create an appetite, but not satisfy a reasonable curiosity.

Give my love to Kitty.   I hope Paula has recovered from her troubles.

Yours aff[tely],
H. Hensley Henson.

★ The Very Rev. W. R. Inge.

13. Kikuyu.

The Athenæum, Pall Mall, S.W.,
June 7th, 1915.

To Mr Worsley Boden *

My dear Jack,

I feel that you have fair ground of complaint against me for not answering your last letters before. But never doubt that my conscience avenges you; only there is a kind of creeping paralysis passing over me, and all the normal duties of life (and I place my correspondence with you on no lower level) are strangely hard to perform when the horrible distraction of the war fills the world. However, don't grow weary in well-doing; write to me as often and as fully as you can, and know that I value what you send.

The "Kikuyu" article had the right ring, and I am glad you wrote it. The Archbishop's "statement" is (as I have told him privately) gravely bad, and must do much harm presently. For the first time since the Reformation an authoritative voice from within the Church of England has disowned fellowship with "the other Protestant Churches", and has indicated that the sacrament administered by non-episcopal ministries is so gravely defective that it were better for an isolated Anglican never to receive the Lord's Supper at all than to receive It in a non-episcopal church. This, of course, makes reciprocity between the English Church and every Protestant Church impossible; and thus prohibits at once and for all every advance in the direction of Protestantism, while leaving to the sacerdotalists an unimpeded course, and an enhanced authority. I understand that the Scottish Presbyterians resent it very much, but will not discuss it so long as the war makes every other business concern look petty. I am in some doubt what to do. My mind inclines towards a letter to the Abp which could presently be published, and which would have at least the effect of shewing that the "statement" was not received with complete acquiescence. Meanwhile the little Romanizing clique, to whom the Bishop of Zanzibar seemed a veritable "Athanasius contra Mundum", are denouncing the Abp for

* A leader writer in India; now The Rev. Dr J. F. W. B. Worsley, Rector of North Wingfield, Chesterfield.

tolerating the occasional communion of unconfirmed persons! But they don't really count.

Yesterday I preached twice—in the Temple, and in the Nave of Westminster. The congregations were very large, and included a good many men in khaki.

Talleyrand is said to have observed that no one who hadn't lived before 1789 knew the sweets of life; and I incline to say much the same about this immense crisis of 1914. Can life ever be again for us, who are old or middle-aged, what it has been? All the pilot-stars of my political thinking seem to have fallen out of the sky, and I have not the ghost of a notion where we all are driving to!

Among other things, the moral collapse of the *Times* is very distressing to me. It is at least a quarter of a century since first I wrote to the *Times*, and it has been associated in my mind ever since with many interests and with many friendships, which I would not willingly let die; but I do loathe this Northcliffe tone and manner. The most threatening phenomenon in the world of literature is the rise of the journalistic millionaire, who aspires to guide the course of the world with no better title than that his millions make him able to buy men's brains and corrupt men's consciences.

Now, my dear Jack, when next you write, tell me everything about yourself, and the way your thoughts move, and remember that I am specially eager to get honest testimony as to native ways.

Very affect^ly yours,
H. Hensley Henson.

14.   *The National Mission.*

Deanery, Durham,
February 9th, 1917.

*To The Rev. A. F. Robson.**

Dear Mr Robson,

. . . .

The "National Mission" seemed to me to be a grave practical blunder, for the time was inopportune, and there were none of the

* Vicar of West Malvern.

conditions of a success. Its only permanent consequences to the Church will be the raising into sudden, and wholly unmerited importance a number of foolish persons, ardent, bigotted, and ill-informed, who would not otherwise have gained a hearing, or been given any authority. The problem demanding solution at the hands of the Archbishops is how to end the Mission without loss of dignity. In order to save their faces they are lending themselves to a whole series of " continuation " movements, crude and ill-considered, which in normal circumstances they would never have sanctioned.

. . . .

15. *Nomination to the See of Hereford.*

Deanery, Durham,
December 17th, 1917.

To Mrs Temple.

My dear Mrs Temple,

I have to thank you for a very kind letter, which it was most good of you to write, and very pleasant for me to receive. I feel that in accepting a bishoprick, I am parting with the last peaceful days of my life. Indeed, there seems some prospect of my figuring as the centre-piece in an Anglican *Auto-da-fé*! It was quite clear to me that, if the offer were made, I could not refuse it. My whole career would make refusal a betrayal of the Cause for which I have stood for 30 years. The great crowd of letters from all sorts and conditions of men expressing joy in my " elevation ", and confidence in me, is almost overpowering : and the laments of the Durham people make me feel a beast. Even the choir boys look at me with an *et-tu-Brute* expression in their eyes which is very trying.

Add that I have been down with a bad chill, and am still such a wreck that I hardly see how to travel to town tomorrow, and you will understand that, for a bishop-designate, I am in a creditably penitential frame of mind.

May I ask you to thank your husband for his kind message? I think there is some malignant confusion which puts us so far apart on the " Life and Liberty " matter. Shall I, as a Bishop, appreciate more favourably his episcopalianism? We must " wait and see ". Meanwhile let him be well-assured that I regard him with something more than a friendly interest.

Yours sincerely and gratefully,

H. Hensley Henson.

16. Consecration as Bishop of Hereford.

Lambeth Palace, S.E.1,

February 4th, 1918.

To The Rev. Preb. A. B. Wynne-Willson.

My dear Mr Wynne-Willson,

I was pleased to receive your and Norcock's † kind message. The Consecration was, as you know, undisturbed: and, though, of course, I could not avoid a certain half-expectation at the crucial points in the service that some Fanatick would place a suitable coping stone to the extraordinary agitation which had preceded, by crying out some protest or insult, and to that extent was distracted in mind, yet the dignity and power of the Function, and its immense significance were not wholly unrealized. I was glad that my consecrators included representatives of all the three traditional schools—the Bishop of Lincoln, the Bishop of Durham, and the Bishop of Southwark may severally stand for the High, the Low, and the Broad—and that both Provinces were well-represented.

The large congregation contained so many personal friends that there was an atmosphere of affectionate good-will in the Abbey, very welcome after the régime of brickbats under which I have been living.

My greatest difficulty at the moment was to forgive the absentee Bishops for their behaviour, which, I apprehend is equally unprecedented, timorous and inequitable: but even this I shall hope to achieve by degrees.

I learned from the Dean that he has fixed the Enthronement for Shrove Tuesday, and that the Mayor has arranged some kind of a

---

* R. D. of Hereford, 1908-20.
† Domestic Chaplain to the Bishop of Hereford, 1916-9.

reception on the same day.   After this I must get back to Durham
and bind up my papers etc.   Also, I have to find time to receive the
Freedom of the City.   Then we must arrange for our exodus from
Durham (a woeful task).   You see, I shall be glad to postpone my
confirmations as much as I can.

I am looking forward to the new work with a vivid consciousness
of the special difficulties heaped in my way superfluously and (in some
cases) wickedly : but with a clear conviction of duty, and a large confidence in the essential justice of the English people.

You and Norcock will, I am sure, be loyal comrades, and we must
help one another to keep the standard of effort high and the levels of
duty too high for petty suspicions and even justified resentments.

After all, there is limitless strength in working with God and for
Him : and that at least we can, if we will, secure.

Yours v. sincerely,
H. H. Hereford.

17.   W. R. Inge's PLOTINUS ; Archbishops' appeal for five million pounds.

The Palace, Hereford,
February 18th, 1919.

To Mrs W. R. Inge.

My dearest Kitty,   .

I had a shock last week when somebody told me that you
were in a nursing home.   So your letter comes as a message of comfort, assuring me at least that you are " in being ", and able to contemplate resuming in a few days that rôle of hostess which you play
so incomparably on the boards of your private theatre. . . .

I am enormously impressed by the range of knowledge, and easy
mastery in its handling, which mark Ralph's *magnum opus*.   I suspect
he would have won his way to the stake with his *Plotinus*, if there
were any effective Catholick discipline left to us.   As it is, we may
read his book, and ask for more with a good hope of getting it.

There is a kind of fatality which makes everything go wrong in
the Church just now.   Here is a case in point.   The Archbishops have,

c

as you know, been led into the folly of floating an appeal for
£5,000,000; and, of course, they are issuing the usual "special
prayers". Now much offence has been given to all right thinking
people by the vulgar and ubiquitous advertizing which has marked
the "floating" of this appeal. Imagine then the feelings with which
the antiphon selected for use in leading in the special petition must
needs be read:

> V.   Not by might, nor by power.
> R.   But by My Spirit, saith the Lord of Hosts.

I simply cannot comply with the request to authorize these prayers for
use in my diocese.

Beeching (who is in rather a bad way with his heart) sends me the
following "Ode suggested by the proposal to amalgamate the
Christian Associations for Young Men and Young Women". I send
it you, as you may find it useful:

Strophe.

Y oung men, who after duty done
M ake Christian sport and recreation
C an your glad hearts be glad alone
A merely male association?

Antistrophe.

Y e maidens, who repair fatigue
W ith tea and toast and Christian tattle,
C an such an Amazonian league
A vail for victory in life's battle?

Epode.

Nay, but be wise; your strengths unite;
Let not prophetic dirges trouble you;
Sun goes with shade, and left with right,
And M is but a form of W;
You will be wiser both with either,
When you have worked and played together.

There, my very dear friend, is the maximum of the comfort I can
offer you in this ill time. Folly prevails, but at least let us laugh at it.

Very affect^{ly} yours

Herbert.

18.   A " Collins" : his description of W. R. Inge at Westminster ; his horror of Disestablishment and Disendowment.

The Athenæum,
March 1st, 1919.

To Mrs W. R. Inge.

My dearest Kitty,

Having succeeded so far in restraining Ella's * lust for spectacles as to induce her to abandon the attempt to witness the enthronement of the Bishop of Worcester, and to travel back to Hereford by a train leaving at a tolerable hour, I find myself in the Athenæum with an hour to spare.   Accordingly I run to the performance of my apparent duty, and send you a " Collins " replete with gratitude for your generous hospitality, which only your enforced absence rendered in any measure imperfect.   That was a shadow, but it was lightened by the news of your approaches to recovery, and dissipated for half an hour by a pleasant vision of you.   And the Archdeacon and Mrs Spooner † have an incommunicable charm of their own.   Ralph did turn up, and vote at the principal division, but he did not speak.   I would have given much to hear him discharge into the Council some of the shafts which he exhibited at the Deanery.   His face was a study ; it indicated a whole armoury of barbed arrows, which no sacerdotalist brass that I have yet come across (and I have come across some potent metal) could resist.   In the end I registered a lonely vote against the whole project.‡   The effect of 4 days discussion is to leave me more than ever persuaded that the scheme is quite inconsistent with the National Establishment, and that, if it is persisted in, it must needs precipitate the disaster of Disestablishment and Disendowment.   It seemed to me important to keep my hands free for future fighting, though I am very doubtful whether I shall be available for the arena, when the next conflicts occur.   For it seems probable that I must accept the necessity of having " extensive alterations and repairs " in my dental system ; and I am provisionally booked to an operation for April 29th.   That will not improbably make me incoherent or at least inaudible for the rest of my days !!   The bother is that I am due

* Mrs Hensley Henson.   † Mrs Inge's parents.
‡ The Enabling Bill.

to preach to the University of Cambridge on May 11th, and how an orator, who has lost his teeth at the end of April, can persuade academics within the fortnight following is an anxious problem! But until Easter, I am committed to an endless succession of Confirmations, which cannot be postponed. So I keep my teeth for that business!

Ralph and you must manage to visit us this spring. The ill times draw rapidly near, when Bishops will be outcasts, and their palaces the abode of female-clerks and public officials. In the brief interval before the deluge, we must do what we can. (N.B. At this prospect my feelings were too strong for me; my trembling hand plunged the pen in the pot with unconsidering vehemence, and shed its intake on my page. Forgive the blot!)

We must go and see Kate * reigning in Hartlebury Castle, before those halls are also vacated.

With renewed thanks for your kindness, and exulting in your friendship,

I am always

v. affect^{ly} yrs,

Herbert.

19. Bishop Percival.

The Palace, Hereford,
May 13th, 1919.

To The Rev. Canon William Temple.†

My dear Dr Temple,

I had seen an announcement that you were going to undertake the task of Bishop Percival's biography, and I am glad that what must needs be a work of considerable importance should be in such competent hands. It needs no saying that you are heartily welcome to any assistance that it is in my power to render: but I fear that this will be very slight, for I had only a very slight acquaintance with my predecessor, and, though we agreed on some theological issues and in regarding with profound distrust and dislike both the Tractarian

---

* Miss Pearce, sister of Bishop E. H. Pearce of Worcester.

† Canon of Westminster; consecrated Bp of Manchester 1921; afterwards Abp of York and finally Abp of Canterbury.

movement itself and its latest developments, yet we had little in common on other questions. I respected his independence and courage: I thought him very ill treated by the reigning clericalist faction: and I held (and still hold) that he ought to have been translated to York. Since I have come to sit in his chair, and been in a position to appreciate the tradition he left in the diocese, it would be true to say that my respect for him has been increased. His political views went far to neutralize his religious attitude: and to strengthen the hands of the narrow factions, who insulted and thwarted him as much as they dared: but he was brave, manly, and generous. He was also extremely liberal, and there was a magnanimity about his action which impressed even his opponents.

He took great interest in the Jarvis Trust, and I think you should refer to Mr Nield of Leominster, with whom he was closely associated in the attempt to establish an agricultural school in Staunton-on-Wye, one of the 3 parishes benefited by the trust. Presently, you might come to Hereford, and, if you and your wife would so far truckle with heresy, spend a few days with us. You could meet Nield and some others who knew Bishop Percival well.

Yes: I regret very much to be in the opposite camp: but the longer I live the more convinced I am that on the lines of denominational autonomy there is no real hope for spiritual life or liberty. I think the Nonconformists are beginning to realize this, though the octogenarians and the politicians will loudly deny the fact.

With kind regards to your wife,

I am,
ever sincerely yrs,
H. H. Hereford.

20. To a young friend in the Merchant Navy: Preaching at Eton College.

The Palace, Hereford,
July 1st, 1919.

To George Minnis, Esq.

My dearest George,

When I returned from London last night, I found your letter from Port Said, and was most pleased with it. That kind of letter is not only most interesting, but it gives me a comfortable assurance that I have a place in your thoughts every day, which is a great thing to have. For, as I get older, the love of my " old boys " is more precious, and of them all you have become the nearest. I am afraid my record is not so interesting as yours, and it is certainly less <u>moving</u>; but you will be interested in it for my sake.

The Peace was signed by the Germans last Saturday, and there were great rejoicings in Paris and London. In all the churches there were hymns of thanksgiving, and special sermons. I was spending the week-end at Eton, where I had promised to preach to the School. My sermon had been prepared, but it had to be " chucked " at the last moment, and I wrote another about the Peace, taking for my text the words in the 90th Psalm : <u>" Show Thy servants Thy work, and their children Thy glory."</u> The congregation of so many hundred school-boys, gathered from every part of England and representing our historic families, is very impressive : and I could not but feel what a different kind of world they would have to grow up in from that which their fathers have known. I told them that there would be no place for idlers and wastrels, and that respect would only be given where it had been clearly earned. More and more I am persuaded that the best thing a young man can have to face the world with, (always taking for granted that his heart is right,) is <u>a useful trade mastered and exercised.</u> Of all the means by which men earn their livings there is none more useful or more honourable than that which belongs to <u>" those that go down to the sea in ships and occupy their business in great waters."</u>

I was amused at Eton by hearing about Marshal Joffre's visit. He was motoring to Oxford to receive a degree from the University, and the boys got wind of his coming, and swarmed out to meet him. They surrounded his motor, climbed on the roof of it, and amazed the great man by their familiarity and uproar. One cheeky youngster thrust his head into the car, and asked " *Parlez-vous Français ?* " which was probably all the French he knew ! Now boys in France are not so free with great and famous men, and Marshal Joffre appears to have been not a little perturbed. However, he was comforted at Oxford, where he was made a D.C.L. with much ceremony, and cheered to the echo by the undergraduates. He went back to London and lunched with the King, who gave him the O.M. (Order of Merit) which is, perhaps, the greatest of all the honours which an Englishman

can receive from the Crown, and which must be particularly gratifying
to a foreigner.

.   .   .   .

You say that there is no service on your ship, nothing to mark
Sunday. You have your Bible and Prayer Book, and you must make
use of them. You have your memories, and the way to God is always
open. I never fail to pray for you, especially at 8 o'clock on Sunday
mornings when I am at the Holy Communion. I trust you always to
pray for me. The assurance of your prayers is a real help to me.

May God bless and protect you wherever you are!

Yours v. affectionately,
H. H. Hereford.

21. Description of Swedish Consecration of Bishops; description of Söderblom (Primate).

Berlin,
October 2nd, 1920.

To The Dean of St Paul's.

My dear Ralph,

We finished our visit to Sweden on Thursday last, and are
now on our homeward journey, breaking it here in order to visit the
Thelwells and to get an impression of this city. If our pace be not
expedited by the coal strike—of which the latest reports are again
threatening—we shall hope to arrive in England on Saturday, the 9th
inst., but if the strike breaks out, we shall immediately proceed hot-
foot to my diocese. It will not be decent for me to be absent, though
I cannot be of any real use.

Our time in Sweden was interesting but rather strenuous. The
specific business with which we (i.e. the Bishop of Peterboro and I)
were charged was accomplished on Sept. 19th when we assisted in
consecrating two Swedish bishops. The ceremonial was very magnificent. I have never seen such a display of medieval vestments—
copes, chasubles, mitres, and pastoral staves. Our Convocation Robes
looked almost Puritanical by comparison. You will be amused to
learn that our relative simplicity of aspect has had a reassuring effect
on some Swedish minds, which were troubled lest the Archbishop of
Upsala's Anglicizing tendencies should have a Romanizing effect on

the Church of Sweden. All doubts as to the genuinely Protestant character of our Church were set at rest by our unquestionably Protestant appearances. The splendour of the service did not pass uncriticized. A vigorous correspondence has broken out in the Swedish newspapers, under such headings as, " Would Jesus Christ have been in the Cathedral of Upsala on Sept. 19th? " In this wordy warfare the Swedish Primate takes a prominent part, rather to my surprise, for, applying English standards of fitness, I assumed that he would have felt it beneath his dignity to cross swords in the newspapers with all manner of correspondents. Söderblom is a really remarkable man. He reminds me of the famous Samuel Wilberforce, and he is playing a rôle in Swedish ecclesiastical life not unlike that played by " Soapy Sam " in the years 1850–1870. He too is *persona grata* at court, and at the same time an advocate of popular opinions in politics. Combine in your mind Bishop Wilberforce, Gore, and his present Grace of Canterbury, and you will have formed a just notion of the Swedish Primate. He is an astonishing linguist; an indefatigable preacher and speaker; an author of recognized distinction; and an ecclesiastical statesman of outstanding importance. Add that his wife is no less able than himself, that they have a remarkably promising family of 10 children, and that he is only 54 and she 50 years old, and you will agree that this Archbishop is a man to be reckoned with. I had an interesting interview with the King of Sweden, and preached with an interpreter beside me at " High Mass " (i.e. the ordinary morning service) in a Swedish Church; but of this and other things I will tell you when I meet you.

With love to Kitty from us both,

I am,

Affect^{ly} yrs,

Herbert Dunelm.

22. *His charming way of saying No.*

Auckland Castle, Bishop Auckland,
November 26th, 1920.

To Mrs W. R. Inge.

My dearest Kitty,

I hardly know what to say. On the one hand, it is quite abysmally base to refuse you anything; on the other hand, it is hard

AT AUCKLAND CASTLE, 1920.

[Facing p. 24

to see how I can undertake anything at 4 p.m., when I shall probably be held at Westminster until 5 p.m., which means appearing in your dining room about 5.30 p.m.   Besides, I want to seize any opportunity that comes to me when I am in London of being in the H. of L., where (until the " Reform " of that Chamber) I possess a seat.

Add, finally, that the subject you suggest is neither edifying, nor attractive.   I have the misfortune to be thoroughly at cross purposes with the present temper and method of ecclesiastical administration; and it is only by a miracle of self-suppressing humbug on my part, and of plusquam-apostolical charity on the part of my fellow-Anglicans that I am tolerated at all !

So it is almost certainly the case that I could not speak decently about the Lambeth Conference, in which so many characteristic tendencies and policies of modern Anglicanism found expression. And why should I give pain to your kindly parsons' wives without necessity?

On the whole, then, Dearest Lady, I think I will do violence to my heart in the interest of my conscience, and say No.

Durham is another kind of diocese than Hereford in the article of work.   I am mightily hustled.   Indeed at present (my house being in disorder, and nearly every face being strange) I am somewhat puzzled as to the best ordering of life.

Ralph has been a burning and a shining light—a blend of Sinai and Vesuvius, which is somewhat enigmatic, if also extremely wholesome.   Give him my love, and be sure that

> I am always most affect^{ly} yrs,
> Herbert Dunelm.

23.   The 39 Articles.

> Auckland Castle,
> February 27th, 1923.

To E. Gilbert-Wood,* Esq.

Dear Mr Gilbert-Wood,

In reply to your question " whether a literal belief in the Articles is by law insisted on ", I can have no hesitation in saying that it is not.

* Now Rector of Beckbury, Shifnal, Salop.

By the Clerical Subscription Act of 1865, the form of subscription was modified with the object of granting relief in this matter. The present form of subscription runs thus:

> "I assent to the Thirty-nine Articles of Religion, and to the Book of Common Prayer, and to the Ordering of Bishops, Priests, and Deacons. I believe the Doctrine of the Church of England, as therein set forth to be agreeable to the Word of God" etc.

It is universally allowed that the 39 Articles are not a Creed, but the official Platform of a Church. In a divided Christendom, every particular Church must "show cause" for its independent existence. In the XVIth century when the unity of Western Christendom was broken up, every fragment of the whole issued its statement of justification. The Church of Rome issued the Creed of Pope Pius IV and the Tridentine decisions; the Lutheran Church put forward the Augsburg Confession, and variants; the Calvinist Churches did as much. And the Church of England, subject to the same necessity, framed the 39 Articles.

None of these "platforms" can be taken to decide questions which have only been raised since they were framed. Thus the questions raised by physical science and Biblical Criticism are not properly answered by reference to the 39 Articles, which had no reference to them. On the other hand, as against the Church of Rome—the governing ecclesiastical issue then and now—the Articles do state authoritatively where the Church of England stands. To subscribe them would mean that you accept the English side in that continuing conflict. You would not be pledged to every statement in a long, and partially obsolete Confession; but you would be endorsing the version of Christianity which the Confession as a whole embodies.

．　　．　　．　　．　　．　　．　　．　　．　　．　　．　　．　　．

There is a great sphere of hard work for a sincere man in Durham, and I shall gladly receive you, if you can satisfy the requisite conditions.

Believe me,

Very faithfully yrs,

Herbert Dunelm.

24. Crown Patronage.

August 31st, 1923.

To Geoffrey * S. Fry, Esq., C.B.
10 Downing Street, Whitehall.

My dear Mr Fry,

I hope to return to Auckland next week, and I will take leave to postpone until then my reply to your letter of the 29th inst.

But I take occasion to make a general observation, to which I attach great importance. The Crown should, if possible, appoint to the livings in its patronage from without the diocese. There are practical reasons which make the Bishop's patronage mainly diocesan; and the patronage of the D. & C. is statutably so. It follows that a diocese can only be rescued from the complete dominance of local claims by the action of private patrons, and of those public patrons whose action is unshackled. Of the latter the Crown is incomparably the most important. Of the 265 benefices in the diocese of Durham, about half are in the patronage either of the Bishop, or of the Dean & Chapter. It becomes very difficult to exercise this patronage satisfactorily if the Crown and other public patrons draw on the diocese for their nominees to parishes within it. The main channel through which " fresh blood " can pass into the diocese is thereby closed: and the diocese is shut up to a régime of parochial " inbreeding ". While, then, I appreciate very highly the courtesy which leads the Crown to consult me on its appointments within my diocese, I do feel a growing apprehension as I observe the tendency to appoint from within the diocese.

You are yourself so friendly and considerate, that I do not scruple thus frankly to confess my fears.

Yours sincerely,
Herbert Dunelm.

* Now Sir Geoffrey.

25. *The Bishop of Exeter (Cecil).*

November 26th, 1923.

To The Dean of Exeter.★

My dear Gamble,

I have read your Bishop's letter with much interest. It is a curious illustration of the man himself—an odd, and in my experience unparalleled blend of acuteness and absurdity, knowledge and *naïveté*. I attribute the combination to his career hardly less than to his character. He has a fair share of Cecilian ability, but combined with perhaps an exaggerated portion of Cecilian ὕβρις and idleness. As Rector of Hatfield during his Father's period of political ascendancy he was in a *milieu* of great and various distinction: and his mind is full of half-remembered *mots* and half-digested ideas! As one " born in the purple ", he has been too much surrounded by adulatory syco- phants and social inferiors : and the supremacy inherent in the episcopal office has fitted in but too easily to the general disposition to play the autocrat, and ignore counsel.

This fatuous election can only do harm to the country. Personally, I cannot think that the Government succeed in making out their case : and although it is not impossible, some people would even say not improbable, that Mr Baldwin may get a majority, I must needs think that he will owe his electoral success to any and every cause except the soundness of his policy. But I cannot think that the Nation will repudiate Free Trade so summarily.

Yours aff^{ly},

Herbert Dunelm.

26. *Quakerism.*

December 10th, 1923.

To The Hon. Faith Pease.

My dear Miss Pease,

My wife showed me your letter, and it occurs to me that I may take leave to send you the assurance, which you will not need,

★ The Very Rev. H. R. Gamble.

that I am very glad to know that you desire to be baptized and confirmed. The Quakers, among whom you have been brought up, have departed from the general tradition of Christianity in rejecting as superfluous or even unlawful the external ceremonies which were appointed by Christ or His Apostles. Their error (for such I must needs hold it to be) was certainly determined by no conscious disobedience to Christ's commandment, but rather by an excessive reluctance to associate spiritual gifts with material channels. Therefore, the Quakers have been conspicuously rich in spiritual graces, but as a Church conspicuously unable to evangelize the world. We may, I think, hold that their history illustrates both the value of their spiritual witness, and the defect of their ecclesiastical polity.

What I want to suggest is that you should come over, and have some talk with me on these high matters, and arrange when and where you may be baptized and confirmed.

I hope you will give me good notice of your marriage day, because I should be particularly distressed if any tiresome duty hindered me from being at your service then.

With kindest regards,

I am, most sincerely yours,

Herbert Dunelm.

27. Rashdall.

February 10th, 1924.

To Mrs Rashdall.

My dear Mrs Rashdall,

I have just read the announcement which for some while past I have been dreading, and I make not a moment's delay in writing to you a few lines of very sincere condolence. Your husband has been my friend for all but forty years, and there is no man for whose character I have a greater affection and esteem. His great learning, sterling honesty, courage and loyalty are hard to equal. He seemed to me in some respects the best Christian of my acquaintance, and I have no doubt at all that the numerous company of those who opposed, and sometimes traduced him, knew well in their hearts that he stood above them in the essential things of the spirit. His death is a heavy loss to the Church of England, and to his friends a very great calamity. His long sickness, and the sore physical distresses of these last years, will have familiarized you with the thought of his departure; yet the blow of the final severance is a crushing one, and you must suffer deeply. "The heart knoweth its own bitterness", yet, even so, the knowledge that the sorrow of bereavement is shared by friends is not wholly valueless. His work will survive him. If there be left in the Church of England any respect for independence or any regard for sound learning, it is greatly owing to his toils and his example.

May God bless and comfort you!

Yours in deep sympathy,

Herbert Dunelm.

28. *Religion in the Schools.*

April 6th, 1924.

To Major John H. Sandham Griffith, J.P.
The Grove, Haverfordwest.

My dear Sir,

I have to thank you for your letter of March 22nd, and for the enclosure.

The whole question of "religious teaching" in schools has to be considered with reference to a new and waxing factor—the professional *amour propre* of the teachers. They will no longer, or only for a little longer, tolerate any arrangement which seems to place them "under the clergy". They are often better educated: and better paid: they are always better organized. They know themselves to be, both politically and socially, a more considerable force. For good, or for evil, they are determined to be "masters in their own house", i.e. supreme inside the school.

It follows that, if religious teaching is, in any worthy sense, to survive in the schools, it can only be by the consent of the Teachers, and by entrusting it to them. Hence the practical futility of trying to maintain the "dual system", and the wisdom of centring effort on the Training Colleges. For everything turns on the religious competence of the Teachers, and this in some degree may be determined by their training.

But I am not hopeful: the drift seems to me running very strongly towards secularism in the Teaching profession.

> Yours v. faithfully,
> Herbert Dunelm.

29. Evening Communion.

August 24th, 1924.

To The Rev. James E. Perry.

Dear Mr Perry,

. . . .

2. As to your duty with respect to Evening Communion, I cannot relieve you of a responsibility which attaches to the Incumbent; but I will say for your guidance in arriving at a decision, that in any case you should continue the present practice for a year, in order that you might become acquainted with the people, and with the parochial conditions. If you should decide, after acquiring such knowledge, that there was no real justification in practice for an arrangement which you honestly think is normally unedifying, then, I think you would be right in changing it; but if you found yourself obliged to admit that there was even but one parishioner, fit and desiring to receive the Holy Communion, who could not reasonably be expected to attend a morning Celebration, or who could not fairly be required to change the habit of a life-time, then I think you ought to provide for an Evening Celebration at suitable intervals. I propose to say something about Evening Communion in the Charge which it is my intention to deliver in October.

The really essential thing in going into a new parish is to win the trust of the people. It is not so much divergence of habit and point of view that drives a wedge between priest and parishioners as the sense that they have not been dealt with fairly, which the parishioners cannot but have when changes are made which they dislike, the reason of which they do not know or which they misunderstand, and with respect to which no effort was made to gain their approval. The Parochial Church Council ought to provide a channel through which a new Incumbent could get into touch with the parishioners, and get them to understand his drift and object.

I pray that you may be rightly guided in what must be for you an important decision. At least you know where to look for guidance.

Yours sincerely,
Herbert Dunelm.

30.   Discipline.

October 20th, 1924.

To The Hon. and Rev. J. G. Adderley.

My dear Jimmie,

I do not think it possible that I could be of any assistance in the case you describe; and even if I could, I doubt if I ought.

1. My mind tends to the conclusion that there are offences which are prohibitive of ministry; and, if there be such, adultery would certainly be of the number. Not indeed that I think that the clergyman, guilty even in that gross degree, would necessarily be a more utterly depraved man than his respectable, that is, unconvicted fellow; but only that the offence itself is properly incapacitating, so that where it has been admitted, there may be a *locus pœnitentiæ*, but there can be no restoration to office.

2. I should quite certainly be personally unable to give the man precisely the kind of spiritual assistance which, I infer from your letter, he would be likely to expect and need. For I am not what is called a " Catholick ", and my conceptions of repentance, discipline, etc. would probably be found unintelligible, unattractive, and unhelpful.

3. I could not keep up any close and continuing relation with him; and, short of that, I should not feel morally free to authorize his ministry in my diocese.

There is no part of my duty as bishop that perplexes and distresses me so much as the treatment of clergymen who have fallen into some gross impurity. It seems intolerable to close the door on them, and yet how can I do anything else ? Parishes ought not to be the victims of a perilous experiment.

Alway, my dear Jimmie,
Yours affectionately,
Herbert Dunelm.

31.   *Note in pencil : " To Nancy aged 9 years."*

Auckland Castle,
November 8th, 1924.

To Miss Nancy Wynne-Willson.

Three times twenty and then add one,
So old is the BISHOP at sixty-one.
An old, old, very old man.
So long is the time since he began
His way in the world to pick and choose,
To pick the nice, and the bad refuse.
So when NANCY sent him a kiss and her love,
He returned the kiss, and he kept the love.
For kisses won't keep, but Love keeps ever,
When Bishops and Birthdays have passed for ever.

H. D.

32.   *The Crucifix.*

December 5th, 1924.

*To The Rev. Canon A. H. Cruickshank.**

My dear Cruickshank,

I am torn by conflicting emotions when the project of introducing a Crucifix into our Cathedral is proposed.   On the one hand,
I have ever regretted that the Crucifix was thrust out of our churches
at the Reformation, and I incline to think that if, like the Lutherans,
we had retained it, we should not have been disturbed by an indiscriminating re-introduction of images.   And I suppose, Sir Lewis
Dibdin's recent judgement on " Images in Churches " may fairly be
thought to legalize the Crucifix in the churches.   On the other hand,
I must needs think it highly inexpedient at the present time to do anything, especially in a Cathedral, which could not but have the effect of
encouraging Anglo-Catholick lawlessness.

I note with surprise and regret that the Dean and Chapter of York
have seized this time for introducing the certainly illegal " vestments "
in the Minster.   We are in a very difficult position and responsible
authorities must consider the probable effect of the action they take.

* Professor of Greek, Durham University.

D

If, as perhaps is not improbable, the great and protracted effort at Prayer Book Revision is going to peter out in complete failure, a new situation will have been created, in which many things may have to be re-considered including crucifixes and vestments; but I think until the necessity has thus arisen, we should stand on the old ways.

As to the form of the Crucifix, I think personally I prefer the un-mitigated familiar, rather than the modified and modern. It is what Gibbon calls " the most repulsive object ever offered to the groaning admiration of mankind " that appeals to me, and I suspect to most other sinners. There is, if I mistake not, a clothed Crucifix in stone in the new Liverpool Cathedral, and I didn't like it. But this is a personal opinion, which has no kind of authority. Bishop Westcott's dislike of the Crucifix as " excluding the idea of glorified humanity " will probably be shared by many.

You mention " the anonymous donor ". I have ever felt very sensitive as to persons who shall be allowed to be donors to our great churches. Not everybody can fitly be allowed that character; mere largeness of contribution is not a sufficient title; and when the gift (as in this case) cannot be separated from religious procedures and points of view, which cannot be regarded as universally, or even generally, accepted by English churchmen, I think it is particularly important that the donor, whether anonymous or not, should be clearly entitled by position, association, or family to have the honour.

You have invited an expression of my opinion, and, therefore, I have written thus freely; but, of course, the question must be considered and answered by the Dean and Chapter without interference, always, of course, within the limits of the Law.

Yours aff^{ly},

Herbert Dunelm.

33. Total Abstinence.

December 6th, 1924.

To the Rev. Westley Bothamley.*

My dear Mr Bothamley,

I am obliged to you for your letter which (if I do not discuss its contents adequately for lack of leisure) I understand and appreciate.

* Vicar of St Nicholas', Durham.

It is, of course, the great difficulty about getting the Church generally to break away from the traditional " Temperance " policy, that the existing situation has so connected in the popular mind the consumption of alcohol and all manner of undesirable things, that good men, and especially clergymen, shrink from even appearing to condone or assist what is apparently and confessedly so perilous and bad.

For this reason, there is a kind of inhibition laid on the more thoughtful and informed people, and they give a tacit (though unconvinced and reluctant) support to the policy of Manichæan intolerance.   Meanwhile the area over which the Churches have influence shrinks rapidly; the Nation is taking its own way, and that way will not be towards Total Abstinence, and its true political expression, Prohibition (which will survive as the distinctive morality of a sect) but towards moderate drinking in better public houses, and in a healthier state of public opinion.

I think it important at some cost to do what I can to hold the Church back from tying itself up with the sham science and partial morality of " total Abstinence ".

Ever sincerely,
Herbert Dunelm.

34.   The Horse.

December 29th, 1924.

To The Marquis of Londonderry.

My dear Lord,

I must thank you for a very beautiful and unusual form of Christmas card.★   The beauty of the race-horse is a beauty of complete adaptation to the object of its existence, and so far (though it may, perhaps, be a strange) it is certainly a very faithful symbol of a perfectly disciplined human life.   To be in harmony with one's environment, and to be equal to one's duties—is not that the very picture of a completely satisfactory human life?   Having then—after the cunning tradition of mine Order—clothed your Race-horse with didactic significance, I exempt myself from seeing it in any less edifying

★ On a copy of this letter Hensley Henson notes : " Lord L. had sent me as a Christmas card a picture of one of his horses."

associations, and thank you much for the good wishes, which it brings.

.   .   .   .

May God's blessing be on you in the New Year, giving you wisdom to choose, and strength to pursue, the right course in this strangely-tangled world!

Be sure, my dear Lord,

    that I am ever most sincerely yrs,

       Herbert Dunelm.

35.   *Suggestion for a Tuberculosis Sunday.*

       February 20th, 1925.

My dear Miss ——,

  I am really sorry that I cannot support your request to the Archbishop.   The fact is that I am strongly opposed to the modern fashion of allocating and naming Sundays for specific purposes.   It has gone great lengths already, and now threatens to ship-wreck the Church's appointed scheme for teaching and worship altogether.

  The cause in the interest of which you advance your request is altogether admirable, but I do not think we must add Tuberculosis Sunday to our list of holy days.

      Yours ever sincerely,

       Herbert Dunelm.

36.   *The value of letter-writing.*

       Auckland Castle,

       April 26th, 1925.

To George Minnis, Esq.

My dear George,

  Your letter, dated the 22nd March, arrived last week, and is now before me.   It is a grave condition of modern correspondence that at least two months must elapse before our minds, as expressed in our letters, can meet.

.   .   .   .

What in these circumstances is the value of letter-writing? I suppose there are four purposes which the correspondence of friends may still serve, and which, if that correspondence were to cease, could hardly be served at all.

1. The love of friendship is kept strong by contact. " Out of sight, out of mind " is a bitter proverb, which, by keeping in touch by means of letters, we rob of relevance.

2. Interest in familiar places and persons is kept alive. In private letters we treat of matters which the papers ignore, and which could not otherwise be sustained in our interest.

3. We secure one of the greater objects of friendship, viz. confession and counsel. Lord Bacon in his great Essay on Friendship writes well and truly thus :

> " No receipt openeth the heart but a true friend, to whom you may impart griefs, joys, fears, hopes, suspicions, counsels, and whatsoever lieth upon the heart to oppress it, in a kind of civil shrift or confession."

4. We can give information through private letters which is not accessible from any public source.

I think all these purposes are being served by our letters to one another, and that, though so long a time must elapse between the letter we write and the answer which we return, our correspondence grows in interest and value.

.   .   .   .

May God bless and guide you, my dear boy!

Yours v. affectionately,
Herbert Dunelm.

37. Spiritual Healing.

Auckland Castle,
May 2nd, 1925.

*To The Rev. Canon F. C. Macdonald.**

My dear Macdonald,

. . . I have been horribly pressed with work, for, on the top of everything else, I got drawn into promising a small book on

* Vicar of Christ Church, W. Hartlepool, 1909–24; Rector of Purleigh, Essex, 1924–35.

" Spiritual Healing ". This has necessitated reading an immense amount of drivel, all the more tiresome since the futility of superstition is linked to the dullness of " science ". The notion gathers strength in my mind that this much vaunted psycho-analysis is mainly nonsense. Certainly nothing could be more contemptible than the blethering of Freud and Jung on the subject of dreams.

The bother of it is that the greedy credulity of the religious public creates a veritable gold mine for any rogue who will pretend to banish pain and get behind death. This man, —— is suddenly famous, and the Anglican hierarchies fall before him like Jericho's walls before Joshua's ramshorns : but that cycle has too often been run before for me to be much impressed by it. . . .

I am, Yours affly,

Herbert Dunelm.

38.   *William III.*

June 18th, 1925.

To Mrs Arthur Long.★

My dear Madam,

I have to thank you very heartily for your valuable and interesting Essay, " Luctor et Emergo ", which I have read with much enjoyment. The belittlement of William III, so fashionable in some quarters, must needs be very offensive to a serious and candid student of the age, which witnessed his career. It is extraordinarily unworthy of considering and patriotic Englishmen.

May I take the opportunity of thanking Miss Marjorie Bowen for the great pleasure and profit I have gained from her historical romances ?

Believe me,

Yours v. faithfully,

Herbert Dunelm.

★ Marjorie Bowen.

39. *Bishop Burge.*

June 20th, 1925.

To The Hon. and Rev. J. G. Adderley.

My dear Jimmie,

Nothing would please me more than to answer Goudge, whose letters seem to me in equal proportions irrelevant, sophistical, confused, and mischievous.   But in the situation as it has now developed, when the Bishops must shortly address themselves to their business of determining how much of the mass of decisions taken by the clergy and laity shall be made definite, and sent forward for final acceptance or rejection, I judge that Bishops cannot cross swords with anybody, even the most inviting of presbyters!

I am sorry on many grounds that Burge has gone. He was a true man, though a weak ruler; and his weakness arose, not so much from any fault of character, as from a too emotional temperament, and an intellect more sympathetic than discerning. I shall never forget that he stood by me in a Day of general Desertion; and we had drawn very close together latterly. He was in despair over this Anglo-Catholic movement which he could not approve, and yet had not the nerve to oppose; and undoubtedly he unintentionally helped it greatly.

Yours aff.,
H. D.

40. *Scotch Songs.*

July 19th, 1925.

To The Hon. Diana Darling.

Dear Di,

Your father was so good as to send me *Ventures in Verse*, into which, after the manner of a greedy boy at a school-feast, I dug seeking the plums for my primary delectation. The four pieces over the signature " Diana Darling " pleased me, especially " To a shaft of sunlight ", which I think very good indeed. But I am of no account as a critic of verse, whereas I reckon myself good as a judge of Scotch songs, and the singing of them.   And I need not tell you to whom I give the first prize in that class.

Yours affect^{ly},

Herbert Dunelm.

41.   *The fallacy of class politics.*

October 8th, 1925.

To Frederick J. Smith, Esq.

Dear Mr Smith,

I have read your letter with much interest and appreciation. It provides me with a confirmation of my belief that the emphasis on the economic aspect of class is unreasonable and mischievous.   For look you, what real truth is there in pretending that you and I belong to different classes?   We are interested in the same things; we read the same books; we look at many things from the same angle; and, in short, we are mutually intelligible and sympathetic.   So far, surely, we are men of one and the same class.   But we are diversely placed in the hierarchy of social life; and we see different aspects of economic life.   That is a strong argument for holding us together in order that our distinctive types of knowledge may be combined to our great advantage, for you see and understand something that I may miss, and vice versâ.   The notion that we should be plucked violently apart, thrust into the prison-house of our economic status, and labelled variously, seems to me as dishonouring to us both as it must be disadvantageous to the nation.   We should both be better citizens by being as far as possible released from class limitations.

I think it is a fair inference from your letter that you also are a Christian man.   If that be so, then we are again much nearer to one another, by our common discipleship, than we are alien by our diverse economic situations.   The dreadful doctrine of " class-consciousness " ties men down to one, and that the lowest, aspect of their life.   As patriots, thinkers, students, Christians, they are united with their fellows, but all these unities are to count for nothing in face of the single, sombre fact that in the economic process, we are variously grouped! It seems to be madness.

And note to what lengths of absurdity this doctrine of class is carrying its advocates. All the great heritage of literature, art, and science is suspect, because, forsooth, it comes from a past which was not communist. So—it would be pathetic if it were not grotesque—"Labour" is actually calling for "class-conscious" universities, a re-writing of history, etc. in the interest of class: so that there may be no understanding of the past possible to the wage-earners, and a total breach of fellowship be effected within the nation.

Along these lines I can see nothing but disaster; whereas in fellow-ship and cooperation I can perceive the potency of limitless gain to our poorest people.

Again thanking you for your letter, I am,

Sincerely yours,

Herbert Dunelm.

42.   A Golden Wedding.

October 15th, 1925.

*To The Rev. Canon H. M. Spooner.**

My dear Friend,

I have learned—too late for the payment of my homage—that you and Mrs Spooner have been celebrating a "golden wedding"; and I am in two minds whether I can decently hand in so belated a felicitation as this sheet must carry. And yet I love you both too well to acquiesce in the total absence of any tribute from me on such an occasion; and I am the more emboldened to adventure a message, since my ignorance was involuntary; and even the cruel Church of the Papists concedes a measure of hope to the involuntarily (and invincibly) ignorant!

Fifty years is a long time on any estimate, but when one adds the consideration of quality to that of number, these fifty years are an epoch, and with possibly one exception—the XVIth century—the most deeply revolutionary epoch of human record. To have lived

---

* Archdeacon of Maidstone, 1900-21; father of Mrs W. R. Inge.

through it, and to have kept faith and love—these are great achievements.

I find myself falling out of accord with the time more and more irreparably; and I cannot see anywhere any signs of hope. Perhaps for that reason I cling to my friends, and insist that they shall not leave me, though I grow as amiable and wholesome as a wounded bear in a corner!

With much love to you and my dear Mrs Spooner,

I am,
Alway affect^{ly},
Herbert Dunelm.

43.   *The Fourth Gospel.*

February 7th, 1926.

To Lord Charnwood.

My dear Godfrey,

I would not write to you in acknowledgment of your gift of *According to St John* until I had read it, and thus informed myself of its value. Now I can send you my hearty thanks for an extremely informing book, full of insight and devout wisdom, which carries the promise of much good influence. I hope it will have the large circulation which it certainly merits.

Some 35 years have passed since I settled my opinion respecting the 4th Gospel in the phrase—" It is not history, but the first and best commentary on the Gospel "—and there I stand still. I think we should be quite unable to conceive of an intelligible person in the Christ as this Evangelist pourtrays Him, if we had the 4th Gospel only; but with the historical Person already clearly presented by the Synoptics, we do find—at least I do—in the narratives and discourses of the great Supplement an illuminating and satisfying Interpretation of the Person.

You have certainly disclosed an unusual capacity of theological understanding; and it is a notable sign of this disordered time that a layman should voluntarily do so well what most of the clergy professionally do so ill.   I think you have a more religious temperament than I, who am really, for all my lawn sleeves, a born sceptick.

I notice that you are evidently in close accord with Gore, and find his books attractive.   Here—and this discloses the spiritual inferiority of my mind—I differ.   Gore is, in my belief, one of the most sincere, godly, and intellectually alert men whom I have ever met; but he impresses me as essentially a sophist.

But I did not mean to get off into criticisms, only to thank you for your excellent book, which I do think is really a good piece of work.

Yours affect^{ly},

Herbert Dunelm.

44.   Sir Oliver Lodge.

April 14th, 1926.

To The Rev. Dr R. J. Campbell, D.D.

My dear Campbell,

I ought to have written at once to say that it will, of course, give me pleasure to meet Sir Oliver and Lady Lodge, for (though I regret that, like Solomon in his old age, he has gone after strange gods), I have a liking for him, and cannot but think that so imposing a façade of a brain case as his, must contain a better and ampler brain than is commonly given to man !

I am mainly handicapped now by the abominable process of substituting Art for Nature between my jaws.   The pundits condemned my teeth as active poisoners !!   It is difficult enough in this false world to speak sincerely, but when one has a mass of self-created fiction planted in one's mouth, it must be vastly difficult to speak the truth, and speak it plainly.   However, as long as the lie is not in the soul, one refuses to despair.

I go back to the Castle after this week, and come on to Brighton on Tuesday.

Yours ever,

Herbert Dunelm.

45. *Religion of the C.L.B.*

Scotland,
April 15th, 1926.

To The Rev. J. Duncan, ★ *O.B.E.*

My dear Duncan,

I am glad to have your conception of C.L.B. There is nothing in what you say which seems to call for comment, still less for adverse comment, although, of course, much must needs turn on the sense which words bear, and on the perspective in which duty is perceived. The efficiency of C.L.B. could hardly consist with any weakness in the military aspect of its work, and would certainly be defeated by any neglect of its religious character and purpose.

The type of religion which the C.L.B. ought to promote in the boys is that which the Church of England has been distinguished for creating in its true members—not a weak or mawkish type, but one which is manly and simple, which gives a kind of primacy to duty, and regards ecclesiastical divergences with a large tolerance. The use of terms which are highly controversial, and therefore misleading (e.g. Mass, Catholick, etc.) would in my view be very undesirable. The traditional language of Anglican piety should be adhered to; and the straightforward simplicity of boys' consciences preserved from the melancholy confusions of partisanship. This would be right in any diocese; but in the diocese of Durham it is essential, if C.L.B. is to make successful appeal to the general conscience. "Take thought for things honourable in the sight of all men" is one of St Paul's counsels which we who bear Christ's commission must ever keep in mind. "Definitely Church lines" means to my mind that the boys will be led forward to Confirmation, carefully prepared, and encouraged in a regular reception of the Holy Communion, and the habit of religious observance. It does not mean that they are taught to sneer at Mattins as something unworthy, and to dissociate the Holy Communion from their reception of the Sacrament.

I do not doubt that you will do much to build up in C.L.B. a strong manly religion which will express itself naturally and happily in the system of the English Church.

★ Vicar of Dawdon, nr Sunderland.

I am really very anxious that C.L.B. should develop in the best way; and I think you can help to that end.

May God bless you in this effort also!

Yours v. sincerely,
Herbert Dunelm.

46. Bishop Ryle.

Auckland Castle,
April 27th, 1926.

To The Rev. Maurice H. FitzGerald.

Dear Mr FitzGerald,

Your letter of April 13th ought to have been answered before, but I have been indisposed, and, for the last week, absent from home. I hardly need to say that it would give me pleasure to assist you in your biographical task as far as I can: but I doubt whether I have it in my power to do much. My personal relations with Bishop Ryle were always of an affectionate character, but our correspondence was infrequent, and generally limited to immediate concerns, of which the interest did not survive the occasion. I do not preserve letters, even from my friends, which have no permanent importance: and, therefore, I doubt if I have any of his which would be worth your looking at.

When, in the teeth of much public agitation engineered by the English Church Union and carried to strange lengths of violence, I was consecrated to be Bishop of Hereford, Bishop Ryle was one of the two Bishops—the other was the late Bishop of Oxford, Dr Burge— who "presented" me for consecration, but he was careful to explain to me beforehand that his consent to do so was conditioned by the Archbishop of Canterbury's approval.

He knew that I disliked the development of ritual and ceremony which took place in the Abbey services during his government as Dean, but this divergence of opinion never interfered with our personal friendship: and I had an unfeigned admiration for the graces of character, which gained for him such wide, and indeed universal regard. When he first arrived in Westminster as Dean, he nominated me, on Canon Duckworth's death, as his sub-dean, and this position brought me into very constant and intimate association with him during the first year of his decanate. I recall the time with unalloyed pleasure. His tact, sympathy and wisdom made a great impression on me.

I fear this is little use to you, and I wish it were in my power to be more serviceable.

Believe me,

Yours v. faithfully,

Herbert Dunelm.

47. Sunday Observance.

May 5th, 1926.

*To The Right Rev. Bishop Frodsham.**

My dear Bishop,

Thank you for your letter. I think the Commissioners have been overborne by the " Life and Liberty " nonsense which now carries all before it at the centre. Because the old Sabbatarianism is untenable in theory and often objectionable in practice, it does not follow that the preservation of Sunday from normal handling (i.e. the obliteration of all difference between Sundays and weekdays) is [n]either reasonable or expedient, [n]or religiously defensible. I have long held, and, as occasion offered, maintained, that the great increase of movement, noise, and distraction which marks the life of modern society, (and which beyond all question brings a cruel and waxing strain on nerve, heart, and brain), has clothed the tradition of Sunday observance with a new importance, and, indeed, made it one of the most precious of our civic possessions. Just as British birds, menaced with extinction by the increased mobility of the masses, and their enlarged leisure, are being preserved by the method of sanctuaries (i.e. places exempt from the normal conditions), little islands of safety in the stormy ocean of national life, so I picture the Sunday as providing a kind of protected enclosure within which the imperilled sanctities of character and home can be guarded against the menace of modern

* Vicar of Halifax, Yorks.

life. And, therefore, I think the greatest caution ought to mark our handling of Sunday.

Christians will not lack special and very cogent considerations which will, and ought to, determine their personal treatment of Sunday; but the considering citizen need not go beyond arguments of the higher expediency to bring him into a working alliance with the religious advocates of Sunday observance.

In the case of the Eccl. Com^{rs} there are two further considerations, viz. (1) they represent the Church of England, and ought therefore to respect the general conscience, (2) they are not authorized nor qualified to direct the spiritual policy of the Church.

With kind regards,

Yours very sincerely,

Herbert Dunelm.

48. Parochial Missions.

Auckland Castle,
May 6th, 1926.

To The Rev. A. Silva White.*

My dear Mr Silva White,

I will sanction your Mission and grant leave to the Rev. Hinton Knowles of St Paul's Church, Middlesbrough, to act as Missioner.

I notice with some concern the multiplication of Missions of one sort or another in the Diocese. When I was a parish clergyman, it was generally said, and I think, with substantial truth, that missions were " superfluous in a well-worked parish, and mischievous in an ill-worked one ". I wish in the Diocese generally that there was a greater confidence in steady parochial work, visiting from house to house and teaching, and less resort to this modern fashion, in which Nonconformists so freely indulge, of keeping the people in a state of constant surprise by repeated " stunts ".

Yours sincerely,

Herbert Dunelm.

* Vicar of St Peter's, Bishop Wearmouth.

49. *Intercommunion.*

September 23rd, 1926.

To The Rev. A. A. Boddy. *

My dear Vicar,

I understand that your invitation to the Holy Communion is not addressed to all without discrimination, but to those serious and good-living Christians who, being already admitted to the Sacrament in their own branches of Christ's Church, are able with a good conscience to respond to the invitation addressed to Communicants in the Communion Service.

So conditioned I must needs approve of your action which seems to me to stand in line with the true Anglican tradition, and to be the inevitable expression in action of the decision reached by the Lambeth Joint Conference, viz: that the Free Church Ministries are to be recognized as true ministries of Christ's Word and Sacraments in the Universal Church.

I trust that the Blessing of God will be with you next Sunday evening when you distribute to your friends and neighbours the most comfortable Sacrament, and that the unity of Christ's family in the parish may be deepened and strengthened.

Yours sincerely,

Herbert Dunelm.

50. *Bishop Weston of Zanzibar.*

November 5th, 1926.

To The Rev. Canon H. Maynard Smith.

My dear Canon,

It is really very kind of you to send me your Life of the Bishop of Zanzibar, which I have been reading with much interest. You have succeeded to a remarkable degree in what I always think is a very difficult kind of composition—biography; and I certainly have

* Vicar of Pittington, Co. Durham.

no fault to find with your references to myself. Of course I regret that the impression should be given, perhaps inevitably given, that he and I were habitually conflicting, whereas we never came into touch before the Lambeth Conference, and his denunciations of me were as unexpected as they were unwelcome. He had formed a picture of me in his mind as an " arch-heretick ", which was strangely remote from the truth. In some sense, I suppose, we are all hereticks now. Certainly he himself did not escape the charge. But in purpose and temper I was never a heretick, but a demurely orthodox and unimaginative person who, in a difficult place, aspired to stand between the parochial congregations and the academick criticks; and that work of interpretation, carried on for 12 years in St Margaret's conspicuously, as it had been for 13 years previously inconspicuously, was as sincere as it seemed to be justified by results. I have lived to become what the Americans call a " back-number "; and to see procedures and teachings, for which I was vigourously denounced, taken to be " matter of course " among Anglican leaders.

Again thanking you,
I am,
Sincerely yours,
Herbert Dunelm.

51. *Advice to an ordination candidate.*

November 7th, 1926.

To William Suthern, * *Esq.*

My dear William,

I want to supplement what I said briefly to you on Friday, when I approved you as a candidate for Ordination who will, if all goes well, be working as a clergyman in this famous diocese of Durham.

The next five years of your life will be devoted to preparation for the Christian Ministry—physical, mental, and spiritual. It is greatly important that you should act rightly with all three. Physical exercise must not be neglected if your Body is to be adequate for its great duty in the career which you contemplate. Health is indispensable to the

---

* Now Vicar of Newsome, Huddersfield.

E

parish clergyman, and it is ordinarily gained or lost between 18 and 23.

You will take a high view of your work for the Schools. A clergyman is a teacher, and his competence to teach depends on his knowledge, and, still more, on his will and capacity to learn. Try to understand your work, not merely to " cram " for your examination. Seek the grace of loving Books, and the habit of reading them. Nothing can make up in later life for wasting these priceless learning years, which now are yours.

And, then, there is the highest matter of all, the disciplining of your character, your spiritual life. Avoid all that stimulates what is censorious, polemical, and partisan. Be very honest with yourself, and by personal prayer and devotion, keep very close to the Source of all true Religion, our Lord and Master, Christ.

It would please me if you would write to me every term, and thus keep in touch with one, who must needs accept a measure of responsibility for your career.

May God's Blessing be on your life in Durham!

Your sincere friend and Bishop,
Herbert Dunelm.

52.   *Thanks for a book.*

December 21st, 1926.

*To The Bishop of Worcester.**

My dear Ernest,

The butler has just brought to me a sumptuous volume on Hartlebury Castle, which (and this is much to say) is entirely worthy of its subject. There are many pegs on which a bishop may hang a lasting reputation—he may be an eminent scholar like Lightfoot, or a " saint " like Moule, or a " scandal " like some others who shall be nameless, or an antiquary of his see. I am not sure whether the last isn't the surest peg of all; for scholars become obsolete, saints fall out of the calendars, and scandals are forgotten, but antiquaries, tying themselves to places and histories, garner something of the perennial interest

* The Right Rev. E. H. Pearce.

of their subjects. And, indeed, it is a great service that you have rendered to your (mutilated) diocese, and to the Church as a whole.

It is kind of you to send it me with an inscription. I shall value it greatly.

I send you as the commissioned carrier of my affectionate good wishes a small book which I purchased from Bishop Ryle's Library, and which is adorned with his bookplate. It will serve to link up in your thoughts, Westminster and its personnel.

I have been reading two apologies for Anglo-Catholicism—one by ——, and the other by ——, two as sophistical knaves as ever perplexed a Church. They seem to think that when they have made out a plausible statement of Anglo-Catholicism as a tenable version of Christianity, they have vindicated their right to hold office in the Church of England and to enjoy the emoluments of such office. Whereas the only thing that matters is, whether, whatever theory they cherish, they can be trusted to obey the laws and teach the established doctrines of the Church of England. The factions are evidently preparing themselves for battle.

Give my love to your sister, and be sure that I wish you both a happy New Year.

Yours v. affect^{ly},

Herbert Dunelm.

53. *Influenza.*

Auckland Castle,

February 18th, 1927.

*To The Rev. J. B. Purvis.**

My dear Vicar,

I am very sorry indeed to hear that you and Mrs Purvis have been attacked by that odious plague. I used to say years ago when first we made its acquaintance, that there were only two things in the world I feared, one was influenza, and the other fanaticism. I really think I am of the same mind still. When I read the statistics of influenza victims on the one hand, and the speeches of the opponents of the Revised Prayer Book on the other, I feel that both of these plagues are with us in their pristine vigour.

* Vicar of Holy Trinity, Stockton-on-Tees.

I fear I cannot come to you on March 28th as I shall probably be in the train. I very willingly approve of General Kenyon speaking in the Churches.

Yours sincerely,
Herbert Dunelm.

54. *A Birthday Letter to an Octogenarian.*

July 18th, 1928.

To J. G. Wilson, * *Esq.*

My dearest Wilson,

I understand that tomorrow is your birthday, and that its arrival will carry you into the small but important company of our " Elder Statesmen ", the Octogenarians. I take leave to send you a few lines of sincere and affectionate congratulation.

Congratulation—yes; I think, on reflection, that that is the right word; for to have traversed all those years, and come out at the end still brave and kind, with spirit unbroken and heart unspoiled is truly one of God's *magnalia* for which we who are your friends may, indeed, congratulate you, and for which we must humbly thank God.

1848 was a wonderful year to be born in; and, as I glance over the list of its memorable happenings, I incline to think that it is nearer to 1928 than, perhaps, any other year in the whole series which links the two.

It is more than 15 years since you and I first made acquaintance, and our acquaintanceship soon became a genuine friendship, which has deepened and strengthened with the passing of the years.

The failing of your eye-sight reminds you and me that Time carries us forward to the unpenetrated mystery of the End; and you would not be the man you are if you did not recognize this. But you are of those, my friend, who, as some quaint poet sings, have so lived that their life can

> Send a challenge to its end,
> And when it comes say,
> Welcome, Friend,

* Hensley Henson's Legal Secretary.

and you will always know how much we all love and honour you. I think you are one of the very few persons, of whom it is true to say that I have never heard any one speak except in terms of respect, and in most cases with a touch of genuine affection.

May God bless you in the Time of Age, and grant you yet some years in which to cheer and help us!

Very affectionately,
Herbert Dunelm.

55. *Preparation for Ordination.*

November 8th, 1928.

My dear Ken,

Your affectionate letter with its freight of Birthday wishes was very welcome to me; and I accept with confidence your promise to play the man, and to be true to your profession.

.   .   .   .

There are 3 things I have it in mind to say to you, and which I hope you will heed.

1. Be regular in your religious observance. You are looking forward to the career of a Christian Minister. The discipline of religious habit is really essential to that career. Be at the Holy Communion every Sunday, and look well to your daily prayers. Work and prayer can never be safely severed.

2. Work steadily and never worry. You are required by your Creator to make the most of the powers and opportunities He has given you. You are not called to be something bigger than you are; or to do something beyond your powers. Worry is wrong as well as foolish, when we are in the way of Duty.

3. Play games. Your mind will be the fresher, and your body the stronger. Also, the intercourse with your contemporaries, which games make possible, will be good for your character. The walk, especially the solitary walk, is not enough; and presently when, by God's permission, you are a clergyman, you will find knowledge and skill in games a really valuable asset in your equipment for pastoral work.

I have set these things down in their order of importance: spirit, mind, body. None may be neglected without sin, and without loss.

I send you the *Bishoprick* as I promised; and I hope that you will find time to read it.

May God bless you, my dear Boy, and lead you forward in His service!

Yours v. affectionately,
Herbert Dunelm.

56. *Pageants.*

November 27th, 1928.

*To The Right Rev. Bishop Talbot.**

My dear Bishop,

It is really very kind of you to send help to the unemployed miners. I have sent on your cheque to the Lord Mayors' Fund, earmarking it for Durham. The prospect for the winter is certainly very black, and I cannot see any lightening of the gloom.

The bustle of organizing Enthronement pageants for our new primates afflicts me with a kind of spiritual nausea. Fisher said the other day that the Democracy, having stripped the nobility of power, was jealously preserving it for its own amusement (or words to that effect). I think we might say the same of the Hierarchy.

When Laud's policy crashed, he was duly, and quite properly, inducted to the block. When Davidson's comes to grief, he is loaded with compliments, given a peerage, and presented with a " tribute ". To add a touch of grotesqueness to the paradox, Sir Thomas Inskip, after taking the lead in heaping on the old Primate an extreme humiliation, comes before the public to solicit contributions to the " Tribute ", thus transforming it from an act of friendship to a " last straw " of belittlement! We live in strange times.

I trust that your voyage and visit will be entirely pleasant. No, I have not seen Neville's book; but my life recently has been so hurried, that much has been omitted.

Believe me,
my dear Bishop,
Always most sincerely yours,
Herbert Dunelm.

* E. S. Talbot.

57.   *His view of his own character.*

December 27th, 1928.

To Lord Davidson of Lambeth.

My dear Lord Archbishop,

. . . .

It has been my misfortune in the course of my life to disappoint every person who has followed me, and every party that has allowed itself to build hopes on me; and the accusation of inconsistency (not to use a harsher word) has been hurled at me from many sides.   Yet I am conscious of so little change in my fundamental positions that I endorse the judgement which has sometimes been passed on me that, like the younger Pitt, I " was cast, and never grew."   A kind of Quixotic honesty, a fatal trick of lucid speech, and a temperamental indifference to the impressions I make, may, perhaps, explain the paradox I seem to be.   Anyway there it is; and it is too late now for this particular leopard to seek to change his spots.

. . . .

58.   *A request to dedicate Silver Bugles.*

January 16th, 1929.

To Lieut.-Colonel F. W. Cluff,
  Barclay's Bank Ltd, Durham.

My dear Colonel,
    I hardly think a religious dedication of the silver Bugles would be suitable.   A line has to be drawn somewhere in these things in order to prevent " our good being evil spoken of."   A few years ago I was asked by a triumphant Football Team to dedicate the shield which was the prize of victory, and I felt bound to decline.   The Bugles have a stronger claim, but not strong enough.

With kind regards,
Yours sincerely,
Herbert Dunelm.

59.   *A Bittern found at Wynyard Park.*

February 15th, 1929.

*To Viscount Castlereagh.**

My dear Robin,

How very exciting! I am indeed pleased to hear of a Bittern at Wynyard, and greatly pleased that you should have reported it. I turned to Thorburn's *British Birds* on receiving your letter, and found a beautiful plate of the " Common Bittern "; and a very interesting account of its fortunes in Britain.

It seems to have practically died out in the last half of the XIX century, and then begun to recover its position;—

" Again, after another 25 years, the Bittern was found in the same county (Norfolk) in 1911 and under careful protection the birds have now so increased that a fair number of pairs now occupy the old resorts, at least 12 nests having been noted this year (1925). Elsewhere in our islands the bird is known as a winter visitor as well as a migrant in Spring and Autumn, and would increase still more if it could obtain better protection at these times."

I rejoice to know that at Wynyard that " better protection " will not be lacking, and that the Bittern's Protector will be the Heir Apparent himself.

I had not realised that the Bittern was so large a bird. Thorburn gives its length as 28 inches and its wing 13 inches.

Always, dear Robin,

Affectionately your friend,

Herbert Dunelm.

60.   *Confirmation candidates.*

May 5th, 1929.

My dear Rector,

I note with considerable surprise that only two girls were presented for Confirmation from your parish, and I think that there

* Now Lord Londonderry.

must be some circumstance unknown to me which can do something to explain so disconcerting a fact.

When I was myself a parish priest, it was commonly accepted that 20 persons reached the age of 14 every year in a thousand people, and this was held to be an indication of what we had to undertake.

The population of —— is stated to be 2,304, which would suggest that not less than 45 persons arrived at the age for Confirmation during the year. Making large allowance for Roman Catholics and Nonconformists, it seems difficult to believe that there were no more than two girls to be brought to the Bishop for Confirmation.

I should like to hear from you what explanation occurs to you as adequate.

With all good wishes,
I am,
Sincerely your Bishop,
Herbert Dunelm.

61. *To a young friend aged thirteen.*

Auckland Castle,
September 17th, 1929.

To Miss Kitty Wilson.

My dear Kitty,

Yes, I hope to be here on Friday : and though all the world and his wife be about me like Wasps about an overripe plum, we will manage to say, Goodbye. School sounds rather alarming : however, I suppose we <u>must</u> go through that too.

Yours always affly,
Herbert Dunelm.

Give my love to the rest of my Quartett.

Written in Kitty Wilson's Autograph album.

> Kitty and Betty and Peter and Dare,
> (A quartett of jewels both rich and rare)
> Peter and Dare, and Betty and Kitty—
> Two of them nice, and two of them pretty.

For girls are all pretty, and boys are all nice,
You can tell the difference in a trice;
And Herbert Dunelm is never pretty.
And as to his niceness, you just ask Kitty.

                                                        H. D.

62.   *Marriage of the Clergy.*

December 12th, 1929.

My dear Rector,

Before I can admit Mr —— into this diocese, I should like to have an interview with him, and thus to have an opportunity of forming an estimate of him. The Bishop of —— tells me, that though " undoubtedly an advanced man ", he has " become engaged to be married ". If, in such a cardinal point of discipline as the marriage of the clergy, he voluntarily prefers the English to the Roman system, it would seem not chimerical to hope that his preference would extend to ceremonial.

                    With kind regards,
                        I am,
                            Sincerely yours,
                                Herbert Dunelm.

63.   *To a friend on reaching the age of seventy.*

Auckland Castle,
March 24th, 1930.

To The Rev. Canon F. C. Macdonald.

My dear Canon,

. . . I send you my belated, but none the less sincere congratulations on reaching the canonical age of three score years and ten: and I hope you will be permitted to put to the test of personal experience the Psalmist's statement that " though men come to fourscore years yet are their days then labour and sorrow." That they should be full of " labour ", may be, as in the case of Lord Balfour, a desirable privilege, that " sorrow " should attach to them will largely turn on the behaviour of others. Anyway, may Heaven deal kindly with you!

I have not been well for the last few weeks, and am still " under the doctor ". Of course the invariable prescription (like champagne to an ailing slummite) is impossible—knock off work and take a holiday!

The Confirmations are now in full course: and I have been commanded to preach to the King on April 6th, and spend the week-end at the Castle. This is interesting but involves a lot of travelling, and no small expenditure of time.

We have taken a small house in London for the 5 weeks of the Lambeth Conference. I hate London with as genuine aversion as the parson in " The Private Secretary ": and I have no great expectation of enjoyment in listening to my episcopal brethren from overseas!

With kind regards to Mrs Macdonald, and love to Fred if he is with you.

I am,
ever affectionately,
Herbert Dunelm.

64. Preaching to His Majesty.

May 2nd, 1930.

*To The Rev. Spencer Wade.**

My dear Spencer,

I am very glad to hear that you are to preach before His Majesty. That is a distinction which is justly valued. Since I am responsible for suggesting your name to Lord Stamfordham, it is hardly fair that you should be put to the expense of your railway fare. I enclose a cheque for five pounds to cover your pilgrimage.

In preaching before the King, you should take care about these points.

1. Do not, at most, exceed 15 minutes.
2. Take no notice at all of His Majesty but just preach quite naturally as if it were an ordinary congregation which you were addressing.
3. Avoid " high falutin " and be straightforward and simple.
4. Speak up clearly because His Majesty is getting a little deaf.

* Rector of Gateshead Fell, Co. Durham.

5. It would be quite fitting and would probably be appreciated, if you said something at first hand about miners' lives. The King is much interested in social questions.

The Chapel is small and the congregation is also small, but the occasion is significant; and I hope and believe that you will acquit yourself well.

Affectionately your Bishop,
Herbert Dunelm.

65.   *Celibacy of the Clergy.*

May 15th, 1930.

*To The Rev. Hugh Raynham.**

My dear Sir,

I cannot honestly say that I think the adoption of celibacy would meet our present difficulties. It would, of course, relieve us of some obvious embarrassments; but it would immerse us in others, and probably worse ones. But I do incline to think that marriage should be prohibited for a period of years after Ordination. This would probably have the effect of leading some men to embrace celibacy; and it would secure to the Church some period of undistracted service.

.   .   .   .

Believe me,
Yours v. faithfully,
Herbert Dunelm.

66.   *To a Vicar who had become Master of the Beagles.*

January 13th, 1931.

My dear Vicar,

I learn from the newspapers that you have become Master of the Beagles, and I feel that it is owing to my position and to yours that

* Curate of The Annunciation, Brighton.

I should tell you frankly that the announcement causes me both surprise and distress.

In present circumstances, when our county holds a dolorous primacy among all the counties of England, in the matter of unemployment, there is something unpleasing about the emphatic association of a leading clergyman with mere amusement. That may be matter of opinion, but a far graver issue is raised when the question is looked at from the point of view of Christian principle. "Take thought for things honourable in the sight of all men," says St Paul. Charity requires that we should not wound the consciences of others. Of all men you, as Christian Minister, are bound to take thought for the offence which you must needs give to that large, and, if I mistake not, rapidly growing number of thoughtful and humane persons, who cannot reconcile sports, which inflict suffering and death on animals, with the principles of Christ's religion. Personally, I incline to agree with the Dean of St Paul's (Dr Inge) that "to take a pleasure in killing our helpless cousins in fur and feathers seems to me a disgusting relic of barbarism."

You will claim, perhaps rightly, that you are entirely free to act as seems to you fitting with respect to a matter which lies outside your professional and prescribed duty; and certainly, I have no wish to impinge by a hair's breadth on your proper freedom. But I should be lacking in my duty if I did not remonstrate with you on action which seems to me inexpedient and unfitting.

Believe me,
Sincerely yours,
Herbert Dunelm.

67. Theological Colleges.

Auckland Castle,
April 27th, 1931.

To George Mackenzie, Esq.

Dear Mr Mackenzie,

You need not apologize for writing to me. Every "old Dunelmian" has an obvious right to address the Bishop of Durham :

* Now Rector of West Grinstead, Sussex.

and the subject on which you very reasonably seek advice is one which may fairly be brought to a Bishop.

. . . .

I hold you to be thoroughly right and reasonable when you shrink from bringing yourself into a situation which might seem to attach you to a " party " in the Church, whether " Anglo-Catholick ", or any other : and I think, therefore, that you will be well-advised not to go to any Theological College which is known to have a well-marked partisan character.

Without passing any opinion on other Colleges, I will allow myself to say that there are three Colleges which I have learned to trust, and to recommend to young friends of mine, who are looking forward to Holy Orders.

1. Westcott House, Cambridge.
2. Theological College, Salisbury.
3. S. John's College, Durham.

I think well also, though I have less knowledge of them, of the following :

4. The Bishop's Hostel, Lincoln.
5. Theological College, Wells.

You should, perhaps, consider whether it is wholly satisfactory to choose a College, for your theological preparation, which is situated in a great University, where you would still be subject to the intense and rather distracting influences, which have borne on you during your academic career. There is much to be said for places like Salisbury, Lincoln, and Wells, which are comparatively quiet, and therefore more favourable to reflection and self-examination.

Do not hesitate to write to me again, if you desire to do so : or, if you care to break your journey to Scotland by spending a night here, you will be very welcome.

With all good wishes,
I am,
Sincerely yours,
Herbert Dunelm.

68. *Freemasonry.*

Auckland Castle,
May 11th, 1931.

To H. F. Macdonald, Esq.

My dear Freddie,

I think you would do well if you became a Freemason : and I do not think you need be unduly apprehensive of offence at the ceremonial. The modern forms of Freemasonry took shape in the XVIII century and they have the stamp of that age, its fondness for pompous phraseology, its lack of humour and its rather impersonal Deism. But there is nothing that need offend : and there is much genuine purpose and fraternal feeling in Freemasonry which are morally stimulating. And for your purpose of widening the area of personal experience, I think the Order is well suited.

So join : and if you want to enrich your application with a reference, do not hesitate to use my name. I shall be pleased to be your sponsor.

. . . Always affectely yrs,

Herbert Dunelm.

69. *Episcopacy.*

October 21st, 1931.

*To The Archbishop of Armagh.**

My dear Archbishop,

I find myself quite unable to take any great interest in the efforts, so ardent and so persistent, of a section of Anglican enthusiasts to arrange union with any and every little sect in West and East, however petty in number, however degraded in faith and habit, which yet possesses the "historic episcopate". So long as episcopacy is looked upon as the *unum necessarium* of a Christian Church, I am sure that no reunion with the presbyterian and congregational churches is possible; and I do not think any good purpose is served by entering on negociations which are bound to fail, since, however courtesy and glozing phrases may conceal the fact, the old brutal obstacle remains unremoved.

* The Most Rev. C. F. D'Arcy.

It is more than 30 years since I reached the conviction that in a spiritual Religion such as Christianity certainly is, questions of specific polity can never be primary; and, therefore, any assumption such as that of our episcopal rigorists that Episcopacy is essential to a rightly constituted church must always be fatal to true religious fellowship between the Christian Churches. Indeed, I suspect that these conferences with little episcopal communities are actually harmful, since they serve in some measure to hinder good folk, like the Bishops of Gloucester and Chichester and both the Primates from realizing the intrinsic enormity of their assumption that the Christian Fellowship is rightly linked and limited to episcopally ordered Churches.

A few weeks before his death, Archbishop Söderblom stayed here, and talked much with me on the subject of Christian unity, for which, as you know, he was an enthusiast. He spoke of the Conference at Lausanne, and described the painful impression caused by the refusal of the English members to unite in Holy Communion with their non-episcopal colleagues. It reduced to nothing all the pleasant fraternity of the gathering, and showed that nothing had really been changed.

Personally, I have received the Holy Communion with the Presbyterian Church in Scotland, and if I did not feel free thus to express my spiritual brotherhood with the members thereof, I should not make any profession of fraternity. Many years ago when these discussions on Faith and Order were started, I told the late Archbishop Davidson that I desired to take no part in them as, in my belief, they could not lead to any result until those engaged in them could agree to meet as Brethren at the Lord's Table. The lapse of thirty years has but confirmed me in this opinion.

The Church of England under its present guidance is directed towards the policy of union on the basis of episcopacy; and I feel quite sure that such success as may be attained will be dearly purchased by the alienation of our true allies—the other Churches of the Reformation.

I am not sure whether you have seen what I said on the 39 Articles; and, therefore, I take leave to send you the copy of the *Bishoprick* which contains my letter. It would please me to know that you approved it.

Always, my dear Archbishop, most sincerely yours,

Herbert Dunelm.

70.   *Special Forms of Prayer.*

January 6th, 1932.

*To The Archbishop of York.**

My dear Archbishop,

Your Grace and Cantuar. have not been fortunate in your latest essay at guiding our public devotions; and if you were to draw the inference that a severer economy in such essays were a prudent course, I must needs think you would do well.

I have often asked myself why it is that modern forms of devotion are so woefully unsatisfactory, and I have come to the conclusion that the ultimate reason is the divided objective with which their authors work. Nominally, they are composing prayers to the Almighty; mainly, they are (though probably they suspect it not) writing oblique sermons addressed to the congregation for its instruction and edification. Few political issues command general agreement; and these well-intentioned forms placed in the mouths of reluctant and protesting worshippers, defeat their own excellent, but illegitimate, purpose. Men resent being brought to their knees on false pretences, i.e. being set to confess sins which their consciences do not feel as a burden, nor their reason allow to be wrong.

Wishing you and your wife all happiness in the New Year,

I am,

Always affect^{ly},

Herbert Dunelm.

71.   *Theodore Woods.*

Auckland Castle,
March 3rd, 1932.

To The Rev. L. W. Trotman.†

My dear Lionel,

Your letter of January 28th is before me. It was most welcome. Whether the oncoming of old age is the cause I cannot say, but it is

---

* The Most Rev. William Temple.
† Hensley Henson's Domestic Chaplain, 1925–9.

the case that I grow more covetous of affection as the years pass, and yours is particularly valued.

This morning I have been across to S. Anne's, and (to use the language of our Anglo-Catholics) celebrated a " Requiem Mass for Frank Theodore Woods, sometime Vicar of Bishop Auckland." His death startled me for he was 10 years younger than I. The precedence of our Bishopricks had the effect of bringing us into habitual contiguity. We always sat together at Bishops' Meetings and other official gatherings. We rarely agreed but we never quarrelled, for his large, bland geniality could never reach the point of quarrelling with anybody. He began as a thorough-going Evangelical, and was holding a Simeon's Trust Living, Bradford, when he was made Bishop of Peterboro. His Churchmanship rose with his fortunes, and he wound up as an Anglo-Catholick with Socialist sympathies, which is, I take it, the most popular type of Anglican ecclesiastic. I find it difficult to forgive him for the breaking up of the famous See of Winchester, which I am sure he disliked, but hadn't the courage to oppose. I remember being asked by Baldwin what I thought of him, and replying that his powers of expression were out of all proportion to his powers of thought. This is, I believe, a just judgement. The usual speculations as to his successor are now being vented. I have no doubt that a resolute effort will be made to get —— translated from —— to Winchester : and I think it quite likely that the effort may succeed. . . . If —— does come to Winchester we shall have a considerable addition to our physical weight, and a calamitous diminution of our mental lucidity. He is the most muddle-headed fellow I know.

This is the centenary of Scott's death, and preparations are being made in Scotland for its due celebration. I have rashly undertaken to deliver an address on him in the ruins of Melrose Abbey on September 28th. It has rather a romantic sound, but means a quite unnecessary addition to my commitments.

. . . .

May God bless you, my dear Lionel, and keep you safe!

Always affly, yrs,

Herbert Dunelm.

P.S. I send you the *Bishoprick*. The " Charge " to the Ordination candidates seemed to be useful as an oblique sermon to the Incumbents!

72. Bishop Gore.

March 13th, 1932.

To Albert Mansbridge, Esq., C.H.

My dear Sir,

It hardly needs saying that I would gladly give you all the assistance in my power, for not only did I regard Bishop Gore with genuine affection in spite of the fact that throughout almost the whole of my clerical life we were in disagreement, and sometimes in open discord, but also because I think that his remarkable career and most attractive personality do eminently merit adequate record. But I find it very difficult to write anything about him as Canon of Westminster. He was appointed to his Canonry in 1894 and was transferred to the bishoprick of Worcester in 1902. I did not become a Canon until the end of 1900. So we co-existed at the Abbey for hardly more than 18 months. I have read through my private Journal for that period, and I can only find two references to him. He supported me when I moved in Chapter that the Revised Version should be read in the public services of the Abbey; and he formally protested to the Dean (Bradley) against my announcement on the notice board of the Abbey of the sermons on Reunion, afterwards published in the volume, *Godly Union and Concord.*

I imagine that my appointment by Lord Salisbury came to him as an unwelcome surprise. The story was current that when that appointment was made public, he was asked what he thought of it, and replied by the counter-question—" What was the message which Philip of France sent to King John, when Richard was released from prison?" The answer, of course, was the significant sentence—" Take heed to yourself for the Devil is unchained." I remember being told of this on my arrival in Dean's Yard, and rallying Gore on it.

We did not see much of one another, for his line of country was not mine; nor had we sufficient agreement on the matters which interested us most to make intimacy really possible. We were, none the less, sincerely attached to one another, and though we fought, we never hated.

I do not know whether you propose to include any account of the episode at Birmingham, when Gore sent me a formal Inhibition (dated March 26th 1909) which hangs framed on my study wall. If so, I should like to see what you have written, in order that I may compare it with my own knowledge of the facts, for I have seen so many perverted and extravagant statements that I think the sober truth should be recorded.

Gore was extremely impulsive. He dashed off opinions which he had quickly to revoke. Thus, when I sent him my little book on "Spiritual Healing", he sent me a delightfully approving letter of thanks, which pleased (and surprized) me greatly; but my satisfaction was short-lived; for it was followed almost immediately by a second letter, recalling the first. He had read on, and found himself woefully disillusioned.

I am very sorry to be so unhelpful, but I think you will understand the reason.

Believe me,
Yours v. faithfully,
Herbert Dunelm.

73.   Bishop Gore (cont.).

March 25th, 1932.

To Albert Mansbridge, Esq., C.H.

Dear Mr Mansbridge,

I have thought much over your letter, and cross-examined my memory; but I cannot find any reason for thinking that I can offer you anything serviceable for your purpose. My Journal does not help me much, and naturally the occasions when Gore and I came into open collision are more conspicuous than our more normal relation of personal regard.

He was an aristocrat to the finger-tips, with an aristocrat's contempt for law and tendency to play the despot. He felt intensely for classes, hardly at all for individuals; the wrongs of the one stirred him to prophetic denunciation, the oppression of the other did not greatly perturb him. Religiously, he was utterly a Catholick, to whom the utterance of the rightful ecclesiastical authority was final, but he was too learned and candid to be a Papist. I judge him to have been the most considerable English Churchman of his time, not the most learned, nor the most eloquent, but so learned, so eloquent, so versatile, and so energetic that he touched the life of his generation at more points, and more effectively, than any of his contemporaries.   He was, like a Jesuit diplomatist, the best company in the world, with no sourness of ascetic oddity to mar the frankness of his good fellowship. His humour, and enjoyment of humour, were delightful.   Yet with all this, there was in him an element of steel-like hardness, which, whenever it emerged, you knew it was quite useless to reason with. He seemed to me at the end rather a pathetic figure, for his disciples had gone to the right, and to the left, and he was alone.   He was always listened to with respect, and then—ignored.   Probably this is the fate which overtakes every leader who has outlived his generation, but in his case, it seemed to be emphasized by his tireless industry.

You can see how useless all this must needs be for your purpose, and yet I cannot write anything about Gore which is not thus mingled, and, so to say, critical.

Believe me,
Yours sincerely,
Herbert Dunelm.

I used to say that he was S. Carlo Borromeo *redivivus*.

74. *An Honorary Degree.*

Auckland Castle,
March 21st, 1932.

To Cecil Ferens, * *Esq.*

My dear Cecil,

That ever marching knave, Time, who never grows tired, and quickens his pace, when one would like to call a halt, has now reached a point in his journey, when I must send you the enclosed,† and in doing so, I bind a talisman about it which will transform its sordid message into the currency of a better world than this.   In effect, I love you well, and am grateful for the help you give me.

Affect^{ly} yours,
Herbert Dunelm.

I am a little exalted, for the University of St Andrews is going to make me a Doctor of Laws!!!! on June 28th; and the Society of

---

* Legal Secretary.   † Cheque for salary.

Antiquaries has elected me a Fellow. The alphabet gathers about my name like radiant clouds about a setting sun! And the best of it is that as Lord Melbourne said of the Garter—" There's no d——d merit about it! "

But there is, or one thinks there is, some kindness, and for that in a world not over well-equipped in that respect, one is thankful.

H. D.

75. *The distinctive gifts of Oxford.*

May 15th, 1932.

My dearest Dick,
    .   .   .   .

What you say about being accused of " over-estimating the power of intellect " interests me immensely. There seems to be in your critics a certain confusion of mind. They do not distinguish between discipleship, and the disciple's specific duty. The primacy among the Christian's characteristics belongs, not to what is intellectual, but to what is moral. " Follow Me " is the Master's formula, and in obedience thereto lies the very essence of discipleship. The Beatitudes in the Sermon on the Mount do not include any intellectual qualification. St Paul, who was the intellectual leader of the Apostolic Church and stands in the History of Christianity as the *Doctor Gentium*, was quite decisive about the superiority of the moral over the intellectual factor. " If I speak with the tongues of men and of angels, but have not love, I am become sounding brass, or a clanging cymbal " (I. Cor : xiii. 1). " Knowledge puffeth up but love edifieth. If any man thinketh that he knoweth anything, he knoweth not yet as he ought to know; but if any man loveth God, the same is known of Him " (Ibid. viii. 1, 2). It would be easy to multiply such passages. Moreover, the essential character of Christ's Religion is redemptive; and it is impossible to imagine a pardoned sinner facing the Redeemer in the spirit of intellectual arrogance. The motive of Christian service is a love which has itself been kindled by His Love, Who, for love of us, died on the Cross. " For the Love of Christ constraineth us; because we thus judge, that One died for all, therefore all died; and He died for all that they which live should no longer live unto themselves, but unto Him, Who for their sakes died and rose again " (2 Cor. v. 14, 15).

When from Discipleship we turn to the Disciple's duty, the whole situation is transformed. "Lord, what wouldst Thou have me to do?" was the question which the converted Pharisee addressed to the Lord, who had appeared to him on the road to Damascus (Acts xxii. 10). And, in less dramatic fashion that is the question which every sincere Christian asks his Master *in foro conscientiæ*. The answer is given by temperament, opportunity, and circumstance. Christ requires of us the faithful exercise of our faculties, the intelligent use of our opportunities, the disciplined control of our circumstances. This surely is the moral of the Parable of the Talents (S. Matt. xxv. 14–30). Apply all this to the case of a young Christian to whom has been given the hope of Ordination and the opportunity of Oxford. Clearly, his duty is to exert himself to the utmost to get from Oxford the distinctive gifts which Oxford can give—knowledge and intellectual discipline.

To neglect one's work in order to indulge one's religious emotions may seem to indicate a humble-minded disregard of intellectual achievement. It far more often means a subtle self-deception, a disregard of the Divine leading, and a failure to answer to the Divine Purpose. Read St Paul's words in Romans xii, and see how he emphasizes thoroughness in the performance of immediate duty as the primary obligation of discipleship.

Dearest boy, your path of duty lies plainly before you. Ask God's help that you may walk steadfastly therein. Offer to your Master the daily sacrifice of work honestly done, recreation enjoyed in purity, and a mind lifted up in thankfulness and worship to Him Who loves you, and Whom you love.

I shall certainly try to see you when I come to Oxford next month; and, if I can at the same time see Malcolm and Leslie, my pleasure will be increased. Only we must have some time by ourselves. I want to make Mark's acquaintance. You did not tell me what you have decided about the projected tour in Switzerland.

I hope you will not be over-wearied by so long a letter. Put it aside, and read it at your leisure. I find much comfort and joy in being able to write to you in this way. May God bless you, and lead you forward in His service !

Very affectionately yours,
Herbert Dunelm.

76. *Invitation to wear Cope and Mitre.*

May 26th, 1932.

My dear Cousin ——,

Look you—I don't possess a Mitre, and I've never worne a Cope at a wedding in my life.   Moreover, the spectacle would wake appetites and create precedents which would be awkward in the future.   You see that, if I come to ——'s wedding, he must be content with my red doctor's gown.

You will know that an English bishop has, like Agag, to " walk delicately ".   Moreover, you will explain to ——'s bride that, in giving a short address, I am not performing a distinctively episcopal act; it might, perhaps, be maintained that the Bishop of Southwell in blessing the marriage is acting *quâ* bishop, and might reasonably be expected to be clothed appropriately.   His Lordship will, I assume, wear his mitre and cope very suitably.

If anything more need be added to extenuate the enormity of refusing anything to a Bride, I would add that a cope is a most awkward vestment to pack, and properly requires a case of Transatlantick proportions.   So she will excuse me.

Affectionately yours,
Herbert Dunelm.

77. *Application for Crown Livings.*

July 31st, 1932.

My dear ——,

.   .   .   .

If you desired to have your name placed on the list of applicants for Crown livings, I suppose you had best write directly to the Patronage Secretary at 10 Downing Street; but I should not advise you to do so, for, in my observations, the best men are not those who are on that list.   It contains rather the names of men who despair of preferment in the dioceses where they work, and " pull strings " to secure appointments elsewhere—an unregarded company.

If, as you say, and as would seem probable, you will be before long offered preferment in the diocese of ——, I should advise you to go on where you are, and take what comes. There is great strength in ministry derivable from the fact that one has *not* " pulled strings ", but gone where the way opened.

There are few aspects of clerical life more unsatisfactory, and none more unpleasing, than preferment-hunting; and you would do wisely to hold yourself altogether free from it. I can well understand that you are sometimes tempted to lose confidence in the governing Providence of God; but I am more surely persuaded of this than of anything else, that God's Hand is upon us for good when we loyally persist in the way of Duty, and that outside that way, we may gain our ends, but we lose ourselves.

. . . .

Affectionately yours,
Herbert Dunelm.

78. *Patronage.*

August 3rd, 1932.

My dear ——,

I must not embark on a discussion of the complicated and much debated subject of patronage. All churches are at their worst in their systems of patronage, and I am sure that the Church of England is no exception. We are not responsible for the system we find established, only for our own behaviour. Two things have been fixed in my mind by a long experience of the Church of England.

1. that the best clergymen do not apply for livings;
2. that good, hardworking clergymen of reasonable competence, who do their duty without troubling themselves about " prospects " and " appointments ", are rarely overlooked.

Almost always, in cases which are supposed to indicate neglect of merit by the responsible authorities, there is some sufficient cause, though it may be known to few, sometimes only to the Bishop.

I am myself too much out of sympathy with the prevailing currents of church opinion to be a satisfactory adviser of a younger man, and it is probably best for your professional interest that you should not be supposed to endorse my points of view.

.   .   .   .

Yours affectionately,
Herbert Dunelm.

79.   *The loan of a ruler.*

Ruswarp Vicarage,
September 5th, 1932.

To The Rector's Churchwarden,
  St Mary's Church, Whitby.

Dear Sir,

I beg to return you the ruler which you were so kind as to lend me; and, at the same time, to thank you heartily for your kindness. I have a great dislike of slovenly work, and, as it is my practice to underline texts and quotations in my sermons and other compositions, I find the use of a ruler very necessary, if I am to preserve a regular aspect in my writing.   So your ruler has been of real assistance to me.

.   .   .   .

With renewed thanks,
I am,
Yours very faithfully,
Herbert Dunelm.

80.   *G. Bernard Shaw.*

December 22nd, 1932.

To The Dean of St Paul's.

My dear Ralph,

Thank you so much for your good wishes, which, it needs no saying, I reciprocate heartily.   I have just been reading Bernard Shaw's little, wicked, black pamphlet, and I am at once perturbed and alarmed. This way—the Bolshevik way of making Christianity ludicrous—is extraordinarily effective. Really, it is " hitting below the belt ". You can't argue with a sneer, or appeal against a jest. I wish you would take some opportunity of castigating Bernard Shaw. You are the only clergyman who has the ability to do so at all, and the influence to do it effectively.

Don't trouble to return Bavink's book, but keep it as the only form of Christmas card which could be decently offered to the Dean of St Paul's !

I shall look forward to reading your Cambridge Lectures.

With all good wishes to Kitty and your family,

Always affectionately,
Herbert Dunelm.

81. *The age for Confirmation.*

January 10th, 1933.

To The Bishop of Exeter.★

My dear Bishop,

Thank you so much for your letter, and the proof it provides that you and Lady Florence have got back safely from that degraded, disorderly, murderous, and grasping community which has only the Atlantic between us and its limitless abominations.

You and I are the only Bishops who insist on 14 as the minimum age for Confirmation, therein (as I agree with you in thinking) conforming to the Rubrick. Of the 36 Bishops who have been good enough to reply to my inquiry, 8 fix the minimum age at 13 ; no less than 22 at 12 ; one (Guildford) at 10 ; and three (Birmingham, Bradford, and Newcastle) appear to leave the matter wholly to the clergy. The vast mass of Papistry, with its rule of Confirmation at 7, is having a powerful gravitational pull on the fragment of Anglicanism ; and, although many of the bishops prate about psychological reasons, the key to the tendency towards rapidly lowering the age of Confirmation, the real cause, is precisely the Drift to Rome. Personally, I would

★ The Right Rev. Lord William Gascoyne-Cecil.

prefer to go boldly back to the Eastern absurdity of infant-Confirmation. It would not be more irrational than the Roman practice, and it would be enormously more convenient. We should hear no more of this mischievous nonsense about the necessity of breaking up the historical dioceses, if, with the Easterns, we blessed oil in central caldrons, and authorized the parish priests to apply it to the regenerated Babes!

With all good wishes to you and Lady Florence for the New Year,

Affectionately yours,
Herbert Dunelm.

82.   Colonization.

Auckland Castle,
January 24th, 1933.

To Noel Lamidez, Esq.

My dear Noel,

I am startled to learn that your last two letters have received no reply, and I am reluctant to think that I can really have been so negligent. But you must be magnanimous, and remember that my normal correspondence is of another kind, more urgent and less interesting, and that my private letters are apt to get pushed aside. But, please, don't think that my neglect means either that I don't value your letters, or that I don't think of you with affection.

The account that you give of the condition of affairs in Australia is extremely depressing, but it accords only too closely with what I hear from other sources. There is something extremely wrong in all the English-speaking communities. Partly, we share with all other civilized communities the disease of "industrialism" which is only now disclosing its frightful potencies of debasement; and, partly, the manner of our colonising has given a quite lop-sided importance to the material factors in life. When the ancient Greeks decided to create a colony, they deliberately created a complete society modelled on their own; and thus, from the first, the Greek colonies were as fully equipped morally and intellectually, as they were physically. With us how different has been the method! Companies of adventurers "on the make", pursuing the quest for gain wherever there seemed good hope of success, have flung themselves on the vacant lands of America and Australasia, and improvised a social order which served sufficiently for their needs.   The earlier colonists (e.g. the Pilgrim fathers) were inspired by higher motives, but even they were not the most cultured of their time.   But in more recent times, who can doubt the mental and spiritual penury of the multitudes who have emigrated from Europe?

Here in England the economic crisis shows no mitigation; and it is telling disastrously on our national life at every point.   There are no trustworthy signs yet of any recovery; and yet, unless some recovery takes place soon, it would appear that some form of revolution cannot be averted.   There are said to be now no less than 120,000,000 men, women, and children unemployed in Europe and America.   How long can civilization carry that dead weight?   How long will these multitudes acquiesce in their exclusion from the economic process?

Show that you have forgiven my long silence, by writing to me again, as fully and frankly as you will.

May God bless you and yours, and guide your course through this difficult world!

Affect^{ly} yours,

Herbert Dunelm.

83. Science and Ethics.

January 30th, 1933.

To The Dean of St Paul's.

My dear Ralph,

I am in a quandary, none the less disagreeable, because it is self-created.   In effect, I want to "pick your brains".

Some months ago I was "temerarious" enough to undertake to deliver the Fison Lecture in June.   I disclaimed the character of philosopher and man of science, being in fact possessed of neither; but on the understanding that the terms of the Trust were very widely interpreted, I was fool enough to offer as a subject, " Ethical conditions of Scientific Methods " and to my consternation this was promptly accepted.

It is an unquestioned assumption that science is ethically and æsthetically impartial, but, while this holds of its conclusions, does it involve the consequence that men of science may be indifferent to moral considerations when they determine their methods of research?

This question has, of course, been raised in connection with vivisection. Westcott decided on moral grounds that vivisection was not a legitimate method. I take the other view; and as we have both been Bishops of Durham, I have suffered some inconvenience by being credited with my famous predecessor's opinions.

It was raised recently in the discussion of Voronoff's experiments. You referred to them very briefly on page 202 of your book on Christian Ethics and Modern Problems. Are they permissible, and if not, why not? The question, me judice, is raised in the realm of psychological research, and in Axel Munthe's The Story of San Michele, which purports to be an autobiography, there is a vivid description of La Salpetrière, where Charcot carried on his experiments in hypnotism. Here is a suggestive paragraph;

> " Hypnotized right and left dozens of times a day by doctors and students, many of these unfortunate girls spend their days in a state of semi-trance, their brains bewildered by all sorts of absurd suggestions, half-conscious and certainly not responsible for their doings, sooner or later doomed to end their days in the Sal des Agitées, if not in the lunatic asylum."

Was this procedure, even though adopted in the name of science, morally legitimate?

In the præ-scientific epoch, it was held that there were areas of knowledge into which Christian men could only enter by unlawful means, e.g. trafficking with the devil; may it not be the case that in our scientific age, there may be some parallel limitation of legitimate knowledge?

I am not at all sure that I am not labouring an absurdity; and yet when I observe how two successive Presidents of the British Association have thought it necessary to express alarm at the ethical incompetence of civilized men to use rightly their scientific achievements, and when I reflect on the blood-curdling possibilities of an unconditioned experimentation in the biological and psychological spheres, I cannot but think that there is a real question to be answered.

Do tell me how this strikes you, and on what lines the discussion might best be pursued.

Always affectionately yours,
Herbert Dunelm.

84. *British Israelites.*

March 3rd, 1933.

Dear Mrs ——,

I am afraid that I can be of no service to you. The British-Israelite Movement in my judgement lies below the level on which rational discussion is possible.

It belongs to the numerous class of fatuities which pullulate so rankly throughout the English-speaking world, and are all conditioned by two cardinal errors, viz: Fundamentalism in handling the English Bible, and a complete failure to understand historic Christianity. On the soil of these twin and connected misunderstandings there grows a queer amalgam of British Imperialism, Protestant intolerance, and individualistic pietism, which has a strange attraction for the half-educated.

It is not worth arguing with, for while the cardinal errors I have named hold their place, and clever brains are devoted to the task of building a logical fabric on them as a foundation, argument is absolutely futile.

We can but trust that, as sounder views of the Scriptures are taught, and a worthier version of Christ's Religion is expressed in the Church, Anglo-Israelitism, like so many other kindred follies, will die a natural death.

Believe me,
Yours v. faithfully,
Herbert Dunelm.

85.   Frederick III.

March 17th, 1933.

To Prof. E. F. Jacob.*

My dear Jacob,

You are indeed generous.   Your references will help me much. Since writing to you, my attention was directed to a passage in Coulton's *From S. Francis to Dante*, p. 243, where he quotes from Salimbene a statement which runs on the same lines as my Apocryphal Syndic story :

"He fed two men most excellently at dinner, one of whom he sent forthwith to sleep, and the other to hunt; and that same evening he caused them to be disembowelled in his presence, wishing to know which had digested the better; and it was judged by the physicians in favour of him who had slept."

Life may have had a vividness of interest in the xiii[th] century, which it has lost in the xx[th]; except, possibly, in Russia, where similar eccentricities appear to obtain.

Again thanking you,
Ever sincerely,
Herbert Dunelm.

86.   Nudists.

Auckland Castle,
March 17th, 1933.

To The Rev. Canon F. C. Macdonald.

My dear Canon,

. . . The Nudists propose an odd problem.   What will be the next absurdity which will flourish in the rank soil of secularized Protestantism?   Certainly until the lunaticks are "clothed and in their right mind" they cannot be confirmed or admitted to Holy Communion. . . .

Affectely yrs,
Herbert Dunelm.

* Professor of Medieval History, Manchester University.

87.   *Centenaries.*

August 16th, 1933.

To The Rev. J. E. Pugh.*

Dear Mr Pugh,

In the expressive slang of the English schoolboy, I am " fed up " with centenaries. You will see from the enclosed copy of the *Bishoprick* that I have done my fair share of them. Centenary sermons inevitably carry you far afield from normal homiletics, and for that reason entail an amount of labour in their composition altogether out of proportion to their importance. I am on the brink of taking a pledge of Total Abstinence from Centenaries.

I share your devotion to Tennyson, and in particular to that great and searching poem, *In Memoriam*, which still seems to me filled with truth and wisdom, shrined in perfect music.

These pitiful Georgians affect to look down on the great Victorians, whom in very truth they are not fit to serve as link-boys!

Believe me,

Sincerely yours,

Herbert Dunelm

88.   *When asked to bless oil for Holy Unction.*

Auckland Castle,
October 6th, 1933.

To The Rev. C. E. Goshawk.†

My dear Vicar,

My own opinion about the Unction of the Sick is set out clearly enough in chapter viii of the Volume, *Notes on Spiritual Healing*, which I published 8 years ago, and of which I send you a copy.

I should not myself consent to bless oil for the purpose of anointing the sick : nor should I counsel any priest within my jurisdiction to do

* Vicar of Clevedon, Somerset, where Arthur Hallam is buried.
† P.C. of St Mary Magdalene's, Millfield, Sunderland.

G

so. But I should not think myself required to intervene officially if, in spite of my known opinions, he should adopt the practice.

Do you remember the words which Dutch William employed when he was induced, contrary to his principles, to "touch for the King's Evil"?

As the King placed the medal round the scrofulous man's neck, he said, "My friend, God give thee better health, and more sense." I incline to agree with His Majesty.

With all good wishes,

Sincerely your Bishop,

Herbert Dunelm :

89. Clergymen on the County Council.

October.7th, 1933.

To Malcolm Dillon, Esq.

My dear Dillon,

It needs no saying that in the matter of becoming members of public bodies, the clergy are entirely free to take their own course. They do, however, naturally and generally desire to know whether their action does, or does not, command their Bishop's approval. I have ever advised them to decline an active part in local or municipal politics. They may not legally stand as candidates for election to Parliament; and I think that the substantial (as distinguished from the historical) justifications for that prohibition may fairly be held effective against their standing for election to municipal bodies.

There are three main objections which, in my view, are irresistible :

1. The clergy have, or ought to have, their time fully occupied with their proper work.

2. The interests and excitements of active politics, whether general or local, are very difficult to harmonize with the temper and work of the parish clergyman.

3. It is inevitable, since politics in England proceed on party lines, that the clergyman who engages in politics cannot help acquiring the character and kind of influence which belong to a

partizan, and thus arousing against himself and (which is a graver matter) against his spiritual message, those suspicions and resentments which men commonly feel against their political opponents. The admonition of St Paul—"Take thought for the things honourable in the sight of all men"—is best obeyed by the clergyman's abstinence from activities which must compromise, or seem to compromise, his independence.

Accordingly, if Mr —— were to ask my advice, I should advise him to decline nomination as a candidate for the County Council: but, as I have said, he is perfectly free to take his own course.

Believe me,

Sincerely yours,

Herbert Dunelm.

90. *Unitarianism.*

Auckland Castle,

March 28th, 1934.

*To The Archdeacon of Northumberland.**

My dear Archdeacon,

I think our difference finds explanation in the fact that while you shrink from seeming to pass judgement on individuals who for adequate reasons you hold in high regard, I refuse to allow the claims of individuals to enter into an issue which appears to me to relate solely to the character and credenda of the Church.   We are no judges of individuals; we are officers of the Church, and guardians of its faith and discipline.

The Quakers stand on the same footing as the Unitarians in the matter of membership in the visible Church.   The one by repudiating Baptism altogether, the other by repudiating the universally accepted method of Christian Baptism, have placed themselves outside the membership of the visible Church.   That is a fact which we cannot dispute, and can only ignore by jeopardizing the whole theory of a visible Church.

* The Ven. L. S. Hunter; now Bishop of Sheffield.

Rashdall was a personal friend, whom I held in high regard as one of the best Christians I know. He subscribed the Nicene Creed, and, though he allowed himself a large liberty of interpretation, he was, I think, essentially orthodox. Thus he writes:

> "There have been many sons of God; only one is in a supreme, a unique sense the Son, the Word made Flesh, God of God, God revealed in a human soul and a human life."

Contrast this with Drummond; teaching that "the union of God with Christ becomes, to use the current phraseology, exceptional in degree, and not in kind."

I think it is, in these most difficult times, the wisdom of the Church's authorities to allow a large liberty of interpretation, provided always that the substance of the Creeds be affirmed. I don't want to evict the Modernists as such, but I desire to be assured that they do not lay axe to the root of the Religion itself; and that, I think, many of them are, more or less consciously, actually now doing. And certainly, I should insist that it is precisely when the Person of the Redeemer is in question, that the real question is raised. I will own that I am very greatly perturbed by the temper and contentions of the kind of Modernism which the *Modern Churchman* now represents, and by the kind of criticism, equally arbitrary and destructive, which is now generally applied to the New Testament.

The Episcopate will never become contemptible by having the courage of its convictions; but it cannot avoid the contempt of all honest men if it attempt, for fear of unpopularity, to "hide the light under a bushel."

Is it really fair to ascribe to the Bishops the responsibility for a controversy which assuredly they did not begin, and which most certainly they would avoid if they rightly could? You may be sure that they have no such *arrière pensée* as you suspect.

Do not let us drift apart into antagonisms which are unreal, and may become baleful.

Affect^{ly} yours,
Herbert Dunelm.

91. *Advice to an ordination candidate on reading.*

Auckland Castle,
May 20th, 1934.

To A. L. Morrison, * *Esq.*

My dear Leslie,

I have mislaid your letter, but I remember that in it you asked me for advice on the subject of your reading. In so vast a multitude of books, of which many have an alluring aspect, and some are really valuable, how shall you determine which shall be the volumes to which you will dedicate your attention? Of the books which you must read, I say nothing: these will be told you by your tutors and lecturers; but of the rest which provide your free reading, what shall be said? I cannot go beyond some general counsels, which if they be platitudinous will, by that circumstance, be sufficiently certified to be sound.

1. Have regard to Authors rather than to titles or even subjects. There are certain writers, respecting whom one may say with confidence that everything that they write is worth reading, and that the more you read of them, the more salutary your reading comes to be. You " see light in their light ", and in a true sense grow intellectually, e.g. Bishop Butler, Hort, Lightfoot, Dean Church, and Edwyn Bevan.

2. Read the big books on your subject whatever it may be. The curse of our time is the crowd of little books. I do not mean to suggest that mere bigness is a safe index of quality, but that where a large mind has been dedicated for years to a subject, and uttered itself in a great book, you should read that book, e.g. Hooker's *Ecclesiastical Polity*, Gibbon's *Decline and Fall*, Milman's *Latin Christianity*, Harnack *History of Dogma*, Coulton, Neander, (old Bishop Reichel put me on to him when I was first ordained).

3. Read the crowd of modern books with the object of learning what particular point (if any) they intend to make, but don't bestow on them the kind of close and reverend attention which the Masters command and deserve. You will find good reviews very helpful. Signed reviews indicate by the signature whether they are worth

* Now Rector of Branston, Lincoln.

reading.   Of unsigned reviews those in the *Times Literary Supplement* are by far the best.   Most modern books are only a re-hash of other and better ones.

4. Choose some subject as your " hobby ", and collect your reading about it.   Nothing is more intellectually dissipating than what I call " browsing ", that is reading at large just as inclination and opportunity incline.   *Experto crede*.   I should have been incomparably more efficient as a Bishop, if, as a student, I had been obedient to the counsels which I give you.

Next week will be given up to the Ordination.   There are 13 deacons and 5 priests to be ordained on Trinity Sunday; and the Master of the Temple is coming to give the addresses in the preliminary retreat, and to preach the sermon.   It will be no less than 47 years since (Trinity Sunday, 1887) I was myself ordained by the Bishop of Oxford in Cuddesdon Parish Church.   The retrospect has much in it that is humiliating and that calls for repentance; but Christ, in His limitless mercy, has endured me all these long years, and I cannot doubt that He will be with me to the end.

May God bless you, and make you strong and happy in the way of duty!

Affectionately yours,
Herbert Dunelm.

Keep common-place books: carefully written and indexed.   I wish I had done so.

92.   A " Collins ".

June 22nd, 1934.

To Mrs W. R. Inge.

My dear Kitty,

I may not delay to send you my thanks for your pleasant hospitality in the House which you have bound into my memory by so many associations of kindness.   It has been the scene of the manufacture of one of the most astonishing personal positions on record. " The Dean " has taken his place in the life and literature of our generation with as secure a title as another Dean, more really " gloomy ", and far less luminously spiritual, who gained something like the same solitary preeminence in Ireland two centuries since. He has been singularly happy in having beside him a Partner, so discerning, so devoted, and so delightful. That other Dean was not so fortunate, and, perhaps, the disastrous development of his worser aspects was not unconnected with that fact. But I am degenerating into what the newspapers call " an appreciation ", when really I am constructing a " Collins ". So I will say no more but thank you for your kindness, and pray that Heaven may prolong and perfect in the relative repose of the country, the Great Career and Partnership which are officially winding up.

Always affectionately,
Herbert Dunelm.

93.   Retirement of The Dean of St Paul's.

September 25th, 1934.

To The Rev. Dr W. R. Inge, D.D.

My dear Ralph,

It was indeed kind of you to send me your *Vale*, and to add to its interest and value by an inscription which gives me very great pleasure. And also a most legitimate pride, for to have a personal link with you cannot but breed and justify that sentiment. But, my friend, you must not speak of your hand having " lost its cunning "; for your latest production has all the " *curiosa felicitas* " of its predecessors; and, indeed, for its own purpose, could not possibly be better.

Your retirement from St Paul's is accompanied by every circumstance that can dignify the ending of a great service, and certify its supreme quality. You will have read the review of *Vale* in the *Observer*. It was rather an appreciation of the writer than an examination of his work. Ella read it aloud to us on Sunday night, and we all subscribed it. I hope, and believe, that from your rural retirement we shall yet receive much to illuminate, discipline, and delight us.

Vale brings home to me the necessity of considering my own de-

parture from the fighting line of the Ministry.   I have a certain desire
(if God were to permit it) to complete fifty years of active service;
and that cannot be until 1937.   I shall then be in my 74th year, and
(as many humiliating indications make but too clear) really incompetent for my present duty.

I am struggling to prepare a set of Gifford Lectures alongside the
persistent and unrelaxing strain of the Bishoprick.   The result cannot
but be calamitous to both the new undertaking and the normal duty.

With love to Kitty, and many hopes for your long continuance in
health and activity.

Always most affectionately,
Herbert Dunelm.

94.   Reunion.

February 24th, 1935.

To The Bishop of Eau Claire.★

My dear Bishop,

. . . .

I think there are many signs that the religious world in Great
Britain is becoming weary of discussions about Reunion.   No
progress is made, because the rock on which any advance is shattered
remains, and will for a long time, if not for ever, remain, viz: the
claim of the episcopal government (or the papal as the case may be)
to take rank among the essentials of Church life.   In the xviith century as in the xviiith and in the xixth, and now again in the xxth, good
men lament the obviously mischievous divisions, but they are not
prepared to make any concessions on the main question, with the result
that every negociation ends in failure, generally with some growth of
fresh exasperation.

The Dissenters, being "voluntaryists" are particularly hard-hit by
the economic depression, and this predisposes a certain number of
underpaid ministers to look with favour on projects which might have
the effect of giving them access to the Anglican endowments; and the
Greek churches, since the downfall of the Russian Church, being in

★ The Right Rev. F. E. Wilson (Protestant Episcopal Church in the U.S.A.).

sore straits, follow the precedents of their history, and make fraternal advances to Anglicanism. But there is little sincerity in these interested and interesting developments. The historic roots of separation remain, and determine the situation. Does all this seem to you both discouraging and cynical? Nevertheless, it enshrines a truth which we may not safely or wisely ignore. For the present, Reunion stock is "slumping" in the British market.

Somebody sends me *The Chronicle-Protestant Episcopal*. It is a very unpleasant paper, and I should hope that it has no great circulation. The tone is so dreadful; nothing could be more contrary to the Christian spirit. Protestantism, on both sides of the Atlantic, must be in a bad way, morally and intellectually, if the *Chronicle* gives a true presentment of it.

Your country baffles me completely. The Lindbergh Baby Trial combined every element of the indecent and the iniquitous according to our English notions of the way in which Law should be administered, and the ends of Justice served. "Hollywood" has become a synonym for flagitious and mercenary exhibitionism. What is the matter with you?

You may, perhaps, be interested to see what I have said about General Booth and the S.A.

With all good wishes,
Most sincerely yours,
Herbert Dunelm.

95. *Confirmation.*

Auckland Castle,
April 7th, 1935.

To Miss Veronica Irvine.

My dear Veronica,

I have been thinking much about you, and this morning since, under the rather flimsy pretext of indisposition, I am keeping my room, I propose to write a few lines to you.

And, first of all, I want to assure you of my affectionate sympathy in an experience which must needs cut deeply into the *arcana* of the spiritual life, for your Confirmation cannot but be the climax of much inner conflict, and the making of one of those cardinal decisions which determine the future. I have no doubt you are acting rightly in desiring to be confirmed, and to order your religious habit on the lines of the Anglican tradition. I say this, not because I have the smallest doubts that the Presbyterian Church of Scotland is a true and living branch of the Church Catholic of Christ, but because I think that, in the Providence of God, the Church of England has been able to preserve some elements of the Christian Tradition of great devotional value, which the other Reformed Churches, in the desperate circumstances of the Reformation, have lost, to their real spiritual impoverishment. I do not think that your Confirmation ought to create any sense of alienation from or breach with the Religious Tradition in which you have been trained, while it will, I think, deepen and strengthen your own discipleship.

And how shall you prepare yourself for Confirmation in my chapel on Sunday the 26th May? It hardly needs that I should advise you to make very special and continuing prayer that God's Blessing may be given you. Confirmation is closely and confessedly linked with Baptism, of which it is in some sense the completion. Therein you claim for yourself your place in the Covenant of Grace, of which Baptism is the Seal: and that Covenant is expressed in the words " Draw nigh to God and He will draw nigh to you ". The profession followed by the Laying on of hands declares the two sides of the Covenant. You draw nigh to Him in openly owning yourself bound by the Baptismal obligation: He draws nigh to you with the Gift of His Spirit symbolized by the laying on of hands. And after Confirmation comes the life of Communion. You will have a rule on this subject, but with respect to that, we will have some talks together. Meanwhile, I should like to know what you have read, and how you think about the Blessed Sacrament.

· · · · · · · · · · ·

You will like to associate your Confirmation with my Chapel and with the Bede Commemoration. You will kneel on the very grave of Bishop Lightfoot, whom we revere as one of the greater saints of Durham.

May God bless you and lead you forward in His Service, giving you great peace and happiness therein!

Affectionately yours,
Herbert Dunelm.

96.   A Jewish Prayer Book.

February 8th, 1936.

To Dr C. J. G. Montefiore, D.D.

Dear Dr Montefiore,

I must make no delay in thanking you for the very welcome gift of the Authorized Daily Prayer Book and the Companion to the same. I have but " dipped " into them, and found much to please and stimulate. The Prayer Book is a precious addition to my devotional books.

My book-shelves contain many works of yours, and these are often in my use. You have placed Christian students under large obligation. I trust that, by the goodness of God, we shall yet receive much from your treasury.

It gave me real pleasure to associate myself, in however small a degree, with the Jewish Community in its great efforts to mitigate the barbarous oppression which now proceeds in Germany. It almost makes one despair of humanity—that such things should be possible in the heart of what we vainly call Civilization. But Israel can say with the sure title of its age-long experience what Theodore Beza said to the Persecutors in the XVIth century : " The Church of God is an anvil which has broken many hammers ".

I take leave to send you a copy of the *Bishoprick* because I would like you to see my review of Mr Webb's Book on Russia.

Believe me,

With high regard,

Sincerely yours,

Herbert Dunelm.

97.   Exchange of Livings.

July 6th, 1936.

To The Rev. W. Patrick Dott.

Dear Mr Dott,

I am obliged to you for telling me how Lord Hugh Cecil can reconcile exchanges with the Patronage Measure. I cannot pretend to think that his argument is other than an unworthy quibbling.   The essence of an Exchange is the assumption that the incumbent possesses a property in his cure of souls, and that he is free (no longer to sell, for that outrage is now illegal) to barter it for another.   If the Bishop approve this transaction, he certainly lends himself to a transaction which is intrinsically unsound.

But I must not weary you with an argument.   I have no doubt that many excellent clergymen avail themselves of a casuistry which, if it cannot be considered morally sound, does at least disguise the true aspect of their action.   The unwholesome rigidity of our parochial system inclines men to grasp at any device which, however morally dubious, does at least inoculate the system with a measure of Elasticity.

Believe me,

Yours v. faithfully,

Herbert Dunelm.

98.   *A New Organist of St Paul's Cathedral.*

Auckland Castle,

July 23rd, 1936.

To J. Dykes Bower, Esq.

My dear Dykes Bower,

I must send you my congratulations on an appointment which implies a conspicuous recognition of your professional eminence; but I must also tell you how greatly I regret your departure from Durham, as well on public, as on private, grounds.

Your work at the Cathedral has been a notable service to the diocese, and your personal courtesy and consideration have made all dealings with you extremely pleasant.

I hope that you will find life in Babylon not only full of interest—it cannot fail to be that—but also personally enjoyable.   There is something to be said for, and something against, life at the centre of the world's life.   At your age, perhaps, the pros predominate in the scales of judgement, and in mine, the cons.   Anyway I think St Paul's is much to be congratulated.

May God's Blessing be on you, and your work!

Sincerely yours,

Herbert Dunelm.

99. *To an Incumbent invited to become Bishop of a Missionary Diocese.*

August 11th, 1936.

To The Rev. P. N. W. Strong.*

My dear Philip,

It is a difficult decision that you must make. I have ever thought that, if one prays regularly in the spirit of the Psalmist's words " Shew Thou me the way that I should walk in : for I lift up my soul unto Thee ", and makes a principle of never " pulling strings ", or consciously indulging personal ambitions, then one ought to accept as Divine direction whatever opportunity opens for work which is not plainly outside our competence and duty. Therefore, I shall not doubt that, if you enter through the door that has opened, you will have acted rightly.

But there are elements in your decision which lie outside my knowledge e.g. your health. Obviously, it would be wrong for you to put your hand to work which required for its due performance a measure of physical strength which you do not possess. On this point, you must seek, and follow the best medical advice which you can get.

Then, again, there may be family claims which you could not rightly ignore. Devout persons are ever tempted to repeat the error of the Jews, and attempt to make self-sacrifice in a duty which they like an excuse for repudiating a nearer duty which they dislike. On this point you will act honestly by yourself, but no one save yourself can know the facts, or reasonably advise your course.

I shall be extremely sorry to lose you from the diocese, for you have so carried yourself as to help and not to hinder your brethren. But there is a diocesan selfishness which a Bishop must resist, and I do not think you ought to be influenced by considerations of a local character.

If the Holy Spirit is leading you to episcopal work in New Guinea, He may be trusted to direct the course of parochial affairs. None of us is indispensable; all of us are under orders.

* P.C. of St Ignatius, Hendon, Sunderland; now Bishop of New Guinea.

I fear all this is of little use to you, but it is all I can say.

May God bless and lead you forward in His Service, giving you therein great peace and happiness!

Affectionately your Bishop,
Herbert Dunelm.

100.   To a Curate offered work abroad.

August 27th, 1936.

To The Rev. A. P. Rose. *

My dear Rose,

Your letter did not wholly surprise me, for I received some days ago from the Bishop of Hong Kong a letter telling me that he had offered you some position in his diocese.

I think that you ought not lightly to take your hand from the plough of parochial service, in which, I am encouraged to think, you have made an excellent start. In my judgement the most imperative requirement at present is that we should make stronger the position of Religion here at the centre, where it has become alarmingly weak. The circumference will reflect the quality of the centre; and, if Christianity fail in England, it will be enfeebled everywhere else. If you are happy in your work, and if, as you examine yourself honestly in the sight of God, you feel that your powers can be fully used in His service here at home, then I should refuse the proposal to transport yourself to Hong Kong. There is a certain risk of being led astray by the restless and wandering habit of our time; and I am sure that there is real strength in the steady loyalty which holds on in the chosen path.

Personally I shall be very sorry to lose you from the diocese: but whether you decide to go or to remain, I shall pray that God may bless and guide you.

Affectionately your Bishop,
Herbert Dunelm.

* Curate of St Mary's, Gateshead; now Dean of St John's Cathedral, Hong Kong.

101. *About giving references to parishioners.*

September 10th, 1936.

My dear Rector,

I returned home last night, and this morning I received your letter.

It is, of course, incontestable that you cannot recommend those, whom you do not know : yet, <u>if my correspondent says the truth when she alleges that you had buried her daughter</u> and <u>baptized her twins</u>, I think that she may be pardoned for imagining that (although you had never visited her during the five years of your ministry in —) you yet had some knowledge of her. It does seem to me rather hard on these poor people that it should be generally assumed that their parish priest is acquainted with them, when in fact he is ignorant of their existence. I am, of course, aware of the difficulty of effective pastoral visitation when population is so large as in your parish.

Nevertheless, I do not feel easy in mind when a specific instance of pastoral failure confronts me.

I am, always

Sincerely your Bishop,

Herbert Dunelm.

102. *On admission of an unsatisfactory person to Holy Orders.*

September 17th, 1936.

Dear Professor —,

I am greatly obliged to you for your candid and careful letter. It supplements and confirms the information about Mr — which I have received from other sources. It is to my mind quite clear that no Bishop could rightly consider him a suitable candidate for Holy Orders. His record is unusually and continuously bad. It discloses a character so unstable and perverted that Charity itself can only suggest that he is not mentally normal. His treatment of women argues a moral unsoundness which, if he should finally succeed in being ordained, would almost certainly find expression in lamentable scandal. To Ordain such a man would be little less than an act of treason against the Church itself.

I cannot imagine that any Archdeacon, having Mr ——'s record before him, could be found willing to present him to the Bishop as " apt and meet for his learning and godly conversation to exercise his ministry duly to the honour of God and the edifying of His Church."

It shocks me to think that he should persist in the belief that, being what he has been, and is, he could be entitled to claim that he has a vocation to the sacred ministry.

If *per impossibile* he were to be actually presented to a Bishop for Ordination, would it not be the plain duty of anybody present who knew his record to respond to the Bishop's challenge by " coming forth in the Name of God " and objecting?

I am in the 19th year of my Episcopate, and every year my conviction is strengthened that the root of most of our clerical scandals is the indefensible facility with which men are admitted to the Ministry.

Believe me,

Sincerely yours,

Herbert Dunelm.

103.   *Quality of ordinands.*

November 11th, 1936.

To The Rev. Eric Graham.★

My dear Principal,

I have to thank you for a very kind letter.   You ask me whether I am pleased with the men from Cuddesdon, who have come into my diocese.   The best answer that I can give to your question is to ask you to send as many more as you can.

. . . .

The longer I live, the more convinced I am that the weak point of our *Ecclesia Anglicana* is the quality, intellectual, physical, and moral, of the clergy.   It may surprize you that I include the physical, but it

★ Principal of Cuddesdon College; now Bishop of Brechin.

is the case that the poor physique of the clergy, (especially of those who come from the humbler ranks of society,) is a serious practical embarrassment. But I don't see how this is to be remedied.

Believe me,
sincerely yours,
Herbert Dunelm.

104. Ribbentrop.

Auckland Castle,
November 15th, 1936.

To The Bishop on the Niger.*

My dear Bishop,

I realise with a shock of shame and surprise that I never thanked you for the exceedingly interesting and informing letter which you sent to me some while ago, answering some questions of mine about missionaries and their methods. I have that letter with me, and have found it very illuminating and helpful. Now you write again to preserve me from some dubious mendicant: and the arrival of your letter stirs my conscience into action. Please forgive me my apparent neglect, and believe that I appreciate and value your letters.

Tonight I am going to Wynyard to meet the German Ambassador, Herr von Ribbentrop, who is making a private visit to Lord Londonderry: and I am wondering how I shall succeed in maintaining courtesy without concealing the moral nausea which the Hitlerite regime creates in my mind. There seems a growing expectation that war on the grand scale will shortly break out, and for that supreme disaster, which may well make an end of what we call Civilization, Hitler will be chiefly responsible. He divides the credit with his fellow Dictator— Mussolini. The crime which has destroyed the last vestige of liberty in Abyssinia has opened the door to a whole flood of disasters. I think you saw the pamphlet which I wrote to relieve my own mind. It can be, alas, no more than a wreath placed on the coffin of African liberty. The effect of this successful villainy cannot but be far-reaching. Last week I received from a South African Bishop a letter marked by

---

* The Right Rev. Bertram Lasbrey; now Assistant Bishop of Worcester.

H

considerable apprehension. He thinks that there is a noticeable and increasing alienation of the African mind from Europeans. If this be so, the outlook is dark.

When the world is in this condition of fearful expectancy, how hard it is to go on with our spiritual task! " Have faith in God " said our Master to his disciples : and that is surely the word to us at this time. The heavens are very dark, but we like Moses must " endure as seeing Him Who is invisible." In the long run the Cause of God prevails.

May God bless and strengthen you.

Affectly yours,
Herbert Dunelm.

P.S.   We are looking forward to the King's Coronation with mixed feelings. The Bishop of Durham must attend as he has part in the ceremonial : but I would much rather stay away, for not only do I dread and loathe crowds, but the ceremonial itself is almost too remote from the actualities of modern life.

105.   Appreciation of Anthology ; views on the Abdication of Edward VIII.

Auckland Castle,
Christmas Day, 1936.

To The Rev. Dr W. R. Inge, D.D.

My dear Ralph,

It has been in my mind for some days to send you a few lines of hearty thanks for your admirable Anthology of the Christian Life, which I have not only found most precious and comforting in my personal use, but have also given as a Christmas gift to several of my friends. It is good to have old favourites brought together with the added authority of your choice, but also it is sheer gain to be introduced to new friends of alluring charm. Really, I think that such an Anthology is the most effective form of an Apology for Religion.

What a year we look back upon! With what fears does it clothe our view of the year that is beginning! I cannot shake off a feeling of inevitable and imminent catastrophe. There seems no probable, perhaps no possible, outcome of the frenzied re-arming of Europe except a war of unimaginable horror and destructiveness. Our own strange little sordid domestic crisis has apparently ended without any more serious consequence than a serious shock to monarchical sentiment, and the breaking in pieces of a popular idol. But I wish our Primates would remember that there is a time to keep silent. Cantuar's broadcast address offended me at every point—its bad taste, its arrogant egotism, its affectation of pontifical moralising, its lack of generous feeling. The " man in the street " (who is no fool in these matters) regards it as " hitting a man when he is down "; and, if anything could give likelihood to the ridiculous suggestions of the Rothermere Press it would be the belated and half-jubilant pronouncements of Primate and Bishops. Temple thought it a suitable opportunity for instructing the people on the difference between $\dot{a}\gamma\dot{a}\pi\eta$ and $\ddot{\epsilon}\rho\omega\varsigma$!

Please carry to Kitty and Catherine * my most affectionate good wishes for the New Year and be sure that I am

always affect^{ly},
Herbert Dunelm.

The Preface to your Anthology is in your best form, and doesn't suggest any weakening of the powers of thought and the expression of thought, with which God has endowed you so amply.

106. *Daniel Lambert.*

September 5th, 1937.

To The Rev. S. R. P. Moulsdale.†

My dear Moulsdale,

.   .   .   .

We had a pleasant journey, breaking it at Stamford, where we were comfortably lodged in the George, and spent some hours in viewing that exceptionally interesting town. *Inter alia* we saw the clothes of Daniel Lambert, whose epitaph declares that he " was possessed of an exalted and convivial mind, and in personal Greatness had no competitor." The truth of the last statement will not be contested when it is remembered that he weighed 52 stone and 11 pounds. When

---

* A daughter of Dr Inge.   † Rector of Hintlesham.

he was " delivered from the burden of the flesh " there can be no
doubt as to the magnitude of the enfranchisement!

With kind regards to Mrs Frazer,
I am,
Sincerely yours,
Herbert Dunelm.

107. Divorce.

November 22nd, 1937.

To A. P.* Herbert, Esq., M.P.

My dear Mr Herbert,

I returned home from London this afternoon, and find awaiting
me your extremely interesting book with an inscription on the title
page which could not but please me in no common degree.   And,
then, when I read your pleasant reference to my speech in the House of
Lords, I was at once abashed and exalted, the first by my knowledge of
the inadequacy of the performance you could so generously approve,
the last because, after all, you should think it worth while thus to
express yourself was something on which I might reasonably congratulate myself.   In effect, you are very kind, and I am very much
your debtor.

The Church Assembly did not distinguish itself in its discussion of
the re-marriage of divorced persons : and, had I been present, I should
certainly have felt obliged to deal faithfully with Hugh Cecil.   His
speech was a notable example of Cecilian ὕβρις, and deserved the
castigation which it would, (if my word had honestly expressed my
thought) have received.   But I was out of London, and the foolish
debate was the shorter by one speech.

I was in Oxford for the week-end, Nov. 7–8, and delighted to hear
that your popularity had so waxed in the University that your seat
was thought to be safe.

Believe me,
Very Sincerely yours,
Herbert Dunelm.

* Now Sir Alan.

108. *Indiscipline in the C. of E.*

Auckland Castle,
December 1st, 1937.

*To The Archbishop of Dublin.**

My dear Archbishop,
It really is very good of you to be at the pains of explaining the position which you adopted in conference with the Easterns, and which I must frankly admit I had not fairly understood. It is a real satisfaction to me to be assured that, apart from the brief reference to the Articles " being openly ignored in the discussions of re-union with the Eastern Churches "—a reference which you show to be ill-founded— you find yourself in substantial agreement with what I have written.

The situation in the Church of England is to my thinking deeply disquieting. We are moving like a rudderless vessel over a rock-haunted ocean. Discipline there is really none, for the fatuous notion (which the most part of the Bishops adopted after the defeat of the effort at Prayer Book revision) that the Church could be governed by consent on the basis of the rejected Book, has been proved, as I said it could not but be proved, quite baseless.

There is no order left: no law which the Bishops will enforce: no discipline which the clergy will accept. We stumble along protected by the obsession of the public mind with secular anxieties. *Quo tendimus?* God only knows, but I fear, to no good.

We pay a high price for being " governed " by two ambitious and ubiquitous orators, who talk so much that they have no time to think. The Centre—thanks to B.B.C.—has completely obliterated the Circumference.

There's a grumble for you.

However, I am,
most sincerely yours,
Herbert Dunelm.

* The Most Rev. J. A. F. Gregg; now Abp of Armagh.

109. *On the revival of the Church Congress.*

January 1st, 1938.

*To The General Secretary of the Church Congress.**

The Bishop of Durham was one of those who regretted the revival of the Church Congress, which, in his belief, serves no useful purpose, and adds to the mountainous mass of superfluous verbiage under which the Church of England is nearly stifled.   He regrets, therefore, to be unable to accept the Bishop of Bristol's very kind invitation that he should be a Vice-President.

110.   *Servers.*

Auckland Castle,
May 24th, 1938.

To The Dean of Durham.†

My dear Dean,

Very well, but I think that I will not talk to the Servers.   I am very busy to begin with, and on the whole I think that I dislike Servers increasingly.   I try to think kindly about them, in the spirit of the old woman of Naples who was good to the rats because, as she said, " they also are God's creatures ".   But I won't talk to them.

I have been studying " The Betting Book ",‡ and observe with humiliation that my name appears with scandalous frequency at one time, but I was young then, and, though Youth did not then spell itself with a capital Y, it had its privileges.

Affectionately yours,
Herbert Dunelm.

* Bristol, 1938.
† The Very Rev. C. A. Alington.
‡ The All Souls Betting Book.

111.   *The gift of an electric blanket.*

Auckland Castle,
June 4th, 1938.

To Canon and Mrs E. F. Braley.

My dear, surprising and most generous Friends,

    You have transformed your Bishop and Beneficiary into the similitude of another <u>Montezuma</u> destined to repose on a bed of Fire, save only that in your version the fire is that of the kindest charity and in his by the lurid flames of the persecutor.

Indeed it was kind of you to send me the comfortable sheet. It warmed my spirit not less effectively than its corporal sheath when I sampled it last night.

Thank you.

Ever affectionately yours,
Herbert Dunelm.

112.   *His resignation from Durham.*

October 31st, 1938.

To The Earl of Scarbrough.

My dearest Lord,

    It was indeed, kind of you to write. It has seemed to me my duty to lay down my office now that I have reached the age of seventy-five : but I am distressed at having to sever the many links which hold me to the North of England.

Among the memories which I shall treasure, none will be more precious than that of my friendship with you; grounded as it has been on affection and respect, in the union of which the true cement of friendship must ever be found. I hate going away, and losing all my rights in this diocese. And, though I have been able to make so little use of it, I don't like losing my seat in the House of Lords, where I have ever been received with so much generosity.

But " Time and tide wait for no man " and I have long felt that the Church of England has suffered from the excessive age of Archbishops

and Bishops.   Therefore, I desired by my own example to make plain
my belief, that the latest *terminus ad quem* for episcopal office is 75.

Thank you so much for all you have been, and for all that you have
done for me, all these many years past.

May God bless you!

Always affectionately your Friend,

Herbert Dunelm.

113.   *Pastor Niemöller.*

April 14th, 1939.

To Pastor Hildebrandt.

My dear Pastor Hildebrandt,

I have to thank you for sending me your little book on *Pastor
Niemöller and his Creed* which I have read with deep interest.   I hope
that it will have a very wide circulation.   The whole Christian church
is profoundly indebted to Pastor Niemöller for his valourous stand
for truth and righteousness.   You will know the lines in *Paradise Lost*
where Milton describes the triumph of Abdiel.

faithful found
Among the faithless, faithful only he :
Among innumerable false, unmoved,
Unshaken, unseduced, unterrified,
His loyalty he kept.

Indeed, I could not imagine a juster verdict on Niemöller than that
which the Lord pronounces on Abdiel :

" Servant of God, well done :
Well hast thou fought
The better fight, who single hast maintained
Against revolted multitudes the cause
Of truth, in word mightier than they in arms :
And for the testimony of truth hast borne
Universal reproach, far worse to bear
Than violence : for this was all thy care
To stand approved in sight of God, though worlds
Judged thee perverse."

If you are writing to him, I should be grateful if you would carry to him the homage of my admiration, and assure him of my conviction that, whatever may happen to him, he will finally be vindicated. " They that trust in the Lord, shall not be put to shame."

Believe me, Yours sincerely and obliged,

H. Hensley Henson,

Bishop.

114. On Autobiography.

May 7th, 1939.

To The Rev. Preb. J. F. Clayton.＊

My dear Jack,

Your unceasing activity is only paralleled by that of the spiritual potentate who shall be nameless, who described his normal habit as " going to and fro on the earth and walking up and down on it." Your friends find comfort in the natural inference that only a robust constitution could endure such never-ceasing activity.

.   .   .   .

Last week I succeeded in dining at both my clubs—" The Club " and Grillions. Both were uncommonly interesting. At the Club the Prime Minister turned up and asked me to sit beside him. We had a capital talk. I was amazed at his alertness and vigour. There seemed nothing to indicate the unceasing strain under which he has been living for many months. On the whole I took the impression that the outlook was not quite so desperate, though I cannot see how a war can finally be avoided. It may perhaps be postponed, and, of course postponement gives time for the disclosure of whatever peaceful factors there are in the totalitarian states and there is always the chance that one or other of the gangsters may be " bumped off".

I am seriously considering the production of some kind of autobiography. No less than eight publishers have been at me on the subject, and I have repulsed them all, but time is passing. I am just 75 years and 6 months old, and that means that I may not indulge the senile weakness of procrastination.

Old Lord Midleton sate beside me at Grillions last Wednesday, and

＊ Hensley Henson's Domestic Chaplain, 1921–26.

held forth to me on the necessity under which he had found himself of producing his last volume. He simply had to turn out a certain number of pages every day. My doubt is as to the value of such a book as I could produce. In the case of a man like Lord Midleton, who has been in high political office for many years, there can be no lack of interest, personal and public, in his reminiscences; but in the case of an obscure person whose activities have been in the narrow and shadowed spheres in which parsons live and work, what interest could his record have for anybody? However I think it probable that I shall make the attempt, and see what comes of it.

My book on the "Church of England", which the Cambridge Press is publishing, will please nobody and offend many, but it is quite an honest book, nonetheless. Sir Humphrey Milford would jump at the Autobiography, and I think if it ever is written that he must have it. Of course, if war does come, there will be an end of writing, publishing, and reading books.

Always affectionately yours,

H. Hensley Henson,

Bishop.

115.   "Quiet Days."

June 6th, 1939.

To The Rev. Canon B. K. Cunningham.★

My dear Canon,

It is, indeed, kind of you to invite me to address your students, and if I felt myself at all qualified for the very special ministry of "taking a Quiet Day" with theological students, or indeed, with anybody, I would gladly accept your invitation if a convenient time were available.

But "the quest is not for me", and I have never in the course of my fairly long ministry attempted it. You will, I know, believe that it would give me very particular pleasure to accede to any request of yours which lay within the pinched ambit of my powers, but "Retreats", and "Quiet Days" lie outside it.

I was in Cambridge on May 21st and had hoped to look in on you, but my time was short, the claimants on it were many, and I was

★ Principal of Westcott House, Cambridge.

pledged to preach in Magdalene College Chapel to the youth there: and so my purpose failed.

The three things that I most regret in my episcopate are:

1. The Seat in the Lords.
2. Travelling First Class.
3. Ability to buy Books.

Could you want more convincing evidences of a " carnal mind ", and incidentally, of my incompetence for " Quiet Days "?

Affectionately yours,
H. Hensley Henson,
Bishop.

116.   On an appointment to a Professorship.

June 22nd, 1939.

To The Rev. Canon O. C. Quick.

My dear Oliver,

The announcement which I have been expecting ever since the Chair * at Oxford became vacant, has now been made, and I am free to send you my cordial congratulations. If Durham must lose you, I could not but rejoice that Oxford should have you. Your personal influence has been so great and salutary that its withdrawal is a sad impoverishment of that little University, which, in the teeth of far greater difficulties than are generally understood, is trying to keep alight the Candle of sound learning : but there also the saying holds, that " the Light shineth in darkness, and the darkness apprehendeth it not ".

May you have health and strength to illumine Oxford from your new Chair! I am glad that your departure from Durham did not precede my own. I shall always count it among the good memories of my episcopate, that it brought me the privilege of coming into personal contact with you.

I beg you to carry to Mrs Quick my cordial congratulations. You will all be badly missed in Durham.

Affectionately yours,
H. Hensley Henson,
Bishop.

* The Regius Professorship of Divinity.

117.   A published Interview.

June 23rd, 1939.

To The Dean of Ely.★

My dear Dean,

By all means make any use you will of the notes of my sermon. There are no expenses attendant on my very pleasant visit to your wonderful Cathedral. I enjoyed my visit, and the great Service, and the opportunity of making your acquaintance.

This morning the publishers sent me an early copy of his latest work by Rom Landau, and I am penitently reflecting on his description of myself, based on an interview, which is sufficiently humiliating.

"Altogether there was something of a Rococo sage about him."

I don't know what that means, but I don't like the look of it; nor am I wholly reassured by being told that "my aquiline features together with the self-assured precision of my bearing reminded one of descriptions of Voltaire."

I have always understood that Voltaire was amazingly like an ugly ape!

Believe me,
Ever sincerely yours,
H. Hensley Henson,
Bishop.

118.   Domestic Troubles.

Hyntle Place, Hintlesham, Ipswich,
July 9th, 1939.

To The Rev. Canon E. F. Braley.

My dear Evelyn,

It is, indeed, a very pleasant prospect for us in September. We shall look forward to having Isabel and yourself at the Rectory, and I shall count on getting some good talk with you. *Entre nous*, I am

★ The Very Rev. L. E. Blackburne.

rather starved for lack of good talk; and I have many things on hand which would be the better for threshing out in close talking.

Moreover we need the comfort of your company; for we are immersed in a domestic tragedy. It is the too familiar story of getting servants! We had prematurely congratulated ourselves on having secured two good girls, when suddenly, as a bolt from the blue, both announced their desire to disappear, the one to get married, and the other because she could not face the world (i.e. remain in her place) without the comradeship of her matrimonially minded friend! So there it is. We hope for the best, and do what we can. But servants are hard to find in the country, and hard to keep! To ease the situation, the gardener's wife announces the approaching advent of an infant! In view of the Population Question, I cannot decently object, but it is the fact that the gardener was appointed because he had a domestically serviceable wife, and no family! So you will understand that, as I said, we stand in need of consolation.

I have been invited to become the Warburton Lecturer, and I have (like an ass) accepted the invitation. The holy Bishop who founded the Lecture prescribed that the Lecturer should prove the truth of Christianity from the fulfilment of prophecies, especially those relating to the Apostasy of the Papacy! Happily the Lincoln's Inn Benchers have accepted a latitudinarian exegesis which leaves the Lecturer free to " talk large " on any subject of his choice. So I must do what I can. There are six Lectures, one in each legal term for two years. I must make a start on November 26th.

I have just learned that Havelock Ellis, who came to live in Hintlesham last year, died last night. He was a very old man, and enjoyed a considerable reputation as one of our " psycho-analytical " moralists who are busily at work on their ruinous enterprize of disintegrating morality. I called on the old man with the Rector. He was civil enough, but never returned my call.

The new Bishop of London is reported to have damaged his knee while visiting Fulham, and is recovering from an operation on the damaged knee. Meanwhile his predecessor is, like Charles II, " an unconscionable time in dying ". Indeed, I shan't feel certain that he has really resigned until his successor is enthroned! Talking of Bishops, I discovered in the new volume of the Camden Society's publications—The Letters of Arnulf of Lisieux—an improvement of the well-known cliché about the non-salvability of Archdeacons. Giraldus

Cambrensis, who was himself an Archdeacon " turned the medieval doubt on to the Bishop "—

"*Non dicimus episcopos non salvari, dicimus autem difficilius ipsos his diebus quam alios salvari.*"

I think few modern bishops would be disposed to dispute this opinion.

I am reading the proofs of my book on the Church of England, which will appear, I imagine, in the autumn, always assuming that Herr Hitler doesn't interpose his veto. Last night we had a " Black-out ", and today there are many aeroplanes flying over us. But we go on as if nothing will happen.

Give my love to Isabel and Jane, and be sure that I am ever

Affect^ly yrs,

H. Hensley Henson,

Bishop.

119. *Cancelling orders for periodicals.*

July 27th, 1939.

To Hugh Rees, Ltd,
  47 Pall Mall, S.W.1.

Dear Sir,

I beg to enclose cheque in payment of my account.   Also, I wish to cancel my order for the following publications :

1. *The Round Table.*
2. *The Church Quarterly.*
3. *The Slavonic Review.*
4. *The Journal of Theological Studies.*
5. *The Hibbert Journal.*

I have no room on my book-shelves wherein to place them.

I have no time to devote to reading them.

I have no money to pay for them.

I have no superfluous eyesight to expend on them.

For all these reasons I conclude that it is no longer worth my while to buy them !

Sincerely yours,

H. Hensley Henson,

Bishop.

120.   *Thanks for two pamphlets.*

September 19th, 1939.

To Dr St John Ervine.

My dear Dr St John Ervine,

I have to thank you for sending me your two excellent compositions, of which the scale and aspect are greatly inadequate to the intrinsic value. I have read them both with interest and admiration. You indeed, have your power of packing a great argument into a small space. I appreciate your friendly quotation from my Gifford Lectures.

"*Inter arma silent leges.*" Cicero's dictum is receiving terrible illustration now. And we must expand our notion of "*leges*" far beyond the lawyer's frigid limits. Morality and Religion with their demands and sanctions are hustled into oblivion when civilized peoples embark on mechanized war!

"The wrath of man worketh not the righteousness of God" is the Apostle's equivalent of the Ciceronian dogma. Yet I cannot read that text in the light of the shallow and selfish understanding of our Pacifists. I think the Prophetess with her "Curse ye Meroz" came nearer the truth.

. . . .

I apologise for this intolerable and aimless maundering, and beg to subscribe myself,

Yours sincerely and obliged,
H. Hensley Henson,
Bishop.

121.   *Julius Streicher.*

Hyntle Place,
September 19th, 1939.

To P. C. Tallents, Esq., C.S.I.,
  Great Bealings, Suffolk.

My dear Tallents,

Thank you so much for sending me your copy of the *Times,* which I do not return because I understood that you did not wish to have it back.

The news this morning is very evil. Indeed, the only ray of light which relieves it is the report (in Copenhagen) from Berlin that the infamous Jew-baiter, Julius Streicher, has been arrested by the secret police on Göring's instructions! If there lingered any justice or humour in this miserable world, he would be forthwith hustled into a concentration camp, and, after a sufficient detention therein to enable him to sample and savour its distinctive arrangements, should there be solemnly stifled by the back numbers of his obscene (and semi-official) paper *The Stürmer*, in the presence of a concourse of Hitler Youth, and to the accompaniment of a chanting of the 109th Psalm by a Chorus of Rabbis assisted by the choristers of Niemöller's Church! The rest of us might unite in Milton's lines in *Samson Agonistes*—

> Oh, how comely it is, and how reviving
> To the spirits of just men long oppressed,
> When God into the hands of their deliverer
> Puts invincible might
> To quell the mighty of the earth, the oppressor,
> The brute and boisterous force of violent men.

. . . .

Ever yours,
H. Hensley Henson,
Bishop.

122.   To a "Little Airman".

November 2nd, 1939.

To Air Gunner T. H. Thompson.

My dear "Little Airman",
(However old and distinguished you become, I shall always take leave to address you thus.)   I was really pleased to have your letter, and to learn from it that, though, indeed, you have been "in many and great dangers," you are still safe.   It would distress me if you did not keep in touch with me; and I hope that you will manage to come and see me.   I like the photographs.   They bring you back to my mind very vividly.

You must not, in your most just repugnance to the abominable cruelty and ravage of the war, deprive yourself of the comfort and strength implicit in the knowledge—I should not hesitate to say the certitude—that you are fighting in the cause of Justice, i.e. the Cause of God.

The whole course of human life, as well on the little arena of the individual's record, as on the great scenes of History, is wrapped in mystery. You remember the verse in the Psalms; it often comes to my mind in these dark days: " Clouds and darkness are round about Him; righteousness and judgement are the habitation of His seat."

It must be dreadful for the thoughtful young Germans, who are capable of judging the quality of Nazi government—the perfidy and violence of German policy, the brutalities of the concentration camps, the abominable oppression of the Jews, and other " non-Aryans ", the infamous methods of German warfare—I say, it must strike a chill into a thoughtful young man's mind, when he thinks that he is fighting for all that. The English soldier is in a happier case. He knows that he is out against the most degrading tyranny that ever cursed mankind.

You should keep ever in mind the cause for which you are serving, and for which you are prepared to give your life. There is a sentence in the Bible which is worth thinking over. It is said of Moses in the court of Pharaoh, when he chose " rather to be evil entreated with the people of God, than to enjoy the pleasures of sin for a season ", that " he endured as seeing Him who is invisible " (see Hebrews XI, 24–27). There is a wonderful power in a great ideal: and surely the British soldier, who can see his stern duty in the light of his religion, has the greatest Ideal possible in his warfare.

My dear " little Airman," it has fallen to your generation to have to face a trial of extreme severity, bringing great temptations, calling to terrible risks, and even requiring the heaviest sacrifices. But the " glory is worth it, for you are called to stand in the front of the great fight against wickedness, in which Jesus Christ is the Captain, and to which in your Baptism you were pledged ".

May God be with you in all your ventures, and keep you from sin and danger!

Write to me when you can find time, and are in the mood to write. Never doubt that you are in my thoughts, and that in my prayers I remember you.

Always affectionately your friend,
H. Hensley Henson,
Bishop.

I

123. THE PROBLEM OF THE FUTURE LIFE.

November 5th, 1939.

*To The Rev. C. J. Shebbeare.**

My dear Shebbeare,

 It was indeed good of you to send me your book, *The Problem of the Future Life*, which I have read with much interest, and with a genuine admiration for the lucidity of your language and the fresh vigour of your thought. It needs no saying that I am quite incapable of offering any criticism of your philosophy which could do more than disclose my own incapacity for philosophical discussion.

 I cannot follow you in your speculations. Indeed, there is more Mohammedanism than Christianity in your picture of Heaven. Will the Master of the Wear Valley Beagles have the endless felicity of meeting again, not merely his well-loved hounds, but also the hares which they, and he, delighted to hunt? I am content to remain an Agnostic.

 With kind remembrances to Mrs Shebbeare and your wonderful boys.

I am,

Always sincerely and obliged,

H. Hensley Henson,

Bishop.

124. THE CHURCH OF ENGLAND ; *Evacuees*

December 14th, 1939.

To The Archbishop of Canterbury.†

My dear Archbishop,

 It was extraordinarily kind of you to be at the pains of writing so frankly and fully about my poor book.‡ I feel really distressed

---

 * Rector of Stanhope.   † The Most Rev. C. G. Lang.
 ‡ *The Church of England.*

and ashamed that it should have inflicted work and worry on you at a time when you must needs be greatly burdened.

It needs no saying that I shall consider most carefully what you have written, and, in the unlikely event of a second edition being required, I shall take the opportunity of adding some observations which may perhaps elucidate my meaning, and mitigate the " pessimism " which you deprecate. My original plan included much which is, perhaps, needed to complete my design, but which could not be contained within the limits allotted to me. But I comforted myself with the reflection, that the prophets who " speak good " are always likely to be numerous, whereas Micaiah, the Son of Imlah will always be a churlish rogue, whose message can hardly atone for its offensiveness by being true. Indeed, I think that substantially my *Speculum Ecclesiæ Anglicanæ* gives a faithful picture of an Effete Establishment.

I was surprized that the Cambridge Press decided to publish the book at the present time, when it is hardly to be supposed that it can find readers : and, though I do not imagine that the situation, so far as publishing serious books is concerned, will improve, I should, perhaps, have been better pleased if the book had been held back. There is something almost indecent in seeking to divert attention from the awful concern of the War. But when the War began, the book was already completed, and the proofs revised : and the Press decided to let it go out.

Here we are confronted by the problem of Evacuates (not, I pray you, Evacuees, which must properly mean persons who have taken excessively some opening medicine, but after the well-established English custom, evacuates). We have many similar Anglicisings of Latin e.g. graduate, literate, oblate. In this parish we are fortunate in having had the girls from Barnardo's Cottage Homes, who are at least clean and controlled, but some of the neighbouring parishes complain bitterly, that the evacuated children are dirty, disorderly, verminous, and, in some cases, disgustingly diseased, and that the mothers are entirely worthy of their offspring.

Is this affliction to go on for years?

What is to be done for the unfortunate householders, who have been deserted by their servants? Here we have a —— " Matron " planted on us—an ardent sectary who has been in China, and reads the *Christian* ! It destroys our privacy, and puts a bridle on our complaining tongue. How long, O Lord? Moreover, grumbling has been stripped of its comforting grace : for who can decently grumble about anything when one thinks of Finland and Poland, to say nothing of the happenings at sea?

Let me wish you strength and comfort in the New Year. " They that sow in tears shall reap in joy."

Always, my dear Archbishop,
Affectionately yours,
H. Hensley Henson,
Bishop.

125. Finland.

Hyntle Place,
February 17th, 1940.

To The Bishop of Växjö, * *Sweden.*

My dear Bishop,

It gave me much pleasure to receive your letter, and to have its assurance that you and your wife are well. I have now been more than a year in retirement, but I cannot say that I have reconciled myself to my new situation. I miss my friends badly, and the continuing interest of episcopal duty, and the familiar places which had become endeared to me by many personal memories.

I am not idle; for I have rather rashly undertaken to deliver a course of Warburton Lectures in Lincoln's Inn. They are 6 in number, and the first is due (unless Herr Hitler interposes his veto) on March 17th. Then I have promised to write a small volume for the Home University Library on *The English Bible*, and to preach in some of the great pulpits. It is amazingly difficult to concentrate one's mind on anything which is not connected with the war; and that is a matter, in equal measures, painful, melancholy, and practically futile. To you in Sweden the menace to liberty must needs be felt as something near and probable. The spectacle of courage and fortitude which Finland presents goes far to restore one's faith in human nature, which Hitlerite Germany has so rudely shaken. I read with profound regret, though not with surprize, that Sweden has decided to give no direct help to the Finns, and even to refuse passage through her territory to the forces which the Allies might be able to send to them.

* The Right Rev. Yngve Brilioth.

It will be an appalling tragedy if those heroic people are crushed by the brute force of Russia.   I sometimes wonder whether the smaller neutral powers would not be wiser in their interest to ally themselves with France and Great Britain against the horrible tyranny of Hitler and Stalin.   Sometimes I let my mind travel back to my earlier manhood when first I began to observe and reflect upon the movement of the world.   It is difficult to recover the sense of security in the great assumptions of faith and life which then was general.   Now the flood-gates are wide open, and we are being swept helplessly on a tide of moral and spiritual anarchy, which we can neither arrest nor under-stand.   Whither?

Remember me most kindly to your wife.   May God be with you, and give you strength and joy in service!

Affectionately your friend,

H. Hensley Henson,

Bishop.

126.   *After a visit.*

May 20th, 1940.

To The Dowager Countess of Limerick.

My dear Lady Limerick,

It was a real pleasure to see you on Saturday, and to gain the moral stimulus of your unconquerable courage and cheerfulness in spite of so much to daunt and discourage in the setting of life, as well personal as public.   I could not but recall those familiar lines in which Milton reflects on his blindness, and which may well be adopted by all who, like yourself, dear Lady are withdrawn by bodily weakness from the battlefield of life, and who, in their absence, yet tell on the course of the battle as much as, or more than, the most valourous of the combatants:

God doth not need
Either man's work, or his own gifts; who best
Bear his mild yoke, they serve him best; his state
Is kingly: thousands at his bidding speed,
And post o'er land and ocean without rest;
They also serve, who only stand and wait.

I take leave to send you this little tractate. It grew out of the desire of an enterprising publisher that I would expand into a pamphlet, a letter which had appeared in the *Times* over my signature on January 6th.

We got home without any accident about 9 p.m. and yesterday I preached in Gorleston to the Mayor of Yarmouth and his " tail " of Aldermen, counsellors, and the " Mobile ".

May God keep you, and make you long the joy and envy of your friends, and among them of

Yours affectionately,
H. Hensley Henson,
Bishop.

127. *Advice to a lady on evacuating her daughter to Canada during the war.*

Hyntle Place,
July 5th, 1940.

To Mrs E. F. Braley.

My dear Isabel,

I must not delay answering you on the subject of the Great Jane. If I had to make the decision, I think the determining point would be whether Jane's future was to be ordered on this side of the Atlantic or on the other.

At her age, it would be rather a formidable risk of lasting linguistic perversion that she would be exposed to if she lived in Canada or U.S.A. for two or three years. And that would be an unfortunate handicap in Great Britain; no violence done to the English language could shock a Transatlantick. Having generally accustomed their noses to function as throats, and attuned their ears to the consequences, they are case-hardened; but we have not yet reached that point here. Then I don't think the risk of residence in this beleaguered island is so great as to justify separating the young lady from her parents. Probably, the perils by sea are greater than perils by land.

If Evelyn came to do duty for the Rector, I should imagine that the general restriction on travelling in these parts would not apply; but this is a mere surmise.

Anyway, if you were hindered from coming by Hitler, then I have to add another item to my crowded indictment against him.

The scene in the House of Commons when the P.M. wept, and the members "let themselves go" in sympathetic clamour, must have been impressive. It had a precedent in the delirious approval which Neville Chamberlain evoked when he read out Hitler's hypocritical promise on his return from Munich. But I am glad that most of the French fleet is under our lock and key.

With love to Evelyn and the aforesaid Jane, and of course to you,

Ever yours,

H. Hensley Henson,

Bishop.

128.   A James I Church.

Hyntle Place,
July 6th, 1940.

*To The Rev. C. K. Pattinson.**

* Hensley Henson's Domestic Chaplain, 1929–36.

My dearest Charlie,

. . . A few weeks ago I preached in Kedington, which has one of the most fascinating & interesting parish churches in the County, or indeed, in England. The Church retains the fittings and arrangements of James I's reign, though the building runs back to the Roman times, and every style of medieval architecture is illustrated. The pews date from the XVth century, and the Jacobean pulpit, a noble " three decker " is equipped with its hour glass. This is the second occasion of my occupying a genuine " three decker " (the other was at Whitby), and I am in the mood to start a Society for the Restoration of Three-deckers in the Established Church. Probably one of the contributory causes of the decay of Anglican preaching and the consequent decline of Anglican influence has been the almost universal abolition of the " Three decker " by the Tractarians, and their descendants the Anglo-Catholics. The three-decker presents the preacher in the exalted dignity which his function and office demand; gives the preacher a strategic position for commanding the attention of his audience, and provides an ample and convenient desk on which to place his sermon.

I should like also to restore the use of the hour-glass but it may be thought that the softness and imbecility of this crazy age would not endure that rational and convenient instrument!

.   .   .   .

May God have you both in his keeping!

Always aff^{ly} your Friend,
H. Hensley Henson,
Bp.

129.   The Surtees Society.

July 15th, 1940.

To H. Lawrence Gradon, Esq.

Dear Mr Gradon,

Your note of reminder was mislaid, or the enclosed subscription would have been sent before. I understand from Professor Hamilton Thompson that the Society paid me the high (and wholly undeserved) compliment of electing me to be its President in succession to the late Dean of Gloucester. I value the link with Durham, and with the Society to whose varied and valuable publications I have owed much, and I regret that my power to serve it must needs be so small.

I trust that the Society will not scruple to suggest my resignation, whenever a more suitable President may be available.

"*Inter arma silent leges*" said Cicero. Today we may extend the meaning of "*leges*" until it includes all the grave and gracious interests which unite in genuine culture, and, among them, such studies as those which the Surtees Society embodies, illustrates, and assists. Indeed, from every point of view "the times are evil."

Here we live in a context of daily and nightly air-raids: but they don't do much harm, and, so far as the morale of the people is concerned, they cause more anger than alarm.

With all good wishes,
I am, Sincerely yours,
H. Hensley Henson,
Bishop.

130. BISHOP CREWE.

July 28th, 1940.

To The Rev. Canon C. E. Whiting.★

My dear Dr Whiting,

I have just finished reading your Life of Bishop Crewe, and the process has given me so much enjoyment and information that I feel bound to send you a few lines of appreciation and gratitude. It humbles and exasperates me to realize that, while I sate in Crewe's throne and, like him, resided in Auckland Castle, I never realized that you were the storehouse of such a treasure of local knowledge, and would not have refused your Diocesan access to it. Indeed I should have been, if not a better Bishop of Durham, yet certainly a much more entertaining host to my visitors at Auckland, if I had known what you have told about the Man and the Diocese !

On p. 58 you repeat the opinion, which (though so often repeated as to have become almost axiomatic viz., that the great chapel at Auckland was a new building erected by Bishop Cosin) was conclusively shown to be erroneous by the antiquary Hodgson. In his charming account of Auckland Castle, Bishop Moule refers to Bishop Lightfoot's account of Raine's investigations, which were subsequently confirmed by Hodgson : and I never hesitated to accept it. The Chapel is dated " about 1190 or a little later "—" The present chapel is Cosin's transformation of Pudsey's Hall " (*v.* Moule, p. 59).

One general criticism I will allow myself. You are, I must needs think, unfair to Bishop Burnet. He was a man of many and exasperating faults, and he brought against himself the bitterest resentments, but he was cast in a large mould, physical, mental, moral. No serious student of the XVIIth century would place Crewe and Burnet in the same rank of greatness. After finishing your book I turned to Firth's careful and discriminating " Introduction " to Miss Foxcroft's *Life of Bishop Burnet*. It is in my judgement the fairest estimate of Burnet's

★ Vicar of Hickleton, Doncaster; formerly Professor of History, Durham University.

character and certainly not the least authoritative. Airy's article on him in the *D.N.B.* is also very sound.

Forgive me these impertinent observations, and

Believe that I am,

Sincerely and gratefully

H. Hensley Henson,

Bishop.

P.S.

· · · · · · · · · · · ·

The too-familiar *mélange* of fiction, fraud and fury which Hitler offered in Berlin has been serviceable in evoking 4 speeches which constitute in combination a most impressive statement of the case for Britain. The Prime Minister spoke with magnificent strength, dignity, and eloquence for the English people. President Roosevelt uttered with impressive decision the judgement of non-belligerents. General Smuts spoke, with characteristic distinction of thought and phrase, for the British Empire. And now Lord Halifax has given a noble expression to the Christian conscience. It is not the first time in History that God elects to speak through the Layman rather than through His ordained servants. The fumbling and calculated platitudes of Pontiffs and Preachers count for little before the simplicity of a layman's faith. Is it thus that the Divine Paradox is justified, " Out of the mouth of babes and sucklings, Thou hast perfected praise"?

But I meander, or rather maunder, intolerably. I only started this grossly swollen *post scriptum* in order to apologise for my confusions and corrections. I wish there had been a picture of Auckland Castle included in the illustrations. It played a greater part in Crewe's tenure of the See than Durham Castle, and makes a fair picture.

H. H. H.

131. *Appointment to the Canonry at Westminster.*

Hyntle Place,

September 24th, 1940.

To The Bishop on the Niger.

My dear Bishop,

Your letter of August 11th reached me a few days ago, and interested me greatly. It was a real relief to have my thoughts carried

Hyntle Place,
Hintlesham,
Ipswich.

My dear Isabel.

With the greatest
pleasure in the world. I
stand sponsor for Jane.
Your decision to send her
to Cheltenham seems to me
very wise, & I doubt not
that the young lady will be
much advantaged by her
membership of so excellent
a school.

Always affectionately.

H— Hensley Henson
Bishop

Wm Braley

A LETTER WRITTEN IN AUGUST 1940.

[Facing p. 122

away from the besieging anxieties of the War (which seems now to have reached a critical phase), and settled on calmer scenes where the Church of Christ is still carrying on its blessed task, and still providing unmistakable evidences of its Divine commission for the world's redemption. I read your article " 20 Years of an African Diocese " with much pleasure. It presents a very encouraging picture of patient effort and continuous progress.

I can well believe that you are anxious about the consequences to the quality and fortunes of African Christianity if once it were definitely severed from its connexion with the parent Christianity of Europe, and left to its own direction. The tide of nationalism is running strongly throughout the world. Europe and Asia are now bleeding and wasted by the wars which owe their origin to nothing else, and I cannot doubt that Africa will not escape the general fortune. Indeed, Egypt already exhibits a notable outbreak of nationalistic sentiment. A few days ago I read in the newspapers that the Japanese Church had got rid of its English and American Bishops in deference to the fanatical nationalism of Japan. The results are not likely to be wholly favourable to religion or to morals. And in some ways the risks attaching to the same experiment in Africa are even greater— Christianity in Christendom itself is in a bad array. Indeed this fearful War is *au fond* a civil war fought out on the fundamental principles on which Christendom, in so far as it is an effective unity at all, must needs stand. And that is why the strain of the conflict is so terrible, and the outlook so solemn. This War—a " War of Ideologies " as secular politicians call it, a Crusade or Holy War as Christians prefer to say—must be fought out to the bitter end. There can be no compromise or patched up peace. . . . What Abraham Lincoln saw so plainly when he cast his weight into the scale of war on the matter of American slavery is not less luminously true now in the conflict with Hitlerism. Just as the American Republic could not be permanently based on a double basis, part free, part slave-holding, but must be wholly one or wholly the other, so the civilized modern world must be either based on Christian morality or on Hitlerite principles, it cannot be a combination of the two. " Ye cannot serve God and Mammon."

You may perhaps have heard that I have consented to resume my old place as Canon of Westminster in spite of my age (77 on Nov. 8th). The Prime Minister pressed the proposal on public grounds. It would be a piece of war work!! On that view I could not refuse, but, now that I have crossed the Rubicon, I am over-whelmed with a disabling consciousness of decrepitude. In the way of apparent and acknowledged Duty one cannot look back, but try "to do out the duty", trusting that He Who appoints the burden will not refuse the strength to carry it. Meanwhile, London is being bombed night and day. There is much destruction of life and property, but from the King and Queen downwards there is no sign of trepidation or cowardice. Rather, purpose is strengthened and courage stimulated by the fury of a cruel and ruthless Enemy. Write to me when you are in the mood and have nothing better to do.

Always affectly your Friend,
H. Hensley Henson,
Bishop.

132.   A mistake in names.

October 3rd, 1940.

To The Rev. Dr J. O. Hannay, Litt.D.

My dear Canon Hannay,
That wonderful institution for harnessing human vanity to the advantage of human greed—Durrant's Press Cuttings—appears to have roped us both into the drawing of his Juggernaut car! Anyway, he sometimes confuses one victim with another: and, clearly, he has done so when he sent your parcel to me. . . .

I hope we may sometimes meet. George A. Birmingham has given me so much pleasure in recent years, that I must needs value his acquaintance.

Ever sincerely yours,
H. Hensley Henson,
Bishop.

133. *Canon Storr.*

October 27th, 1940.

To The Dean of Westminster.*

My dear Dean,

We are truly living in a " cloudy and dark day " at our beloved Abbey. The menace to the fabrick is a continuing night-mare of anxiety; and now comes the lamentable impoverishment of the College by the death of Vernon Storr. He was, of all the Canons, the only one whom I have long known, and certainly the only one respecting whom I have the right to say that I both loved and honoured him. His miserable health was a kind of Stylites-pillar from which his intellectual distinction, his tireless industry, and his charming personality were raised into a prominence which none could miss. He came to wield a wide and salutary influence in the Church of England, and his attempt to effect a working harmony between Evangelicals and Modernists was far more successful than either faction imagined to be possible.

I have written to Mrs Storr the sincerest letter of condolence I have ever composed. It is a hard blow for the poor lady, and she has had much to bear. In these darkest hours what mockery words, however well chosen and sincere must needs be! " The heart knoweth its own bitterness."

Your decanate will be memorable for the badness of the time in which it was ordained to pass. And now the removal of your most intimate colleague will be no slight addition to the burden which you must carry. But you have the great consolation—how great only those know who must review the mingled record of a life time—that these specially emphasized difficulties of your office are in no degree due to faults and failures of your own.—You will be carried through this evil time, and in due course be able to say with the Psalmist— " With the help of my God, I have leaped over the wall ".

And I think it may be granted to you that your contemporaries should say of you what was said of another Dean of Westminster who also in his day endured much buffeting of ill fortune—" He was

* The Right Rev. P. F. D. de Labilliere.

among the few excellent men who never had and never could have an enemy."

> Always, my dear Dean,
> Affectionately yours,
> H. Hensley Henson,
> Bishop.

134.   "Reprisals."

November 3rd, 1940.

To The Bishop of Durham.*

My dear Bishop,

Yesterday, I received a very interesting *Bishoprick*, so interesting, indeed, that I read it through forthwith. With what you said about " Reprisals " I am in hearty agreement. It seemed to me regrettable that the Prime Minister, in an otherwise admirable speech, should have countenanced the entirely misleading notion that we are engaged in " reprisals " when we bombard " military objectives " in Germany. There is the same difference between the two procedures as that which separates War, as alone permissible for Christians, and War that cannot possibly be brought within the ambit of Christian duty. But I am really afraid that, as these atrocious bombardments continue, there will develope such an exasperation in the public mind, that the cry for " reprisals " in the true sense of the word will be too strong for the yielding virtue of politicians and ecclesiastics.

The new slogan, " Men, Money, and the Ministry " is about as true and as misleading as the old, " Life and Liberty ". It may, in the general enfeeblement of intellect and inflammation of appetite, which will surely follow this War, as it followed the last, secure a measure of success, but it carries the whole issue on to a plane on which the spiritual interest is quite evidently subordinated to the material. I observe that a Clerical Trade Union *tout court* is already in being. It will recruit its members from the least religious elements of the clergy. It seems to me quite apparent that the programme could only be seriously adopted after Disestablishment. The notion

* The Right Rev. A. T. P. Williams.

that the State will simply hand over the entire national system with the endowments to the church as it now is, without any security, either that effective and satisfactory re-organization of property arrangements will be made, or that discipline will be restored, appears to me altogether chimerical. Nor do I think that it is in itself reasonable.

Moreover, the deeper issues of faith and worship ought not to be evaded in the interest of adding something to clerical incomes.

There is much more to be said, but I have filled my sheet. The clamour for more money does not come from the best of the clergy, and it can never be satisfied on the lines suggested.

I begin to doubt whether at the Abbey, I shall find either a pulpit to occupy, or a house to inhabit. At present my house (4 Little Cloister) shelters two families of bomb-evicted Abbey servants!

Ever affectionately,
H. Hensley Henson,
Bishop.

135. Burial of Neville Chamberlain's ashes.

Hyntle Place,
November 16th, 1940.

To The Rev. Preb. A. B. Wynne-Willson.

My dear Wynne-Willson,

Thank you so much for your kind wishes for my birthday. When a man has actually entered his 78th year, Birthdays are rather sombre Festivals. They cannot possibly be many and (as the world now stands) they are not likely to be happy, so that the conventional Birthday formula of goodwill has lost relevance and sounds more satirical than sincere!

The bombing of Coventry and the destruction of its cathedral are indeed distressing. I have written to the Bishop (for whom I have no common regard) expressing my horror of the crime, and my sympathy for the calamity. I cannot doubt that the new intensification of their air raids indicates rather the exasperated ferocity of a cornered rat, who knows that its fate is assured, than any intelligent and hopeful plan of campaign. The contrast between Taranto and

Coventry leaps to the mind, both in method of warfare and in measure of achievement. I went to London to take part in the burial of Chamberlain's ashes in the Abbey. The service had (by the Prime Minister's special desire) been kept strictly secret, and outside the great Church there was no sign that anything unusual was taking place within its walls, but a considerable congregation had collected, and the service was moving in its solemnity and simplicity. I am glad that he is buried there: for the name of Chamberlain could not rightly be absent from the Abbey record, and I think that (though he made a great blunder in his policy of so-called "appeasement") his character was high, his motives generous, and his sacrifice great. Personally, I liked and respected him.

We shall still make this our home, only occupying the canonical house in Westminster for the 10 weeks of "close residence". At present I am using it to provide housing for two members of the Abbey Staff, who have been, with their families, bombed out of their homes.

Yes: times have wonderfully changed. I could not help reflecting on the significance of the burial of a devout Unitarian with a fully Christian (though not the statutory) service in the Abbey. The old orthodoxies, doctrinal and disciplinary, are as dead as the mysteries of Mithras!

Give my love to your wife and thank her for her good wishes. I am glad to hear such good report of your family.

Always affectly your friend,
H. Hensley Henson,
Bp.

136.   On an O.M.

January 1st, 1941.

To Dr Gilbert Murray, O.M.

My dear Dr Murray,

I cannot refuse myself the pleasure of telling you how delighted I am to know that you have received the great honour of being made an O.M. The fact will be heartily welcomed by all who respect fine scholarship and severe high character. I first came into contact with you more than half a century ago, and, though our paths have been widely separated, I have followed your career with deepening interest and admiration. In this dark and evil time you have kept the standard of honour and personal disinterestedness flying, and it is good to see that you have been publicly recognized. I think that if I were a layman, the O.M. is the one distinction which I would covet, and to no man could it be more fitly given than to yourself.

With hearty good wishes for the New Year.

Believe me,

Most sincerely yours,

H. Hensley Henson,

Bishop.

137. Resignation of the Canonry at Westminster.

Hyntle Place,

September 1st, 1941.

To Noel Lamidez, Esq.

My dear Noel,

Your last letter is dated March 20th, 1941. It ought to have been answered long ago, but there have been many obstacles to letter-writing, and, when these have been surmounted, we cannot exclude the possibility that our letters will never reach those to whom they were addressed.

I kept my first—and last—" residence " as Canon of Westminster for the 2nd time, during last April. Then I had experience of two bombing raids, and shall never forget it. The great Abbey seemed to shiver and shudder when the high explosive bombs fell about it, and in the interval between the explosions there was the sinister crashing of the glass from the clerestory as it fell on to the stone floor of the nave. The windows had to be boarded up with the result that the Abbey Church was so darkened that I could read the services and sermons with difficulty, and only walk with some risk of stumbling. My eyesight had been giving me cause for anxiety; and I betook myself to the oculist. His report was rather disconcerting, for though he thought my eyes would still permit me to do my own work, at my own pace, in my own study, he insisted that I ought to retire from the

K

Canonry.   Accordingly, I made no delay in sending my resignation
to the Prime Minister.   He recognized the adequacy of my reasons,
and wrote to me a very kindly expressed letter.   On May 1st, my
resignation took effect.   My final preachings in the Abbey are to be
published in a small book, under the title *Last Words in Westminster*.
When it appears, I will send you a copy.   Since my retirement the
Abbey has been bombed again, and considerably damaged.

London has suffered badly, especially in its most precious historic
monuments; and much of the damage is irreparable.   But the spirit
of the Londoners has been magnificent.   I am proud to remember
that I was myself born in London, though I was still a baby when my
family retired into the country, and have hardly any right to reckon
myself a Londoner.

Mr Menzies made a very favourable impression in this country,
and his fall from power is generally regretted.   We should be glad to
have him here as the permanent representative of Australia in the War
Cabinet.   The fighting qualities of the Australian troops have been
wonderfully illustrated in this war.

The restoration of the Emperor of Ethiopia to the Throne from
which he was so foully driven by Mussolini is one matter for genuine
satisfaction.   I hope that we shall not "let him down again"; but
his black skin is a terrible handicap, and, for sentimental reasons,
Italian influence in Great Britain is dangerously strong.   The Roman
Catholick Church uses its vast influence against a Christian Church
which does not acknowledge the sovereignty of the Pope.   So there
are many dangers to free Abyssinia ahead.   Nevertheless, I cannot
bring myself to believe that Great Britain will fall to the infamy of
deserting its gallant and long-suffering ally.

.   .   .   .

The outlook in the Pacific remains obscure.   Japan may have
carried herself into a situation from which she cannot escape without
fighting.   In that case, I do not think her prospects are bright.

The meeting between Roosevelt and Churchill was a thrilling
episode, and the 8 points of the "Atlantic Charter" can hardly fail
to affect opinion throughout the world.   I thought the Prime Minister's
broadcast speech was as near perfection as is humanly possible.   We
have, indeed, much reason to thank God for having given us in him
a man of supreme ability, ideally qualified for the stupendous task of
his office.

Australian politics are difficult for us to understand, but they do not impress us well.   At the present juncture the violence of their partisan conflicts seems to us regrettable and morally repulsive.

Next Sunday is to be observed throughout the country as another " National Day of Prayer ", marking the start of the 3rd year of this fearful war.   I have promised to preach in Felixstowe, (where we are staying for a short holiday before settling down for the winter).   It is not easy to speak wisely, sincerely, and devoutly.   As the war progresses, the essential quality of Hitler's warfare becomes apparent.   I cannot recall any adequate parallel to the enormous wickedness of his conduct. . . .

May God bless you, dear Noel, and give you great peace and happiness in His service !

Always affect^{ly} your Friend,
H. Hensley Henson,
Bishop.

138.   *Quill Pens.*

Hyntle Place,
October 26th, 1941.

To The Dean of Durham.

My dear Dean,

I have been going through a bundle of letters which have not been " answered ", and which are, in varying measures, entitled to be ; and, with mingled surprize and shame, I find among them your very interesting letter, dated, as long ago as Sept. 17th.   But, for one reason or another, I find myself becoming a curiously reluctant and unsatisfactory letter-writer.   One reason for this is certainly the practical impossibility of getting quills to write with.   These hateful steel pens destroy freedom in the process and significance in the result of writing ; I loathe the sight of such handwriting as they compel me to produce, and which it humiliates me to acknowledge.   I cannot find a steel pen which serves my turn, and the honest pride with which a well-written sheet fills the writer's mind is no longer a satisfaction within my reach.   It is yet one more consequence of this accursed mechanisation which has given Hitler the Empire of Europe, and which (we are assured) can only be overcome by consenting ourselves to be mechanized like him!

I am committed to the Autobiographical venture, and find my chariot wheels, like Pharaoh's in the Red Sea, moving heavily. If I am candid and possibly interesting, I must be brutal, and certainly offensive. In the case of such an Ishmaelite as I have been, Auto-biography drifts inevitably into Apology, and that cannot possibly be either important, or really worth while! I sustain myself with the reflection that it is the very obscurity of authors and the very irre-levance of their activities that constitutes their value as interpreters of their age; and perhaps my stormy and fruitless career may possibly throw some small illumination on the course of Anglican history during the years in which I played some part, however small, in the foolish affair.

Affectionately your Friend,
H. Hensley Henson,
Bishop.

139.   *After reading Temple's Penguin* *CHRISTIANITY AND THE SOCIAL ORDER.*

Hyntle Place,
April 4th, 1942.

To The Rev. C. E. A. Harford.★

My dear Harford,

The strength of Copec and Malvern derives not from the economic sphere, but from the emotional and religious, wherein men's feelings and passions are strong in proportion to the narrowness of their experience, the smallness of their knowledge and the strength of their prejudices.

The Archbishop's method is medieval. First, determine what ought to be and then plan your world to match your theoretical scheme. The more cautious procedure prefers to start with what you have, and where you are and only to advance as opportunity and

★ Vicar of Bramford, Ipswich.

resources make practicable.   The formula of sound progress is "line upon line, line upon line, here a little there a little ", and nowhere so much as in the sphere of social reform is the dictum better worth keeping in mind " *dolus latet in generalibus* ": which we may broadly render thus: "Men are trapped into the pitfalls of failure, when they indulge in day-dreaming and go over broken ground with their eyes on the clouds ".

Walking and talking are good mind-clearing exercises; we must get some more as the spring advances.

Yours ever,

H. Hensley Henson,

Bishop.

140.   A Book of Poems ; Daily Service.

Hyntle Place,

June 19th, 1942.

To The Rev. J. D. C. Wallace.*

Dear Mr Wallace,

I have to thank you for your gift,† and for the very kind letter which accompanied it.

Your verses interest me greatly, none the less for my total incapacity either to write or criticize poetry.   Beyond an early, life-long devotion to the giants Shakespeare and Milton, and the Victorians, Wordsworth, M. Arnold, Tennyson and Browning, I read little verse, and most of the modern poets offend me by their bizarre conceptions and uncouth forms.

For I have a rooted belief that good poetry must be both beautiful in expression and readily intelligible.

I remember going to preach for Butler at Wantage, when I was beneficed in Essex, and being much, and favourably impressed by him; I cannot wholly share his attitude towards Daily Service, though I always maintained it in my own Church.   But in rural districts where Churches are sometimes far from the parson's house, damp, and

---

* Chaplain and Master of Ravenstone Hospital, Leicester.

† A copy of Mr Wallace's *The Bells of Hugglescote*, *and other poems.*

unwarmed, I think it is difficult to make out a case for insisting on the solitary service, a congregation being hardly possible.

I note with something akin to sardonic amusement that the Church Assembly and the Convocations are still perambulating the much-beaten ground of Bishops' Palaces and Parsons' discipline. They make no advance, but it creates a comfortable illusion of religious activity. And of course, the admirable Hierarchs might be worse employed.

The picture of the Chaplain, and the Chaplain's House add distinction to your very attractive volume.

Believe me,

Yours sincerely and obliged,

H. Hensley Henson,

Bishop.

141.   A Friendship.

Hyntle Place,

September 2nd, 1942.

*To Prof. G. Grey Turner.**

My dear Professor,

It was indeed pleasant to hear from you again, and to be assured that you and Mrs Grey Turner are well. Thank you for letting me see the account of Bishop Shute Barrington's medical requirements : but I must not keep it, as the knowledge has no value for me now since I have ceased to sit in his chair, and it may very likely possess some value in your collection of documents.

In going through my private journal while working at my Auto-biography, I have recently had occasion to read my record of the time when first I came into personal contact with you, and, by your skill and care, received from you an important service, which I can never cease to remember with gratitude. And, on the top of that scientific benefit, you added the immaterial benefaction of your friendship, which I value very highly. If, by God's goodness, we are brought out of our present distresses into a time of peace and waxing prosperity, I

* Prof. of Surgery, London University ; formerly Prof. of Surgery, Durham University.

hope we shall meet again.   I should particularly like to see how Elston has developed.   He will have falsified the promise of his Boyhood if he has not shaped into a strong and kind man, of whom his country and his family may well be proud.

Give our very kind remembrances to your wife,

and believe me,

sincerely your Friend,

H. Hensley Henson,

Bishop.

142.   " Malvern"; moral effect of alliances.

Hyntle Place,

September 13th, 1942.

To The Dean of St Paul's.*

My dear Dean,

I have to thank you for an exceedingly kind letter,† which gave me real pleasure.   It was good of you to write like that, and yours words were so clearly sincere as well as generous that I could not but find them comforting.

I wish, indeed, that I could avail myself of your suggestion that I should visit you, but, while this evil cloud of war darkens the world, I doubt if I shall move, though I am literally hungering for the sight and speech of friends.   Petrol restrictions have immobilized and isolated me, and, of course, my neighbours are in the like case.   The growing disabilities of *dura senectus* disincline me for the exertions and fatigues of travel, and there is a certain patriotic obligation not to add anything to the transport difficulties of the time.   Now there are fresh restrictions on paper, which make one feel guilty when one puts pen to paper, and, well,—why multiply words?—I am trying to reconcile myself to solitude born of self-conscious obsoleteness.

I do not like the drift and temper of our " High Command " in the Hierarchy.   What I felt about Copec, I feel again and, perhaps, even

* The Very Rev. W. R. Matthews.

† Thanking Hensley Henson for his helpful sermons in *Last Words in Westminster Abbey*.

more strongly about Malvern; and again the central Figure is William Temple. I admire his industry and envy his various ability, but I distrust his judgement, dislike his company, and dissent from his reading of ecclesiastical duty. Both he and his predecessor are more astute than wise, more ambitious than faithful. But, while I think and feel like that about him, I perceive the enormous difficulties of his position, and sympathy paralyzes criticism.

I miss the Athenæum increasingly for it brought me so many contacts with friends, kept me in touch with new books, and enabled me to see as much as I wanted of the journals etc. Now, I am reduced to such books as I possess, and such papers as come into the house. And while I have around me much that I want to read, and abundant leisure, my eyes are no longer equal to the demands that I would make on them. I should like to finish the *Retrospect*, and, indeed, am pledged to produce the manuscript by next January—but the task grows more difficult as I advance, and when one is nearing the end of that final decade of life which the Psalmist (who plainly was drawing on his own experience) described as " labour and sorrow ", one does not feel confident about achieving anything. I think the deepening tragedy of the world destroys the courage to attempt, and the strength to persevere : and it protrudes grim questionings into the sanctuary of one's personal faith. How shall I make answer to those who, in their deeper perplexity and affliction, turn to me for counsel and encouragement?

The enormous wickedness which is embodied in Hitler and his criminal associates does at least so far ease my way, that it leaves no possible doubt as to the stark obligation of fighting him and all he stands for. As I read the wonderful lesson in the parish church this morning, I seemed to be declaring our actual situation spiritually discerned—" But if not, be it known unto thee, O king, that we will not serve thy gods, nor worship the golden image which thou hast set up." That is the last word of " Theology *in extremis*."

I wish I could feel happier about the effect of our new intimacy with the Americans. That they are definitely lower than our own people in the two respects of sexual morality and civic quality does not seem to me doubtful; and both they and we are morally at our weakest and worst in the circumstances which compel us into close and continuing intercourse. I think I am more apprehensive of moral damage from America than of economic and political damage from Russia. I am presiding over 3 conferences arranged by the Ipswich Urban Council on the subject of Unemployment after the War. I was asked to preside as being known to stand outside the parties, and we have the subject presented from the "view-point" of the three parties in succession. The Liberal party started with Seebohm Rowntree as its exponent; tomorrow, one of the Labour members is to be the speaker; and we end with Willink, the Regional Director, for the Tories. It is not altogether easy to keep the company within the limits of practical politics. They want to get away into the wide lands of socialistic theory, and to indulge in the rhodomontade, not unfitly described as " Sob-Stuff "—which I cannot endure !

With kind regards to Mrs Matthews, and many thanks for your letter,

I am,

Affectionately yours,

H. Hensley Henson,

Bishop.

143. Bishop Welldon ; Archbishop Temple.

Hyntle Place,

November 1st, 1942.

To The Dean of Norwich.*

My dear Dean,

It was indeed good of you to send me so kind a letter, which was most welcome. Your comments on my poor book are worth having. Edward Lytleton's judgement on Welldon accords notably with that which I have often heard from others, who have known him well in his earlier years. " He has never grown up." My acquaintance with him runs back to my days as Vicar of Barking, and, of course, I came to be closely associated with him in Westminster, and later in Durham. He united a heavy frame and blustering manner, which suggested a truly virile personality, and a sentimental sensitiveness which would have been hardly pardonable in a schoolgirl! And he was found, in the experience of colleagues, to be radically

* The Very Rev. D. H. S. Cranage.

untrustworthy, not deliberately or consciously, but because he could never resist the appeal of the Gallery. He would never fail to sacrifice a friend to a cheer! In my 2nd vol., I must sum him up as equitably as I can; but I fear the result will be hardly pleasant.

I am trying to complete the book, and am even pledged to send the finished manuscript to the Press next January; but my progress is dreadfully slow, for, as the story comes nearer the present time, it becomes more difficult, since so many of the persons who enter into it are living, and must not be hurt in their feelings, and so much of the most interesting material is not available being *sub sigillo* of honourable reticence. However I must do my best, and put faith in the considerate charity of my friends.

I cannot understand how the Prime Minister could have been carried to the puerile blunder of putting German prisoners of war in chains by way of compelling Hitler to take chains from British prisoners. It could not effect anything but the intensifying of German brutality and the lowering of British credit. How to get out of the blunder is not quite easy to see; but the sooner this squalid competition in lawless violence is ended, the better for prisoners and Allies alike.

Is it not comforting for us who are now in " the sere and yellow leaf" of our lives to observe, that even in these days, when Youth is impudently triumphant in the pulpit, the press, and on the platform, . . . the greater Figures—Smuts, Churchill, Roosevelt—are old men?

I like and admire Temple, but I regard his ceaseless pronouncements with deepening anxiety. He, and the sycophantic crowd of clerics which follows him, are running gaily before the wind of Socialism which blows so strongly just now, but he forgets that the really dangerous Revolutions are those which reflect the mood of popular disillusionment; and that by making his important contribution to the volume of swollen expectation in the general mind, he is securing an early emergence of the crisis when the people will be disappointed and disillusioned. Moreover, he is putting too heavy a strain on his wonderful powers of mind and body. I feel inclined to address him in the words which an eminent Scottish Judge (Lord Young) is said to have addressed to Mr Gladstone at the time of the Midlothian Campaign : " Mr Gladstone, you'll have much to answer for in the Day of Judgement." " Why so?" asked the statesman in ruffled astonishment. " Ye speak too much, Mr Gladstone."

I remember once talking about the question of admitting clergymen to the secular Orders. It was at Windsor, and, if I recall the occasion rightly, we were discussing the Victorian Order. I was told that it was the personal insistence of H.M. Edward VII which overrode the objection of Abp Davidson. A kind of compromise was reached. The Order might be conferred, but it was to convey no title to the wife. Personally, I dislike these secular distinctions being given to clergymen. The secularizing influence of the Establishment is always great, and we should not make it greater. I do not think the conferring of secular peerages on retiring Primates is likely to assist their rightful influence. There is no reputation more injurious to religious credit in the Nation than that of a *Curialis*; and the prospect of a peer's coronet as the sign and symbol of Court favour cannot have a good effect on the Primate, or commend him to the people's confidence. From Archbishops to Hon. Canons, and Colonial " dignitaries ", the lust for titles obtrudes itself ignobly!

Give my kindest regards to Mrs Cranage, and believe me,

Always affectionately,

H. Hensley Henson,

Bishop.

144.   On the retirement of the Senior Verger of Durham Cathedral.

Hyntle Place,
December 29th, 1942.

*To Mr Burton.**

My dear Burton,

The Dean has told me that the end of this year will coincide with the end of your official connexion with the Cathedral, which you have served faithfully for so long. You will allow me to send you a few lines of sympathy and goodwill. There cannot but be a measure of regret and sadness in having to retire from active service into the comparative obscurity of private life; but there comes a time even to the bravest warrior when he must leave the Field and

* Senior Verger of Durham Cathedral.

take off his armour. You will have the deep satisfaction of carrying with you into retirement the affection and respect of all with whom you have worked in and for the great Church. The treasures of the Aged are the Memories of their lives; and you will certainly have that treasure in amplitude.

I shall always think of you as a loyal colleague and a faithful friend. May God bless you with health of body, and peace of mind, and give you the happiness of seeing the foul tyranny of Hitler and his gang finally destroyed, and the world brought to just and lasting Peace.

Believe me,
Affectionately your friend,
H. Hensley Henson,
Bishop.

145. Chaplains in the Merchant Navy; Women's Education.

Hyntle Place,
January 16th, 1943.

To L. D. Holt, Esq., J.P.

My dear Holt,

The more I reflect on the project of providing ships of the Merchant Navy with Chaplains, the more apparent it becomes that no general provision is really practicable. The scale and variety of the need, on the one hand; and the paucity of available men on the other, are so formidable as to (*me judice*) impose a veto on the general plan. But I think that a better organization of the arrangements for the guidance and assistance of the crews in ports, especially of the younger members, would be of great value; and the steady insistence on the importance of maintaining wholesome conditions of life on board ship could not fail to raise the standard of seamen's society in the necessarily restricted limits of ship-board life. Beyond such generalities, I can see nothing; and even in setting down these, I feel the absurdity of offering any opinion at all on a matter which, so far as its salient features are concerned, lies so completely outside my know-ledge and experience. I think it is most reasonable to recognize frankly that the problem is so plainly one of practical conditions as to lie outside the range of ecclesiastical organization. The analogy be-tween the Royal Navy and the Merchant Navy is not close enough to provide a basis for argument. There are too many zealous parsons who need to remember the bitter wisdom of the proverb, that " Fools rush in where Angels fear to tread." One genuine Christian's personal influence has more moral and spiritual value than an army of chaplains. If we could secure the presence of that Divine leaven in the ships, we should, probably, have done what can be done in the way of checking the worst evils of ship-board life, and not of that life only.

With regard to the Girls' School, what can I say? I am more firmly persuaded than ever that the treatment of women has got on to wrong lines, and is directed largely to wrong ends. When the Feminists succeeded in giving the political franchise to women, they spoiled more than they gained. It is hard to see how that error can be cor-rected; and the war has enormously extended its influence. The Fall-ing Birth Rate threatens civilized society with utter destruction, and that in no distant future; but unless marriage and motherhood can be restored to their true place as the natural and most noble career of the Female Sex, I do not see how the present tendencies can be arrested. That means, of course, that I have no message to my generation on this vital issue; and must stand aside in self-confirmed helplessness from debating the most urgent social problem of the age. I feel like a latter-day Shimei running alongside the car of modern " Progress ", cursing all the way!—a poor exercise for such muscular activity as re-mains possible for an octogenarian!

It pleases me that you should find my poor book sufficiently interest-ing to gain the compliment of your reading. I had originally intended something more worthy of publication; but the failure of my eyes forced me to acquiesce in a very ill-ordered and non-literary production; and the extraordinary difficulties created by the war have added defects of another kind. However, for what it is worth (which is mighty little) there it is; and I am grateful for the kindness with which it has been generally received.

What a humiliating spectacle of Democracy at Work is being pre-sented by the great Republic of U.S.A. There, I suspect, is the weakest point in the Grand Alliance; and it is so weak that even at the eleventh hour—when Victory is in sight—it has made Defeat no impossible denouement of this fearful and protracted conflict.

> Always, my dear Holt,
> Sincerely yr friend,
> H. Hensley Henson,
> Bishop.

P.S.   Having written this letter, I find myself reluctant to send it because it may well lead the reader to form a false, or at least a lop-sided, picture of my mind on the great subject.   I recognize and admire the marvellous achievements of women in the prosecution of the war; but I can only justify their new activities as justified by the necessity of the situation; and I cannot reasonably base a policy for normal life on procedures demanded by an abnormal crisis.   I should be blind not to see, and fatuous not to recognize the quality of individual women, and I should be irrational and unjust to refuse to such gifted persons the opportunity of cultivating and exercising their unusual powers; but I cannot wisely build a policy for the sex, on the claims of extraordinarily gifted individuals.

Women ought not to be educated on the same lines, or by the same methods, as those which are proper for men; for their distinctive sex aptitudes and functions are different; and in both cases, these ought to determine the character and objective of education.

There is in human life, a natural (i.e. a Divinely ordered) duality, which must be respected.   It reflects itself in the ordering of society. Men must find their sphere of service in the external, women in the internal sphere.   Man is the bread-winner, the Head of the Family. Woman is the prevailing Influence within the Home.

It is not right or politically sound, or morally safe that girls should be trained to contemplate as normally open to them a large choice of careers.   The principal cause of the strange reluctance to bear children and even to contemplate marriage, which is now so strange and familiar a phenomenon among young women, is probably the fact that they have been taught to look forward to professional careers, to build their first hopes and ambitions in the general life elsewhere than in homes of their own, and, indeed, to claim a place alongside their male contemporaries on every plane of social endeavour.   When at last Nature asserts itself, and the sex appeal cannot be ignored, too often the natural mating time has passed, tastes and habits more congruous with masculine than with feminine life have been formed, and the childless wife is frustrated, unhappy, and sometimes scandalous.

But I am old and childless; the primary requisites for a balanced judgement on the subject of Girls' education are lacking, and it is not tolerable that I should formulate opinions and judgements about it. Nor would I have written so much, had you not directly raised the matter. You are incomparably better equipped for handling it than I.

H. H. H.

146. *Lectures to convalescent soldiers.*

To The Rev. C. K. Pattinson.

Hyntle Place,
February 5th, 1943.

My dearest Charlie,

. . . For some weeks I have, on Wednesday afternoons, gone to the Red Cross Hospital in Hintlesham Hall, and given a " Talk " to the convalescent patients on something which is supposed to assist in developing their civic sense, and thus improving their capacity to take a reasonable line after the War, when the process of reconstructing Society has to be taken in hand. The whole business seems rather silly, but it is organised by the Government, and I thought it my duty to volunteer. I am expounding to them the mysteries of British Institutions. I dealt with the Monarchy, and last Wednesday gave a talk on the House of Lords. When my solo has been finished the chorus of interrogation and discussion starts : and it is really rather illuminating. It brings back to my mind the old days at the Oxford House, when I used to have similar experiences in the Clubs. Last week a decent looking young soldier, whose countenance, perhaps, was more good humoured than intelligent asked me with an evident desire for information " What is this Lord's Day people talk about? " He evidently connected it with the House of Lords and was naturally puzzled! He was mortified as well as relieved to learn that it meant nothing worse than Sunday!

Next Wednesday I have to talk about the House of Commons : and rather expect to hear some original comments. . . .

Always affectly your Friend,
H. Hensley Henson,
Bp.

147. A visit of three Durham friends.

Hyntle Place,
September 18th, 1943.

To The Dean of Durham.

My dearest Dean,

We have gone to the Felix Hotel, Felixstowe, for this week, and design to return to the Diogenes-Tub at Hintlesham on Thursday, the 23rd. In our absence we hope that a repulsive but indispensable purgation of the sewer at Hyntle Place will be achieved.

Some days ago we had a pleasant week-end visit from three of my old Durham colleagues—my ex-domestic Chaplain, Pattinson, now Rector of Edmundbyers; Cecil Ferens, my indispensable legal secretary; and Captain Carter, whose "silver jubilee" you decorated with felicitous verse. It was delightful to see them, and to hear their account of the old diocese.

.   .   .   .

I read your very wise and serviceable observations on the proposed improvement of "the Faithful City" by its local Solons. This mad passion for "Planning" is a nightmare and a continuing menace. It may pair off with the endless pratings about "Youth", and what it really wants, and how it is to get its demands satisfied. Both planners and praters are a public nuisance, and probably more seriously mischievous than Hitler's bombers.

I am interested in the visit of Garbett to Moscow, and the probable revival of the ecclesiastical Flirtation with the Orthodox Church which it suggests. By a significant coincidence this flirtation synchronizes with another acute phase of Papal self-abasement. But I am not much impressed by the religious value of these intermittent attempts, now at Malines, and now at Moscow, to get away from our historical character as a Reformed Church, and to effect some kind of a working union with the unreformed churches, Western and Eastern. My own belief is that before any reality can enter into such essays, those churches must traverse an intellectual and spiritual crisis analogous to the Reformation. Both are as yet in the medieval phase; and they must become modern in order to be intelligible.

Stalin follows the Napoleonic precedent by getting into a working alliance with the Church; but it will be in Russia as it was in France. The generation of aggressive and scornful atheism will have broken the essential continuity of the national religion; and there can never be a return to the old loyalties.

How tantalizing have been the reports from Italy! The Nazis seem to outwit us strangely. I suppose the fact only illustrates the Dominical dictum—"The children of this world are for their own generation wiser than the children of light." But we threw up our hats over the surrender of Italy too soon. . . . These arrangements [for Days of Prayer and Praise in the churches] are but too often boomerangs, which return with astounding effect on those who throw them!

Give my love to Hester. Ella and Fearne send theirs.

Always aff^{ly} your Friend,
H. Hensley Henson,
Bp.

148.   Religion and Life Week.

Hyntle Place,
September 27th, 1943.

To The Bishop of Derby.*

My dear Rawlinson,

I meant to have written to you before in order to express my regret that I was not able to "sit under" you in Ipswich last week. I can plead three reasons every one of which can, perhaps, be regarded as sufficient.

(1) I was in Felixstowe with my ladies, securing (at a terrifying cost) a week by the seaside in the Felix Hotel, which, as you probably know, is nobly perched on the shore, commanding the most glorious view of the sea.

(2) I am immobilized by a total prohibition of petrol, and immersed in an isolation, which, like the darkness of Egypt, can be felt.

(3) I am too much out of harmony with the methods of spiritual

* The Right Rev. A. E. J. Rawlinson.

L

" stunts ", illustrated by the Religion and Life Week. The Bishop here was good enough to invite me to take the chair at your meeting, which was at that time arranged for Dr Raven, a man for whom I have considerable regard and some admiration, but whose opinions I disagree with too deeply to make it safe for me to preside over his oratory. I read your speech as it was reported in the local newspaper, and thought it excellent; and, in any case, I should have rejoiced to have sight of you, and speech with you.

I have just read through the papers which were written for the Modern Churchman's Conference in Oxford last July, and they left a very unpleasant impression on my mind. Inge's paper interested me greatly. I have read it three times, and find it deeply unsatisfactory. You will readily understand that I reflect much on the constituents of my own personal religion and, indeed, (if my failing eyesight does not impose a veto) I have some intention of supplementing the two volumes of my worthless *Retrospect* with an epilogue, which will include a personal *confessio fidei*. I am not sure that I can achieve this, even if I have the requisite physical competence, for, as I draw to the end of my life, (and on November 8th next I shall complete 80 years on this sinful planet) I find myself compelled to accept an agnostic position over an ever larger proportion of the ground which is covered by official and conventional credenda.

.   .   .   .

I have been reading with great delight Buchan's *Augustus*. It is really an admirable piece of work, illuminated by very keen and sympathetic studies of the leading characters of the amazing period in which Augustus blazed on the world. My opinion of John Buchan has always been the highest, and this book provides fresh justification for it.

With kind regards to Mrs Rawlinson, and, if he is with you, to Anthony, who must be on the threshold of his University career,

I am always affectionately your friend,

H. Hensley Henson,

Bishop.

149.   *Proposed Education Bill (1).*

Hyntle Place,
November 2nd, 1943.

To The Archdeacon of Doncaster.★

My dear Archdeacon,

.   .   .   .

I am following with much interest the fortunes of Butler's Education effort. I wish he had had the courage frankly to make an end of the Dual System. He is only endangering the cause of educational improvement by retaining it; and he is undoubtedly facilitating the cynical but unconfessed Roman Catholick policy, which has as its ultimate objective the complete secularization of the national educational system in order that Christian folk may be compelled to accept the impudent and indeed sacrilegious assumption that only in the Roman Catholick schools may sound moral conditions be provided. That policy has largely succeeded in U.S.A. and the Dominions, and it is by no means inconceivable that it may also succeed in Great Britain. This is in some genuine sense a Christian nation, but its Christianity is " undenominational ", and if Christian teaching is to become, as it ought to become, an integral part of the nation's educational scheme, that teaching cannot be denominational. The general acceptance of " agreed syllabuses " shows two things, viz. the fundamental agreement of the general mass of non-Roman English Christians, and the possibility of expressing their agreement in the process of religious teaching. There never was a more mischievous phrase than that which fell from the lips of the G.O.M.—that grand master of mischievous phrases—than his description of undenominationalism as " a moral monster ". It pleased him to assume that by undenominationalism nothing else could be meant than the absurdity of a residuum of teaching, respecting which no conceivable difference could exist, whereas, of course, undenominationalism means concentration on the fundamentals of Christianity which must be held by all Christian denominations just because they are Christian, and these, unless Christianity be a misnomer, are neither doubtful nor disputed. The real difficulty in England is the widening discord between the national

★ The Ven. R. W. Stannard; now Bishop of Woolwich.

Christianity and the kind of Christianity which is now being very generally expounded by Anglo-Catholick clergymen in the Church schools.   The National Schools were legally designed to inculcate the principles of the Established Church, and those principles, when the National Society was incorporated, were understood to be something very different from those which the Tractarians succeeded, by a miracle of tortuous casuistry, in extracting from the Thirty-nine Articles.   The Bishop of Gloucester has a letter in this morning's *Times* which may pair off with the speeches of the Bishop of Oxford.   Both these excellent prelates are as the Bourbons, incapable, both of learning and of forgetting.

This little house is a small Tudor building, with something of the indefinable dignity which marked the domestic architecture of the XVIth century, even in its humblest examples.   It has been extremely beautiful this autumn, clad in the imperial vestment of its crimson creeper, but this has now almost vanished before the waxing cold of incipient winter. . . .

I am always affectionately your friend,

H. Hensley Henson,

Bishop.

150.   *Proposed Education Bill (2).*

Hyntle Place,

November 12th, 1943.

To The Dean of Norwich.

My dear Dean,

It was indeed kind of you to take thought for my birthday, and to send me so kind a letter.   There is something almost terrifying about having to acknowledge that one has actually reached the four-score years which the Psalmist regarded as the extreme limit of normal human life, and certainly the most conceited of octogenarians must acknowledge to be a period darkly shadowed by waxing physical and mental deterioration.

I had foolishly allowed myself to frame quite a respectable programme of activity by voice and pen, which should relieve the tedium of senectitude and occupy not unworthily its ample leisure.   But this fearful war has created a situation in which that programme, if it had been practicable, would have been ridiculously irrelevant; and the failure of my eyes has gone far to destroy my capacities for any effective work.   However, I am ashamed even to allude to my private misfortunes, while from every side, near at hand and far afield, comes the miserable evidence of almost indescribable suffering and calamity.

.   .   .   .

I wish Butler had had the courage to build his educational reforms on a definite abolition of the Dual System.   It only blocks the way to the establishment of an effective and generally acceptable national system of education.   None of the Anglican leaders has the candour to admit two facts of quite cardinal importance :

1. The transformation of Anglicanism since the Dual System came into existence.   Most of the Church Schools are held on National Society Trusts, which provide for the education of the children in " the principles of the Established Church ".   Then those principles were well understood to be such as commanded the acceptance of the vast majority of English people.   The Tractarians changed all that, and now " the Church teaching for Church children in Church schools " carries to the English minds, in a great and increasing proportion of the parishes, a meaning which is anything but welcome. There is very little to choose between Romanism and Anglo-Catholicism.   If the National Church were still in 1943 what it was a century ago, a Protestant Church professing that Protestant religion which at the Coronation the King vows to maintain, there would not be that volume of suspicion and dislike which now so generally, and over a widening area, is attached to " Church Teaching " in schools maintained almost entirely by the State.

2. The absolute indifference of almost the whole of the parents of the children who attend the State schools to the imaginary grievance which we are so incessantly assured they feel at the teaching of undenominational religion.   I wish the Government would meet the impudent claims of the Papists with a stern and explicit refusal.   The most that equity can demand, or patriotism concede, is that the state schools should include a conscience clause for both teachers and children, adequate buildings, and sufficient guarantee for efficiency, together with permission under certain reasonable conditions for dis-

affected minorities to "contract out" of the national scheme at their own charges. Democracy certainly does not mean an equality between the majority and the minority of the citizens. I have no doubt that if the Dual System is continued Butler's excellent project for educational reform will lack the saving grace of finality. I am not sure whether you ever saw the enclosed pamphlet which has regained relevance in connexion with the South Indian Scheme for reunion. I think His Grace has probably given that poor little venture in goodwill its *coup de grace*. The policy of "running with the hare and hunting with the hounds" is traditional in Lambeth, but it is not favourable to achievement, nor does it add to the spiritual credit of the Primacy.

My second volume of the *Retrospect* is still delayed by labour difficulties, but I am told that it will appear this month. I shall not believe that it has appeared until I have the volume in my hands.

With very kind regards to Mrs Cranage,

I am, my dear Dean,

Always affectionately your friend,

H. Hensley Henson,

Bishop.

Blakeney sent me a delightful letter, and included some verse which pleased me much. What a good fellow he is!

151.   *Earl Baldwin.*

Hyntle Place,

January 15th, 1944.

To The Rev. Preb. A. B. Wynne-Willson.

My dear Prebendary.

By all means, make public the incident you recall. I have no reason for thinking it apocryphal, and it is less enigmatic (not also to say disreputable) than most of the dicta which are ascribed, with varying measures of justice, to the late Bishop of Durham.

.   .   .   .

I had a very charming letter from Earl Baldwin this morning, in which, after acknowledging the copy of vol. ii, which I had directed the publishers to send him, he added these words:

> " We have both ridden on the crest of the waves, each in his peculiar sea, but I am in the trough now where many a better man has been before me."

There is pathos in this; and, perhaps, a delicately veiled rebuke. It reminds me of the story of Montezuma over the red-hot cinders silencing the groans of an inferior victim of Spanish cruelty with the words " Am I then on a bed of roses? "

There is a kind of humble magnanimity about Baldwin which has always appealed to me.

Always affect^{ly} your Friend,

H. Hensley Henson,

Bishop.

152.   *A letter of consolation.*

Hyntle Place,

March 23rd, 1944.

*To The Rev. Canon J. F. Hughes.**

My dear Canon Hughes,

I am concerned to read in the local paper that you, like so many others in this sad time, have been called to pass into the cloud of bereavment.   You will allow me to send to you and your wife a message of sincere sympathy on the death of your son.   Words are poor messages of consolation, but we have no other.   It cannot but be consoling—the more as Time mitigates the shock of bereavment, and discloses the full magnitude of the Cause in which it befell you— to know that he gave his life for the rescue of mankind from the foul tyranny which threatened the very spirit of humanity.   If the thought thrusts itself on your mind that a young life, full of hope and promise of service, has been cut short by " a pitiless arrow of Death ", you may

* Rector of Sudbury, Suffolk.

rest your heart on the Faith which Faber expressed in his poem, " The Old Labourer ", which is even more fitly applied to a Young Soldier,

> God judges by a light
> Which baffles mortal sight,
>   And the useless seeming
>   man, the Crown has won.
> In His bright world above
> A world of larger love,
>   God hath some great
>   employment for His son.

May God bless you both !

Ever sincerely yours,
H. Hensley Henson,
Bishop.

153.   General Montgomery.

Hyntle Place,
May 13th, 1944.

To Lord Woodbridge.

My dearest Arthur,

I was just about to dictate a letter to you, when your gift of asparagus, and loan of the book arrived. Thank you so much for both : the last shall be returned to you in due course.

I have read with interest *The Miracle of Britain's Survival*—which you gave me. From the author's own point of view it is very effective, and I am sure that it is a good thing to remind our bumptious generation, hypnotized by " science ", that there are limits to its power, and that in the long run the victory lies with those who, like Moses, " endured as seeing him who is invisible ". Nevertheless, I dislike and disapprove the tendency to excessive dogmatism about the procedures and purposes of the Almighty whenever circumstances seem to favour our own policies and preferences. I remember being much surprised and even startled when I visited Belfast in the summer of 1914 by the evident conviction with which I was assured by the leaders of the Ulster Protestants, who were on the verge of open rebellion against the British Government, that the successful introduction of arms from

Germany to Ireland had been made possible by coincidences and happenings which were truly " miraculous ", and could only be reasonably interpreted as proofs of Divine approbation. The voyage of the " Fanny " from Kiel to Ulster had been, so I was assured, divinely directed throughout. When the vessel was enveloped in fog, the commander kneeled down on the deck, and after praying for Divine Guidance, gave his orders at a venture, and these orders invariably turned out to be exactly right. I remember observing at the time to my informant, " You Ulster men are still living in the 17th Century." Montgomery is himself of Ulster stock, and uses similar language. I always feel a little uncomfortable when I hear his blending of religion and patriotism. The two ought to be associated, but the association is not easily preserved from the perilous poison of presumption. I hope you read the article by the Dean of St Paul's in last Sunday's *Sunday Times*. It is headed " Let God Arise ", and it is confessedly a careful commentary on Montgomery's recent oration. I received this morning a letter from the Dean, acknowledging a note of agreement with the article which I had sent him. In this note he says :

> " Montgomery is, I believe, sincerely convinced that the war is a crusade. The danger is that he may take too simple-minded a view of the situation, and give people the impression that he believes in the God of Battles in the Old Testament style. I hoped to do something to underline the truth in his appeal, while suggesting the Christian qualifications."

For my part, I think we should be very slow to dogmatize. The interpretation of coincidence is never easy, least of all when self-interest or political passion or racial prejudice disturbs the balance of judgement. Events which provide for one man the demonstration of supernatural approval suggest to another the demonstration of Divine censure. And both may be fully assured in their own minds that they are (to use Bishop Butler's phrase) " on the side of the Divine Administration ". I think we should weigh much in these times the far-reaching words of Christ to His contemporaries when they interpreted current events in religious terms. You will know the passage. St Luke XIII. 1–5. We do not really know what is congruous with the ultimate victory of righteousness, but we do know that in the long run righteousness will prevail, and that it is our duty and highest privilege to contribute to that ultimate victory by being loyal to our own highest conception

of righteousness. "The spirit of man is the candle of the Lord";
and, if we walk in its light, we shall not go astray, although our path
may lead to secular failure as well as to secular victory.   Wesley's
hymn * hits the nail on the head :

> "God moves in a mysterious way
> His wonders to perform.
> He plants his footsteps in the sea,
> And rides upon the storm."

I enjoyed my morning with you yesterday very much.   The beauty
of your wonderful garden, unfolded under the sunshine of a perfect
day, provided a setting for our talk which was at once interpretative
and delightful.

Always affectionately your friend,
Herbert.

154.   *Proposed Power-Station at Durham.*

Hyntle Place,
July 9th, 1944.

To Cecil Ferens, Esq.

My dear Cecil,

I have not heard from you for a very long time : and now I
want to know what precisely is the situation in the matter of some
project for decorating Durham with hideous chimneys and pylons by
way of promoting its economic "expansion".   Yesterday, I received
from the Dean a letter expressing the utmost concern, and invoking
my cooperation in an effort to withstand what he regards, not without
some reason, as a horrifying desecration.   What has actually happened?
It would surprize and distress me if, indeed, the City Fathers could lend
themselves to any project which could justify being so described.   Yet
I was always aware of a certain subterranean agitation for such an
"exploitation" of Durham's historic and architectural attractions as
would "bring much gain" to the shop-keepers of the Faithful City.
Tell me truly whether there is any serious ground for my alarm.

Demetrius and the craftsmen in Ephesus could at least camouflage
their cupidity with the profession of a pious zeal for the worship of the

* The lines are in fact by W. Cowper

" great Goddess Diana " for whose temple they maintained a lucrative trade in " silver shrines "; but I hardly think any Dunelmian would attempt to describe a plan for desecrating Durham as the outcome of a passionate devotion to Christian worship!

This morning I have officiated at Mattins in the parish church, as —— was too indisposed to do his duty. I preached a sermon which violated every principle of sermon composition which I have ever maintained, being (in old Fuller's phrase) " hot from the spit and raw ", i.e. improvised hastily from notes. The congregation was worthy of the discourse, being hardly more than a score of rustics, mainly in petticoats. . . . Why is the C. of E. so powerless to arrest the attention of the people? . . . The longer I live, the truer to me seems the old saw, " A house-going parson makes a church-going people ". As the lace lengthens on the cottas of the serving boys, so do the parishioners fly from the church! But I see no sign anywhere that this truth is likely to affect the behaviour of your priestlings. I note that it is a growing fashion to speak of " priests " instead of " padres ". That big and rather brainless youth, ——, wrote to me the other day, and the word " priest " flamed from his letter like red poppies in a neglected cornfield! There is a world of potential failure in that word " priest ". I wish we had been content with the more accurate and modest " presbyter ".

Write to me, and comfort my soul.

Always your affect^{te} Friend,
H. Hensley Henson,
Bishop.

155. CHRIST IN THE GOSPELS.

Hyntle Place,
July 16th, 1944.

To The Bishop of Derby.

My dear Bishop,

I have to thank you for your very interesting valuable little book *Christ in the Gospels* which I have read carefully with an appreciation which treads hard on the heels of admiration. The Subject has been much in my mind, and I am grateful for real assistance in the difficult even baffling effort to make clear to mysel f, and even to other what I really mean when I take my stand with the grand assumption of the Incarnation. I am certainly not orthodox in any adequate sense, only so far as I cannot find any more satisfying formulation of my belief than what the Tradition of the Christian Church has delivered.

We have had Noël Davey as an incumbent within bicycle riding distance of this house: and I have found him a very pleasant and thoughtful man, with whom I was hoping to have much profitable converse: but he has been already sought out for the important position of Editorial Secretary to the S.P.C.K. and will leave us in September to my great regret. He shares my opinion of the book of a certain Mirfield Father, named Edwards on *The Virgin Birth*. It is an amazingly impudent specimen of " orthodox " polemic. I was astounded to read a review in the *Guardian* which described it as " an excellent defence of an essential article of the Creed to be highly recommended to any troubled with difficulties about it ". I have rarely come across a worse example of pseudo-scholarly writing. It evoked an effective and very temperately expressed reply by a writer who signs himself " Discipulus ". Who is he? It was a relief to read in your book p. 24 respecting St Luke's Birth Narrative : " The whole constitutes in the scheme of the Gospels a kind of poetical prelude to the story of the Saviour's life in the Synoptic Gospels." I think the connexion between Christology and History needs more careful consideration. The argument of Hoskyns and Davey in their book on the Fourth Gospel did not secure my acceptance. Your chapter X did not succeed in winning my acceptance. The conception of " nonhistorical writing history " eludes me. It ignores the essential issue.

Until History has delivered its verdict on the " Jesus of History " Christian Theology (Christology) does not possess the materials for the achievement of its indispensable task. Only when the historical facts are known can their spiritual significance be fairly appraised. But enough. I only meant to thank you for your book.

I take occasion to congratulate you and your wife on Anthony's triumphal march. May God protect and carry him forward to yet larger ranges of achievement and service !

My eyes handicap me horribly.

Always yours affectionately,
H. Hensley Henson,
Bishop.

156.   *Northern Folk.*

Hyntle Place,
September 26th, 1944.

To The Hon. Mrs Alington.

Dear Hester,

I have been thinking much about you, and hoping that you are making good progress in recovering from the severe accident, which cannot but have been a cruel shock. It distressed me greatly to hear about it.

I received a pleasant letter from the new Chief Constable's wife, which gave me the impression, that she must be an attractive person. In spite of her absurdly flatterous reference to my prose, her letter amused me, and may, perhaps, amuse you. In acknowledging it, I told her what Lord Durham (the present Earl's uncle) told me when I came to be Dean more than a quarter of a century ago—"Don't be alarmed at their rudeness. They are only taking your measure. They probably won't touch their hats to you; but if you touch yours to them, they will return the compliment." And I allowed myself to assure her that she would find in the Dean's wife somebody not only delightful but really worth knowing.

We have these horrible "doodlebugs" over us most nights, and one actually fell in the parish. But we take little heed, holding with the late Lady Londonderry, that it was wisest, "to take them lying down", i.e. to go to bed and stay there.

I have read with great delight and admiration, George Trevelyan's *Social History of England*. He has the sure hand of a great master of historical writing, alike in the choice of his vast material and in its interpretation. Our local Rabbi is *hors de combat* with illness, and I am officiating and preaching in the parish church, to congregations of villagers (mostly in petticoats) more select than numerous.

Forgive me for inflicting a letter on you, and let me know how you are.

Always affectionately
your friend,
H. Hensley Henson,
Bishop.

157. *Modern trends in Education and Theology.*

Hyntle Place,
October 17th, 1944.

To E. H. Blakeney, Esq.

My dear Blakeney,

It is a very long time since I wrote to you, and I hope you will not imagine that the explanation lies in forgetfulness or indifference, but largely, I think, it is because of my failing eyesight that I have found exertion of every kind repugnant; and I think probably it was the consciousness of indefensible inactivity which has arrested my pen, when writing to my friends was in question.   A few days ago I heard from my old chaplain, Jack Clayton, that he had met you at Norwich, and then the restiveness of my conscience became so great that I determined I would write to you without further delay.

I promised Major that I would write an article for his paper, *The Modern Churchman* on "The Archbishop's book" significantly entitled *The Church Looks Forward*, and I am now trying (with humbling little success) to carry out my undertaking.   Temple is on any showing a very remarkable man, and personally he is very attractive.   I have seen a good deal of him, on and off, since I made his acquaintance years ago, when he was a layman, in Westminster; and I have a real affection for him, though a deepening distrust of his wisdom, and a fear that he is giving the Church a lead in directions which I cannot approve. I propose to limit myself to his ecclesiastical polity, which has disclosed itself I think, very unfortunately in his handling of both the South Indian Scheme and Butler's Education Act.   As regards the first, he has thrown his weight into the scale of "Apostolic Succession" and thereby given the *coup de grace* to a project which is only really considerable on the assumption that it involves a repudiation of that fallacy which since Newman's Tract One, has obsessed a waxing number of the clergy.   With respect to the other, his acceptance of the National Society's programme in the matter of the Dual System has, I believe, probably ensured the failure of an honest and promising effort to Christianize effectively the national system of education.   I have read through recently with some care the last series of Bampton Lectures on *The Church and the Papacy*.   It is a meticulously learned attempt to provide a foundation in history for the Papal claims. The author, Dr Jalland, is an incumbent in Oxford, and is, I understand, an advanced Anglo-Catholick. The book illustrates the strong Romeward current which is now running in the Anglo-Catholick party. I think, if I had to choose between defending the Petrine claims of the Papacy and the Apostolic Succession of the Episcopate I would rather undertake the Papacy than the Episcopate. Of course, both are from a historical point of view totally inadmissible, but, if you accept the assumption of both, (viz. a Divinely instituted polity) and trace their working in history, the Papacy makes the better show than Episcopacy; and as an advocate I think I should be on stronger ground in defending the despot on the Seven Hills than in championing the multitudinous despots in episcopal palaces!

. . . .

Last week I had a foolish accident in my study which has confined me to the house with a game leg. Nothing was broken but my movements were rendered difficult.

. . . I hope you are well and cheerful.

Believe me always,

Affectionately yours,

H. Hensley Henson,

Bishop.

158. *On the death of Archbishop Temple.*

Hyntle Place,

November 12th, 1944.

To The Dean of Durham.

My dearest Dean,

Thank you so much for your kind remembrance of my 81st Birthday. It was shadowed by the reports of many deaths of contemporaries, younger than myself. Temple's death was almost tragic. I rarely agreed with him, but I could always admire his amazing gifts and could not but feel the charm of his most attractive personality. I think he is *felix opportunitate mortis*, for he has passed away while the streams of opinion in Church and State, of which he had become the outstanding symbol and exponent, were at flood, and escaped the experience of their inevitable ebb. The enthusiasm will give place to resentment as the chill of disillusion lowers the atmosphere. My estimate of him is a high one, though I think he had some very grave defects, not of character, but of temperament. Davidson once said to me, " Willie's weakness is that he is so kind that he can say no to nobody ". My observation of his career would accord with this. Nevertheless, I incline to think that he is the most variously distinguished of the 32 Archbishops of Canterbury since the Reformation; and, though I think he has given a great impetus to tendencies in the Church and in the Nation which I judge to be largely unsound, still it was a great thing for both Church and Nation that the chief place in the Hierarchy should have been filled by confessedly its most eminent member. Mrs Temple and her father were regular members of my congregation at St Margaret's, Westminster; I liked her, though I did not know her well, and she certainly was a woman of great ability and determination, and I think she succeeded in " making Willie a good Catholick "! It will be difficult to find a successor. I have always had a great desire that Mervyn Haigh should go to Canterbury, but I am increasingly doubtful whether his physical strength would be adequate to that position. Probably Fisher, if he would accept appointment, would be the best, in the circumstances, for the Church of England. A few years ago Bell of Chichester was generally regarded as almost the inevitable successor to Davidson, but many things have happened since Davidson's death. Lang's Primacy was probably not good for the Church of England. . . .

Mr Justice Charles was my Chancellor in Hereford, and I liked him. He is a hearty, impulsive man, who sometimes " speaks unadvisedly with his lips ", a trick which is quite consistent with his amiable character, but rarely admired in a Judge of the High Court.

. . . .

I am very glad that Hester is making good progress to recovery. Your " plaster saint " * will again adorn a more fitting pedestal in the College and Diocese of Durham.

. . . .

With love to Hester
I am, my dearest Dean,
Always affectionately yours,
H. Hensley Henson,
Bishop.

* Mrs Alington had had her legs in plaster for five months.

159. U.N.O.

Hyntle Place,
January 17th, 1945.

To Brig. The Hon. H. C. Cumming-Bruce, D.S.O.★

My dearest Harry,

The newspapers are filled with accounts of U.N.O. which has floated into history on a tidal wave of optimistic rhetoric and a mighty shower of mutual compliment. Yet there is a very disconcerting framework in which we have to contemplate the picture of a peace-making Sanhedrin of the nations. An unmanageable orgy of strikes in Britain and America, an almost acknowledged outbreak of fresh conflict in the Dutch East Indies, and something ominously like a rift between the Great Powers, to say nothing about the ever-worsening situation in Palestine and the revival of the too-familiar phenomenon of anarchy in South America; these must chasten, if not actually extinguish, the enthusiasm even of the most convinced pacifists. I would give much to have a " heart-to-heart " talk with you about the entire outlook, as it must present itself to you in Germany. I own to feeling considerably in need of consolation in England. I feel badly about Winston's exclusion from power at this juncture. If ever he, with his personal prestige, his amazing power of interpreting great situations greatly, and his unequalled capacity for uttering noble thoughts in noble words,—I say, if ever he, being what he has been, and what he is, was needed by Britain, by the Empire, and by mankind, this is the time. . . .

I imagine that the appalling problem of feeding Europe has been rendered somewhat more easy to solve by the destruction of life during the war. Putting together all the casualty-lists of the combatant nations, and their victims, and adding a reasonable estimate of civilian casualties, the sum of mortality must be very large, large enough to reduce importantly the amount of food-supplies needed for the continued sustenance of the populations.

What is your own opinion about the education of the Germans? I read statements about the great numbers of school-teachers, who are being dismissed as too perilously tainted with the Nazi poison, but I

★ Commandant, B.A.O.R. Training Centre.

M

have not hitherto observed any reasonably adequate plan for providing substitutes.   The shortage of trained teachers in Great Britain is very alarming.   I don't see how we can provide any large body of suitable men for service in the schools of Germany.   Is there any likelihood of raising a sufficient number of trained Germans who could be trusted to carry through the job?

Do you see the *Spectator*?   If so, you will have noticed the numerous letters which deal with the problem of bringing Religion effectively to " Youth ", as well military as civilian.   I cannot say that I have been favourably impressed by most of these letters, nor have I found them either informing or illuminating.   I wish we could talk over this subject also.   We are both agreed on its importance, and I think we both approach it as ourselves (albeit so unworthy of the " honourable name ") claiming to be Christians.

May God keep you, and lead you forward in His service!

Always affect^{ly} your friend,
H. Hensley Henson,
Bishop.

160.   *Thoughts on the War.*

Hyntle Place,
January 22nd, 1945.

To The Rev. Dr W. L. Sperry,★ *D.D.*

My dear Sir,

I have to acknowledge receipt of a very kind letter, and two copies of the Harvard Divinity School Bulletin which included a review over your signature of my book—*Retrospect of an Unimportant Life*.   Please accept my sincere thanks for both.

It pleased me to have my thoughts carried back to the Sunday evenings in 17 Dean's Yard when I had the satisfaction of meeting in a free, informal intercourse so many and such various persons, who had an interest in St Margaret's, and its witness.

I am greatly interested to learn that you were acquainted with

★ Dean of the Harvard Divinity School (Rhodes Scholar, Queen's College, Oxford, 1904–7).

Albert Saxton.* For many years now, he has passed out of my knowledge; and now I don't know where he is, or what he is doing. One of the shadows of life, as one recalls it in old age, is the reminder of so many individuals who were once near and dear, and have somehow lost touch and passed out of knowledge.

Your spiritual movement interests me, and adds rather special value to what you say about me and my career. Indeed, I must needs be grateful for a review so understanding and so evidently inspired by generous feeling.

I was surprized, indeed almost startled, by the kindness with which the book has been generally received in England, even in quarters where resentment might not unreasonably have been expected. Its relatively large circulation has seemed to me remarkable at a time so fully charged with absorbing anxieties, which might well disincline men for books of such a limited range of interest and importance.

Perhaps the fact may be taken to indicate that the questions which have exercized my mind so persistently throughout my life are pressing in varied measures and forms on the minds of many others.

I have not abandoned the hope that I may be able to add a supplemental volume, in which (after the manner of St Augustine) I might include some *Retractationes*, by which I imagine that he meant, not recantations, but re-considerations of some questions in the light of larger knowledge and longer experience. But the failure of my eyesight compels me to realize that the prospect of my succeeding in achieving my purpose is lessening; and no man in his 82nd year can wisely indulge in framing projects.

This fearful war has brought into debate so much that seemed settled, and gone so far to blurring, or even blotting out, what seemed to be the firmly fixed barriers and boundaries of Reason and Faith, that no considering man can wholly escape the chill and enfeeblement of doubt. "The foundations have been cast down" says the Psalmist, and adds the despondent question, "What hath the righteous done?"

The war has been so widely extended, and waged with such atrocious violence, that the prospect of the problems which Peace will propose is hardly less terrifying than that of war. I have never for one moment wavered in my conviction that in 1939 Great Britain took the right decision, when it resolved to fight rather than acquiesce in the Hitlerite aggression. Now, in the sixth year of the conflict, with the wreckage

* A protégé of Hensley Henson's at St Margaret's, Westminster.

of its violence apparent on every hand, I feel more than ever sure that we were not mistaken when we regarded the conflict as truly a Crusade, to which as a nation we were divinely called.   The deepening infamies of Nazi warfare—infamies so horrible as almost to shake one's faith in the essential Divineness of Humanity, have added confirmation to my original conviction that Great Britain was being called to " come to the help of the Lord against the mighty."   But there are so many indications of persistent evil, unrebuked and unrestrained by the fearful experiences of the war, that I am sometimes filled with a great fear, that the Peace will inaugurate not (as our Christian Socialists seem to think) the " Kingdom of God on Earth ", or at least a morally purged and strengthened civilization, but rather one more epoch of cosmic conflict.   So I take refuge in the Psalmist's conviction, " The Lord is King, be the people never so impatient " and I seek grace to " tarry the Lord's leisure " and " do out the duty ".

Dr Edward Moore and his family showed my wife and me much kindness when we visited Harvard, and we retain an affectionate memory of him and his.   I have not heard from him or about him for a long time; and should be glad, if he is still living, to get into touch with him.

I owe you an apology for so long and rambling an acknowledgement of your very kind letter, and review of my book, and remain,

Sincerely and obliged,
H. Hensley Henson,
Bishop.

161.   The Grace of Resignation.

Hyntle Place,
January 23rd, 1945.

My dear Dashwood,

    .   .   .   .

I have now been taking duty in this parish for nearly 4 months, and am beginning to feel that I am entitled to resign again.   But, as I have often observed in bishops and in incumbents, the grace of Re-signation is of all the Christian virtues the one which finds most difficult acceptance.

The story of Arthur Foley's second acceptance of the Bishoprick is, if not true, yet *ben trovato*. I am sure that a just view of Anglican history during the 20th century will have to attribute great importance to the character and duration of Ingram's Episcopate in London. Emotional anarchy in the one, and crustacean tenacity in the other destroyed discipline and confused the normal progress of "preferment".

I was on the whole pleased with Fisher's nomination as Archbishop, but if I had seen the picture of the Primate of all England with a pipe in his mouth, shamelessly published in the semi-official paper issued under the title "the Spiritual Issues of the War", I might have hesitated before writing a letter of congratulation to him! However, as I had not seen it my letter was quite sincere. But I do loathe and lament the modern "democratic" fashion of parsons smoking publicly. It is in line with the other and worse exhibitions of secularized pastorate. This dreadful weather shrivels me with helpless cold: and I am in my 82nd year!

I do feel with you in your anxiety for your son: but he is in God's Hands, and so are we. *Sursum corda!*

Always affectely,
H. Hensley Henson, Bp.

162.   *The Title of the* RETROSPECT.

Hyntle Place,
January 30th, 1945.

To The Dean of Norwich.

My dear Dean,

Thank you so much for your very welcome and interesting letter, which ought to have been answered before this, but this arctic weather has not only chilled my miserable carcase, but also gone far towards blunting my moral sense, and paralysing such relics of intellect as have survived contact with this queer world for more than 81 years.

I am really glad to know that you are well advanced with your autobiography. With regard to a title, I think you would be wise to postpone choosing it until your work is substantially completed. You will then be in a position to settle the title page with some reasonable measure of relevance to the character and contents of the book. That book cannot fail to be interesting, for it will be the garnered product of an interesting life, and it will assuredly be well constructed and well expressed because it will be arranged and composed by a man of proved literary power and good taste. I may confess to you that the much-criticized title of my *Retrospect* was not really deliberately chosen. When I sent the stuff to Milford, I just scribbled the title as a suggestion, and he took it *au grand sérieux*. On the whole I felt that it would serve as well as any other, and so it has remained.

It is pleasant to hear that Blakeney thinks kindly of me. I greatly appreciate his friendship, and admire his literary judgements and happy power of graceful verse. I do not forget that I owe his friendship, among other good things, to you.

This wonderful news from the Eastern Front seems to justify the hope that the end of the war may be nearer than we have dared recently to think possible. It is, however, impossible to avoid a feeling of anxiety, which is almost a foreboding, that we shall not have done with Russia, when the " Cease Fire " is sounded. Whenever I look at Stalin's picture, I feel that we have in him one of those dynamic, semi-civilized prodigies, like Theodoric and Charlemagne, who may be set for the regeneration of society, but who may be, like others of the same type, raised up for its destruction. We must wait and see, as Mr Asquith sagely said. We must "tarry the Lord's leisure ", as the Psalmist phrased the same thought religiously.

With kind regards to Mrs Cranage,

Believe me always,

Sincerely your friend,

H. Hensley Henson,

Bishop.

P.S. I hardly think it would be worth your while to include a photographic reproduction of Temple's letter, unless of course it was of unusual interest. You do not need the assistance of anybody's Foreword; and the amiable Temple had done more than most men to " debase the coinage " by undue minting, in the matter of " Forewords ". But on this matter you alone can give a reasonably considered decision.

H. H. H.

163.   *Lloyd George.*

January 31st, 1945.

To *The Rev. Preb. A. B. Wynne-Willson.*

My dear Wynne-Willson,

.   .   .   .

I can feel for you and with you in the dolourous consciousness of failing memory. It is, perhaps, even more practically paralyzing than the disconcerting fact of failing eyesight.   How often do I lament the fact that I was never taught in boyhood to keep a " common-place book ", and how to index it effectively !   When I think of the accumulation of varied and valuable knowledge, garnered from a relatively wide extent of reading, which would then have been at my service now, I feel so indignantly remorseful that I could do myself some penal injury !   As it is, I am continually baffled by being unable to give " chapter and verse " for things that linger in my mind, and cannot be used because they cannot be verified !   This consciousness of self-imposed frustration is one of the darker shadows of old age.

When Lloyd George's earldom was announced in the *Times* on New Year's Day, I wrote a letter of congratulation in which I reminded him that we both were born in the same year, 1863, which Austen Chamberlain once described as a " vintage year ", adding that he could recall a Government in which no less than 8 Cabinet Ministers were born in it.   I observed that L.G.'s nomination of me to Hereford had affected my career, not unimportantly, though it could have had no importance in his.   This morning I received a very belated acknowledgement from the Welsh Wizard, expressed with much kindness, and including the following, which has an interest of its own :   " There is no act of my public career which fills me with greater satisfaction than the two appointments of Hereford and Durham.   And as events show, my action has been completely justified."

It is not uninteresting to remember that my first contact with L.G. was the receipt of an angry protest, rather rudely expressed, which I received from him at the time of the Welsh Disestablishment conflict, when he was a protagonist for the Bill, and I an opponent. Now on that issue, I have " crossed the floor " !

With kindest regards to your wife,

I am, always affectionately
your Friend
H. Hensley Henson,
Bishop.

164.   The Servant Problem ; Professor A. M. Ramsey's book on the Resurrection.

Hyntle Place,
July 1st, 1945.

To The Dean of Durham.

My dearest Dean,

We were charmed with the Bishop of Jarrow,* and would have been pleased if we could have seen more of him. What an unusually interesting career he has had ! That he should have emerged from it with such admirable balance and good sense, discloses qualities of a high order, and he has a taking aspect and manner to provide a suitable " shop-window " for the goods behind the counter !

When will the " servant problem " find a tolerable solution? The tradition of indispensable personal loyalty, without which a genuine domestic discipline is really impossible, has been broken ; and I cannot see how it is to be restored. The multiplying crowd of social " reformers " have their faces set in the wrong direction, viz. towards a complete assimilation of domestic service to the hateful type of " organized labour "—the Trade Union ideal with its appropriate methods and manners is to cross the threshold of private life, and, within the ruined " Home ", the constituent factors are to confront one another as suspicious, reluctant, and even openly hostile associates, bound together with knives in their hands like Swedish duellists ! It is a hideous prospect. Perhaps it is as well that its prodigious cost will exclude pensioned ecclesiastics from enjoying it.

In the latest issue of the *Modern Churchman* there is a strong, and

* The Right Rev. Colin Dunlop.

even severe criticism of Ramsey's recent book on the Resurrection. It confirmed a certain misgiving about him, which his inaugural lecture (which he very kindly sent me) stirred in my mind. Does he really understand historical method? Does he imagine that History can be seriously handled under the domination of theological assumptions? To my mind Theology cannot begin its work until History has provided so much of its material as is properly called " historical ". The weakness of " orthodoxy " modern and ancient has ever been its habit of subordinating History to Theology, for the Religion of the Incarnation is bound into the historical process, and cannot be safely " developed " except on a sound basis of historical science. It is the historian's primary obligation to cleanse his mind from prejudice, whether friendly or hostile, to the orthodox theory; but " prejudice " does not mean the natural and unavoidable bias or tendency of the student's mind; it does mean his subordination of the historical argument to the requirements of a theory. But I must stop; or I shall weary my eyes, and spoil your admirable temper!

We are tied to this house by the practical impossibility of finding a place where we might get a change. Our solitary domestic must get her holiday; and in her absence we shall have to make shift as best we can. For myself, it matters little, for probably I am more comfortably placed in my own house than anywhere else; but I am concerned that my admirable ladies should get no change, although even in their case, I doubt whether the gain of getting away would outweigh the fatigue of travelling, the discomfort of inferior and overcrowded hotels, and the exorbitant cost of the experience. The difficulty of transport and commissariat is as great as ever; and one needs to accept Carthusian discipline within the confines of a Cynic's " tub "! Then, I am now reduced to the extreme limit of sartorial decrepitude, and, in the brutal prose of unwelcome reality, am not fit to present myself in civilized society. My humble ambition soars no higher than to avoid the ignominy of " indecent exposure "! So, I suppose, we shall moulder here for the rest of the summer.

Always my dear Cyril,

very aff[ly] your friend,

H. Hensley Henson,

Bishop.

165.   *After a dinner-party at Hyntle Place.*

Hyntle Place,
October 2nd, 1945.

To Lord Woodbridge.

My dear Arthur,

The enclosed lines written on a sheet of paper may have been picked up on the dining room carpet after the Goose had been consumed by the company in Hyntle Place on Sept. 30th. The verse is poor, but the intention is evidently good, and the substance obviously sound.

Ever aff^{ly} your friend,
Herbert.

TO A GOOSE

O famous Bird, by Roman writers hailed
Rome's guardian once, when other guards had failed,
Whom shallow mortals, heeding but thy hiss,
Thy subtle wisdom must for ever miss.
* Thy stately march, when, plucking grass, before thee
Thou mov'st in pride of conscious royalty
Thou dost recall our former joys, foretelling more.
When autumn brings again St Michael's Day
O Goose, thou com'st in festival array,
And gloom flies from thee, as the Night from Day.
Gift of my Friend, for me thou gild'st the close
Of Summer's warmth and out-of-door repose.
O Blessed Bird, I love thee, while I eat
Remembering ARTHUR, and his praise repeat.

* The author at this point appears to have omitted a line. In attempting to supply his omission, I seem myself to have fallen into some confusion.   However, I trust to your forbearance to allow me, in view of the present shortage of paper, to send the stuff on, without making a fair copy.—H. H. H.

166.   *Thanks for a birthday message.*

Hyntle Place,
November 8th, 1945.

To The Rev. B. B. F. Westcott.

My dear Basil,

I take it as a very kind thing that you should remember my birthday. Many of my friends sent me very good wishes; and did much to mitigate the inevitable sadness of a commemoration which attests so clearly the passage of time and the near approach of that *hora fatalis* when I must hand in my account to the " Great Taskmaster ", an account of my long life. Nothing consoles me and cheers me so much as the continuing affection of men whom I was privileged to ordain.

Affectionately your friend,
H. Hensley Henson
(Bp).

167.   *AN UNIMPORTANT LIFE.*

November 10th, 1945.

To The Rev. Canon D. E. Sturt.*

My dear Canon,

The title has been much criticized, but I think its justification must turn on the kind of importance which the descriptive adjective has for its root.   In some ways I can imagine that it might be thought, and indeed has been thought, that my career has exercised considerable influence ; but I myself was thinking of the objects for which I have contended ; and I am compelled to admit that most of them seem now to be more remote than they were when I began my ministry. The Establishment is discredited, and, *me judice*, has become morally indefensible ; the lawlessness in the Church is more impudent and extensive than ever ; socialism is now the reigning temper of the time, and carries all before it in Church and State ; episcopalian exclusiveness now reigns in the Theological Colleges ; and the old Anglican

* Vicar of Norton, Stockton-on-Tees.

ideal of the " Parson " has been almost everywhere replaced by the misleading and invidious description " Priest ".   The temper of the Church has steadily deteriorated, and I do not think that there is any reason to hope that the war will have improved it.   Nevertheless I do not despair.   *Temporis filia veritas* ;   Time will take its time, but in due time will provide its justification for truth which in its own time was obscure, or denied, or repudiated.

Yours affectionately,
H. H. Henson (Bp).

168.   *On the death of Archbishop Lang (1).*

Hyntle Place,
December 6th, 1945.

To The Dean of Durham.

My dearest Dean,

It seems a long time since I heard from you.   Probably the fault is mine.   If so, be generous enough to forgive it, and to be sure that it has its cause in the imbecility of old age, never in the faltering of my regard.   Lang's sudden death brings home to one, the old, old verity which nobody disputes and everybody forgets, that " in the midst of life, we are in death ".   I have read through the obituary notice in the *Times* with much interest.   It is, of course, very laudatory, but it is not indiscriminating in its eulogy, and to anyone who has followed Lang's career from his undergraduateship to his purple dénouement in the royal retreat in Kew, indicates a fairly close knowledge and no common insight.   His personal gifts were exceptionally great, and his opportunities extraordinarily many and ample.   He had what I sometimes call " the Scottish genius for success ".   And, in his case, and in that of other Scots who also have notably succeeded in England, I have reached the conclusion that to be Scotch is a positive advantage in England.   The Scotch are naturally physically tough, intellectually interested, socially adaptable, and immensely ambitious beyond the normal English of comparable type.   And—this is of cardinal importance, they do not provoke the envy and suspicion which a successful Englishman commonly arouses, if he chance to be in any respect, personal or circumstantial, odd.   Lang was handsome, gifted with an admirable voice, a fine presence, and the hereditary power of facile and eloquent speech.   He had, like most Scots, an unerring instinct in the choice of friends, drawing towards the titled and socially or professionally influential, with the sure procedure of iron moving to a magnet.   He was bound to mount quickly whatever was the profession he should choose.   He exchanged the relatively unimportant church of his forbears, for the relatively splendid Church of England; and when he had domesticated himself in his new spiritual home, he instinctively attached himself to the prevailing section.   He was a born prelatist, and " reared his mitred front in Court and Parliament ".   Had he adhered to the Bar, he could not have avoided the Woolsack.   There, too, he would have been carried forward, not only by his own great qualities, but also by the patriotic assistance of " kindly Scots ".

I recall that it is now 60 years since first I met him in the old historical Seminar, where he read a paper on Burke.   I remember how he impressed me by his handsome face, and the amazing facility of his sonorous eloquence.   I was five years his senior in All Souls, 3 years in Ordination, and 1 year in age.   We were very closely associated, especially after I migrated from the Southern to the Northern Province in 1912, and especially when, as Bishop of Durham, I was always sitting beside him in Convocations and Conferences.   We were always civil enough, but, I think, that both he and I were conscious of a certain inner dissidence which made friendship difficult.   We were temperamentally severed rather sharply.   When we came closest together at the time of the R.P.B. conflict, I thought he did not play a creditable part.   No doubt he regarded me as a precipitate and violent person.   My last letter from him came a few weeks ago, and in it he emphasized the excellence of his health, and the pleasantness of his life in retirement.

I wonder whether History will endorse the extraordinarily honourable judgement which their contemporaries have pronounced on 3 successive Archbishops of Canterbury—Davidson, Lang, and Willie Temple.   They were very different, and two of them were Scots.

The Bishop of Coventry sent me two days ago a proposed " explanation " of his Cathedral scheme, which is shortly to be published.   It does not appear to me to make the scheme more intelligible or more religiously valuable.   It seems to express architecturally the view which I hold to be essentially un-Christian. Christian unity is to be reached by collaboration of Christians in all kinds of non-committal social and economic experiments on the understanding that they agree to acquiesce in limiting admission to the Altar to those only who have received Episcopal Ordination. But that exclusion is confessedly the result of the Apostolical Succession theory of the Christian Ministry, and that theory is notoriously abandoned by most serious historical scholars outside the unreformed churches. Yet, as Willie Temple said, the essential scandal of Christian division is the inability of devout Christians to meet at the Lord's Table. The new Coventry Cathedral will embody in a very significant way the disgust of Christians as such with existing divisions, and the refusal of Anglicans to abandon an untenable position.

.   .   .   .

Give my love to Hester, and be sure that I am always,

affect^{ly} your Friend,

H. Hensley Henson,

Bishop.

169.   On the death of Archbishop Lang (2).

Hyntle Place,

December 22nd, 1945.

To The Rev. Dr D. H. S. Cranage, Litt.D.

My dear Dr Cranage,

Thank you so much for sending me the charming picture of your house. It looks most attractive. You must, I think, be not far distant from another friend of mine, the very distinguished surgeon, Professor Grey Turner, who lives at the old Evelyn house, Huntercombe Manor, near Taplow. I made his acquaintance when he operated on me for appendicitis. I always tell him he is the only man who knows me in and out! We stayed there in 1936, but I hardly dare to hope that I shall repeat the very pleasant experience. A purblind octogenarian can hardly contemplate much travelling, even if conditions become much more normal than at present they seem likely to become.

Archbishop Lang's sudden death came to me as something of a

shock. He was almost exactly one year my junior in age, three my junior in Holy Orders, five years my junior at All Souls. We were brought closely together on many important occasions, and always maintained a friendly correspondence. Though we were, I think, *au fond*, temperamentally divergent. My last letter from him, received a few weeks before his death, dwelt on the felicity of his retirement. A beautiful house, private entrance into Kew Gardens, an honorary trusteeship of the British Museum, abundant good talk at the dining clubs, Grillions and the " Club ", and, to crown all, a seat in the House of Lords, which enabled him to express himself effectively on public affairs when he wished to do so. I am disposed to add yet another felicity, which he did not foresee. What could be more enviable than to crown one's active life with a death so painless and so swift?

I was very much surprised to read in the *Spectator* a thoroughly un-deserved criticism of Lang's successor as being inferior to his two distinguished predecessors in the matter of extra-ecclesiastical pro-nouncements. Surely, neither Cosmo Lang nor William Temple added to his influence by his excursions into politics. In my judge-ment, the present Primate is a far sounder guide to the Church of England at this most difficult juncture than either the Scot or the Socialist.

Give my affectionate remembrances to Mrs Cranage,

and believe me,

Affectionately your friend,

H. Hensley Henson,

Bishop.

170. *Bishop Strong of Oxford.*

Hyntle Place,

January 10th, 1946.

To The Dean of Durham.

My dearest Dean,

.   .   .   .

I suppose there is no need to be surprised that the Prime Minister cannot make up his mind as to the appointments which he must make to several important positions in the Established Church. I did not like his selection for ——, because the policy of translating clergymen from the Dominions to English Sees seems to me of doubtful wisdom. I gather that —— is an extreme Anglo-Catholick. . . . I cannot see any reason for thinking that he has anything of value to contribute to the discipline of the —— churches or the guidance of the English Church, but beyond that I cannot say anything about him. I have never read a line of any book he has written; I have never met him; nor have I a notion what he looks like! I should have preferred the appointment of the Dean of St Paul's. It seems to me very surprising that a man of his evident ability, astonishing industry and, so far as one can judge from his public pronouncements, soundness of mind and breadth of sympathy should be ignored when so many bishopricks have to be filled up. Harold Anson tells me that he has undertaken to write some kind of a biography of Strong of Oxford, and appeals to me for some material. I was very fond of Strong, and had much to do with him in the course of my life. He and I were gazetted to bishopricks in the Northern Province at the same time, when he was moved from the Deanery of Christ Church to the Bishoprick of Ripon and I was translated from Hereford to Durham. I had a great regard for him, and often consulted him. We very generally acted together; but, of course, he was definitely an Anglo-Catholick, though his humour, knowledge and sanity were hard to reconcile with that character; and I was quite definitely in no sense so to be described. I was always surprised that Strong did not count for more in the central policies of the Church. He very rarely took a definite line on any question of importance; but whenever anything which might be called important emerged, his vote would pretty surely be cast with the Anglo-Catholick bloc, of which Bishop Talbot of Winchester was the recognized and venerated head. I did my best to provoke him into indiscretions, but rarely succeeded. He crowed and chuckled to himself, but emitted no coherent opinion. During the discussions on Prayerbook revision his opinion was felt to be very important on all matters on which church music was concerned, and he was a recognized intermediary between the episcopal bench and the University Press. He was, I gather, eminently successful as a Vice-Chancellor during the first World-War. He was fond of undergraduates, and liked to be in their company; but I always doubted whether in his complaisance, he did not acquire a style and a habit which concealed his real strength and militated against his rightful influence. I had a good deal of intercourse with him, over Buchman's groups, and I think we were fundamentally in agreement; but I could never goad him into any helpful public statement. He was, perhaps, overmuch impressed by the apparent devotion and sincerity of some of Buchman's victims. I think, perhaps, it would have been good for him to have been translated from Oxford to one of the primacies, though it is unlikely that he would have shaken off his academic habit. He was a very loyal "Old Westminster" and I used to see a good deal of him when I was living in Dean's Yard, and I think he ought to have counted for more in the Church than he did. The last phase of his life was to me very distressing. His memory failed, and when his sister died, and he was left quite alone, he became a pathetic figure, haunting the Athenæum like the phantom of some deceased philosopher, who could hardly remember for ten minutes what he had said. Certainly, Lang is much to be congratulated on his swift and painless departure before he had time to obscure and discredit his distinguished past.

I am glad to be informed from several sources that Mrs Alington is wonderfully active and cheerful in spite of her accident. She is a great person, and I blend my affection with the homage of my respect.

Always, my dear Dean,

Affectionately yours,

H. Hensley Henson,

Bishop.

171. Christian Doctrine.

Hyntle Place,

January 19th, 1946.

To The Dean of Winchester.★

My dear Dean,

I seem to have omitted to acknowledge your very kind letter of January 4th. Probably this is one more consequence of my em-

★ The Very Rev. E. G. Selwyn.

barrassing trouble with my eyes, and you will condone it. Thank you so much for your good wishes for the new year, which I heartily reciprocate.

It is a very real satisfaction to me to know that you approve what I wrote in the *Times* under the heading, " The Creeds ". It seems to me that the advocates of simplification lie open to the charge of greatly under-rating the intelligence of those whom they aspire to assist, and, at the same time, gravely over-rating their own competence for the task which they have allotted to themselves. I have had a fairly long innings as a Christian minister, and in the course of my life I have encountered many attempts to justify the repudiation of the Christian claim, but never (except as a transparent excuse for a repudiation obviously based on far other grounds) have I been compelled to conclude that the language of the creeds is really the obstacle to faith; and I think much harm is done by elaborating the assumption that nothing else is really the key to the rapid and apparent decline of Christianity. I don't think sufficient importance is attached to the language of the Eighth Article, " Of the three Creeds ". There the authority of the creeds is based on the assumption that they " may be proved by most certain warrants of holy Scripture ". If, it would seem to follow, the language of the creeds cannot be so regarded by the sincere modern student of Holy Scripture, then the authority of the creeds is to that extent for him withdrawn. The whole question is thrown back from the formulary to the Scripture. If then it be the case that the modern student of Scripture, if he be sincere and honest, will find himself compelled to take into his reckoning a great accumulation of knowledge, scientific, historic and critical, which was not accessible to former generations, and was quite notoriously inaccessible to those who compiled the ancient formularies, it would seem to be inevitable that these formularies can only be competent to serve their purpose at the present time when explained and interpreted in the light of modern knowledge. The process of explanation and adaptation has proceeded far since the great chasm between traditional formulations of faith and the accumulations of relevant modern knowledge disclosed itself. The Clergy Subscription Act of 1865 was intended to be, and has been generally regarded as being, a sufficient authority for the legal subscription, which Anglican clergymen are required to make to the Creeds and Articles in the Prayer-Book. So far as the difficulty which the Headmaster of Malvern has stated, is a fact, that current irreligion must be largely attributed to the incorrigible Fundamentalism of Christian teachers, disclosed as well by the crude literalism of the Evangelical party as by the irrational exaltation of Patristic exegesis by the Anglo-Catholicks. I welcomed the Report of the Archbishops' Commission on Doctrine, because it did seem to me to go a long way towards admitting all this. Not the pictorial language of the creeds, but the didactic incompetence of the Christian pulpit is mainly at fault, apart, of course, from those deeper moral and spiritual difficulties which have ever clouded the vision of the " natural man " when he has to face the Christian claim. I await with considerable interest the episcopal appointments which must shortly be made. I do not envy the Prime Minister his task in selecting suitable men; for, indeed, suitable men, as suitability might be reckoned by Labour politicians, are not numerous, unless, of course, the standard of suitability for episcopal office has been dramatically changed. I could name, perhaps, as many as four men whom I should like to see " elevated " to the Bench, and, perhaps, a dozen about whom I should be glad to have assurance that they would not arrive at that eminence !

I have not yet read the Report on the Conversion of England, but such notices of it in the press as I have seen do not encourage me to think that it will assist the Church to discover a solution of that immense and terrifying problem.

I have a great regard for Blakeney. He has a fine and just mind, and a genuine gleam of poetic insight along with an unusual power of giving effective and dignified expression to his mind.

My eyesight is a great problem. It is not quite clear what I ought to do about it. . . . I have had to make a final end of public ministration, and I find dictation less fatiguing than handwriting, and that must be my excuse for addressing you in typescript.

Always sincerely yours,
H. Hensley Henson,
Bishop.

P.S. I am very glad to know that your edition of I. Peter will soon issue from the Press. A good edition and commentary on that epistle is greatly needed. If Hort had completed his edition, we should have been in better case. The fragment which he left us is priceless, but it is only a fragment. Blakeney told me that your book was on the way, and he said enough to stimulate my appetite. I hope you have followed the admirable example of Bishop Lightfoot by enriching your edition with dissertations on some of the leading problems which the epistle raises.

H. H. H.

172.   Appointments to the Episcopate.

Hyntle Place,
January 30th, 1946.

To The Dean of Durham.

My dearest Dean,

If, as you assure me, the Bishop of Jarrow's arrangement of the Commemoration Service justified itself in experience, I have no reasonable ground for objecting to it, and the less since in itself it appears to be admirably conceived.   The liturgical trick of breaking up forms into fragments, duly introduced with more or less appropriate tags from the Scripture, is now so well established that (after having successfully played its part in discrediting the Revised-Prayerbook), it may very well determine the procedure in other compositions!!!!!

I am glad you had Matthews to preach.   I wish he had been made Bishop of London, or at least Bishop of Gloucester.   I await with some curiosity the next batch of episcopal appointments.   Somebody tells me that Attlee will make a rule of insisting on parochial experience as a condition of episcopal office.   If that should be so, I think a great blunder will have been made; not only would a great number of very inadequately equipped clergymen be carried on to the episcopal bench; but also the personal quality of the bishops, (which is the basis of such influence as they possess), would be seriously lessened.   The parochial clergy would incline to discount the authority of their superior by judging him as probably no better than themselves.   The Evangelical proverb—" No prophet is without honour save in his own country "—would in some sense and measure apply.   I do not think experience favours the elevation of parish priests.   Schoolmaster Bishops, professorial bishops, and even decanal bishops, have a better record as bishops than the waxing number of exhausted missionaries and popular parish priests.

Thank you for Lavinia's address. We are very glad to possess it. With love to Hester,

I am always affectionately

your friend,

H. Hensley Henson,

Bishop.

173.   Thanks for the loan of a book.

Hyntle Place,

May 14th, 1946.

To Lady Thurlow.

My dear Lady Thurlow,

I have been reading *So Few Got Through* with great interest, and an ever strengthening impression of the marvel and mystery of the British officer's character and achievements. Of course, I was nowise surprised to find our dear Harry * disclosed as a magnificent example of the type, but it was delightful to find so fresh and evidently sincere a revelation of a colleague's mind respecting him. It must be a profound satisfaction to you and his father to see him marching forward with such well merited homage and, we may add, such remarkable professional distinction. At the same time, the book brings home to me how grievous is the price which Britain has had to pay in the loss of so many of these gallant and chivalrous young men, and how pitiable appears the degraded haggling of the international market to which the cosmic idealism of U.N.O. has now degenerated. I do not think it would be possible to exaggerate the moral squalor and political cynicism of the discussions of the " Big Three " and the " Big Five ", and their subordinate collections of Foreign Secretaries. However, the history of mankind shows that the most valuable results have sometimes been garnered from strange sowing. When I was Canon of Westminster nearly half a century ago, I used to say that the glorious Abbey was " a violet growing on a dunghill ", for the money requisite for the architectural work of Henry

* Brig. The Hon. H. C. Cumming-Bruce.

III and Edward I is said to have been provided by the fines levied on the Jews by those sapient monarchs who tolerated the money-lenders in order from time to time to confiscate for the benefit of their own exchequer and the edification of their Christian subjects the usurious wealth of their commissioned victims!! How truly did the poet sing

> " God moves in a mysterious way,
> His wonders to perform."

. . . .

We have arranged (at vast cost) to get rooms in the Hotel de Paris, Cromer, from June 17th to July 1st, and we hope that during our absence this house will be painted. It has much the appearance now of the old " Great Eastern " after it was finally scrapped and presented a marvellous spectacle of submarine accumulations on its much travelled hull!

With kindest regard to Lord Thurlow,
Always affectionately yours,
H. Hensley Henson,
Bishop.

174. Friendship.

Hyntle Place,
June 2nd, 1946.

To Anthony Lightfoot, Esq.

My Anthony,

Your letter gave me very real pleasure, and I have read it several times, and always with a stronger assurance that a true friendship links us together. It sets me thinking about the marvel and mystery of friendship, whence it comes, and why, and how, and whereto it leads. There is the sudden and spontaneous attraction which discloses itself incalculably. The classic record of this emergence of friendship is, of course, the sacred record of Jonathan's and David's :

" And it came to pass when he (David) had made an end of speaking unto Saul, that the soul of Jonathan was knit with the soul of David, and Jonathan loved him as his own soul " (I Samuel XVIII, 1).

Christ described His disciples as His Friends; and it is surprizing, suggestive, and profoundly significant that the name has never been generally adopted by His followers. Even the Quakers, who so described themselves were, perhaps, intending the reference rather to their co-religionists than to Him, whom they all worshipped and in whom they discovered the power and principle of their friendship for one another. Yet we cannot be mistaken in thinking that "the disciple whom Jesus loved, and who so described himself, was in some deep sense His friend, as none of the other Apostles was felt by Him to be; for in St John Jesus found an understanding of His character and purpose truer than theirs, and a response, more prompt and unreserved to the quality of His Personal influence.

Friendship, however begun, is a voyage of discovery, full of perils and surprizes. As the friends have intercourse, which deepens into that fullness of mutual trust, which is implied in their union, they learn more of one another, are startled, perhaps, by finding unsuspected defects, and cheered by unveiling unrealized powers, but as the cementing force of community in hopes and interests tells on them increasingly, their original venture of faith finds consecration in experience.

You speak of the inadequacy of letter-writing as a method of self-expression, and compare it with the freer and more self-revealing method of conversation. I agree with you wholly in this matter, and allow myself to hope that the time may not be far distant when we may clasp hands again, and in the Psalmist's words "hold sweet counsel together as friends". Meanwhile, till this tyranny of untoward circumstance is overpast, we will keep touch in the exchange of letters, and in community of heart and mind. It greatly pleases me that we shall both make daily use of the collect which we both find so rich in spiritual comfort. To be agreed in that inner sphere of the spirit is to be possessed of the very secret of mutual understanding.

.   .   .   .

I am glad to be out of the noise and crowd of the "Victory" celebrations on June 8th. In spite of Mr Churchill's approbation, I cannot but think that the celebration is unreal, unwanted, and sinfully wasteful of food, money, and productive power.

Always, my Anthony,
Affect^{ly} your friend,
H. Hensley Henson,
Bishop.

175.   *Vivisection.*

June 25th, 1946.

To E. H. Blakeney, Esq.

My dear Blakeney,

Thank you so much for your letter and for the Whitsuntide *
hymn, which I liked so much that I have copied it into my journal (a
fly in Amber?) and for the loan of the Apocrypha lectures.† I am
nearly half through them, and find them so interesting that I mean to
finish them before telling you what I think about them.

On the subject of Vivisection, I have thought and read much and
I cannot but sympathize with the generous sentiments which determine
your refusal to admit its right to the acceptance of considering Christian
men.   And yet I cannot but think that a repudiation of a method which
seems indisputably essential to the advance of medical and surgical
science in the interest both of men and animals, cannot finally be
sustained.   I think we must not regard the non-human creatures as
merely the tools of human interest, lying outside the concern and
protection of morality, but rather as only so far lying outside, as their
lack of personality necessarily implies.   They must be treated responsi-
bly and where their lack of personality makes it impossible to require
their voluntary consent to procedures requisite to the higher interests
of mankind, the decision must be taken for them by their natural
governors, Men, but always taken in their interest, as well as in that of
mankind, and never for frivolous or immoral purposes.   I find it far
more difficult to reconcile " blood sports " with Christian morality,
than to reconcile vivisection;. and I hold it to be morally requisite to
bring vivisection under such effective control that it cannot be bent
to the service of idle curiosity and cynical callousness.   I am not
satisfied with the argument which yet has to serve *faute de mieux.*
The castration of animals for their better adaptation to human needs,
and their deliberate extirpation as a method of colonial development
are procedures not less repulsive than vivisection, but even less apparently justified by the ambiguous but never wholly negligible
casuistic dictum " The end justifies the means ".   Perhaps all turns on
the quality of the end, and how far that of the means is really congruous

* Now published in Mr Blakeney's *Collected Hymns* (Winchester, 1949).
† Delivered at Winchester (unpublished).

and indispensable.   But the ramifications of the Argument are limitless; and one is driven back at last to a rough and ready solution of the practical problem on a balance of expediencies as conditioned by Christianity.

.   .   .   .

Always your friend,
H. Hensley Henson,
Bishop.

176.   *Two seaside sermons.*

Hyntle Place,
July 4th, 1946.

To The Dean of Durham.

My dearest Cyril,

.   .   .   .

I . . . remember —— mainly by the sermons which I heard in the parish church by two strange preachers. . . . [The one] opened his sermon with the declaration that he was about to preach on a text on which he had never heard a sermon during a long life.   The text was none other than the very famous one, which has been my favourite text and on which in the course of my life I have probably preached more than on any other—" Jesus Christ is the same yesterday, today, yea and for ever."   He argued from the narrative of the Pentecostal phenomena described in Acts II—the rushing, mighty wind, and the cloven tongues as of fire——and understood in the light of Christ's unchangeableness that these signs still followed them that believe.   " I believe the Bible," he shouted, " every word of it.   These signs of the first Pentecost, I have myself witnessed in India, where I have seen cloven tongues of fire sitting on the heads of the converts, yes, fire, so real that the native attendants endeavoured to extinguish it with water." As the congregation was leaving the church, he flew after me, and addressed me a question, " Was my sermon too unorthodox for you?" " Sir," I replied, " it was not the unorthodoxy of your discourse that impressed me most, but its incredibility."   That seemed to surprise him. " But I must say the things that I have heard and seen," he protested, " I am a sincere man." " Well, sir, sincerity is the salt of genuine preaching, and I may not question yours," I said. " I am an old man," he said, " 78 years old," but I mercilessly left him no ground, for I replied, " Ah, I can give you points there, for I shall be 83 before the year is out."

Now, my dear Cyril, if I may adopt the formula of the late Mr Tom Crevy—" did you ever? " The other sermon [was] . . . delivered by a clergyman . . . described on the poster at the church door as " The Singing Parson ". I was agreeably surprised to see not an improvised negro, such as one naturally associates with seaside resorts, but a good looking young clergyman with a pleasant tenor voice, who, when the anthem was due, stepped forward and sang Mrs Alexander's hymn, " There is a green hill far away ". I have always disliked anthems in parish churches, and was pleased with the singing Parson's performance. The sermon was an emotional rant of the familiar evangelical mission type, which I should have supposed had lost its appeal to considering folk, but the congregation listened with apparent avidity, and, I suppose, were edified, but I came away from the church reflecting on the " Conversion of England ". I was not surprised to learn from the Rector himself that he was a friend of Dr Buchman's.

I am always your friend,
H. Hensley Henson,
Bishop.

177. WILLIAM TEMPLE AND HIS MESSAGE.

Hyntle Place,
July 24th, 1946.

To The Bishop of Chichester.*

My dear Bishop,

Thank you so much for the gift of the Penguin Book *William Temple and his Message*. I have read your Memoir with very great

---

* The Right Rev. G. K. A. Bell.

interest, and some gratitude, for it provides me with an effective answer to the not infrequent remonstrance against the description of my *Retrospect* as the record of an " Unimportant Life ".

Here is the story of an important Life, one moreover which was strictly contemporary with my own throughout its entire course, and which touched my own very closely and frequently at many points, and yet appears to have been entirely unconscious of my existence. It brings home to me the essential unimportance of my own career, which yet seemed at the time strenuous enough. Your excellent memoir belongs to the category of biographical eulogies in which the XVIIth Century provides so many and such admirable illustrations.

I do not dissent from the eulogy, while yet I cannot wholly endorse the approbation. " The worst fault of Willie is that he is so kind-hearted that he can say NO to nobody "—that was said to me by Archbishop Davidson, and was a judgement which my own observations inclined me to endorse. He was magnificently endowed by Nature, and all the circumstances of his life favoured him. Most of all, perhaps, the temper of the time in which his course was run. He found himself in hearty accord with the prevailing tides of opinion in Church and State, and moved forward with the winds behind him. How far the verdict of History will be as frankly favourable as your own, it is too soon to say; but that his personal influence on the course of national development was very important, perhaps even in some measure decisive, will not, I think, be disallowed.

He was *felix opportunitate mortis*, for he passed from the scene when the " Socialistic " tide was still running strongly, and the inevitable ebb had not yet clearly emerged.

I am growing to be so blind that what is called " literary " work is becoming outside my range.

Thank you again.

Always affectionately,
H. Hensley Henson,
Bishop.

I am pleased with the appointment of Charles Smyth to the Rectory of St Margts We. and (though I don't know him) of Dr Chase to the Bpk of Ripon.

178.   Sydney Smith.

Hyntle Place,
September 29th, 1946.

To Mrs St Johnston.

My dear Mrs St Johnston,

You somewhat alarm me by suggesting a parallel between the late Bishop of Durham and that inveterate and vastly corpulent jester—Sydney Smith.   At least in the physical sphere I cannot think that I shall ever justify the suggestion; but I think that without excessive effort I might become, if I have not done so already, a fairly efficient bore.

I expect the great man did become rather afflicting by his irrepressible jocosity especially when one was not oneself in the mood to laugh.   But you are not the first to find a likeness.   Many years ago, when I prepared Alfred Lyttelton's daughter, Mary, for confirmation, he gave me Sydney Smith's works, because he felt that I was in his succession, but I refuse to believe that he held me to be so addicted to jesting, for he knew me best as one of my congregation in St Margaret's, Westminster, and at least in the pulpit I never sink to jesting.   I hold with the Puritans who presided over my youth that, at least for the preacher " the House of Mourning is better than the House of Joy " though in that opinion he rarely commands the assent of his hearers !

I shall be both pleased and honoured if you can visit my Diogenes Tub, and give me the privilege of making your personal acquaintance.

My eyes are a great nuisance just now, and they must provide an excuse for the deplorable handwriting of this letter.

Mrs Braley will be able to tell you where this House is placed.   It is not difficult to reach from Ipswich.

Yours very sincerely,
H. Hensley Henson,
Bishop.

Do you know *The Smith of Smiths*? *
It is an extremely amusing account of the great Sydney.

* By Hesketh Pearson.

179.   *An incident in Durham Cathedral.*

Hyntle Place,
November 8th, 1946.

Dear Dashwood,

Thank you so much for your letter.   I will cap your " Group "
story with the record of a happening in Durham Cathedral.   At the
recent celebration of the Thanksgiving for Founders and Benefactors
in the Cathedral, the special preacher was the late Bishop of Gloucester,
Dr Headlam, who took occasion with questionable taste, and unques-
tionable offensiveness, to criticize severely the University of Durham,
which was officially included in the congregation.   The severity of his
criticism was, however, mitigated, and its effect sufficiently reduced,
by the following incident.   He began his sermon with a fit of coughing, in the course of which he evicted his false teeth with some violence.
However, he just managed by a very creditable effort to catch the
errant treasure, and then *coram populo*, indulged in the difficult and
gradual process of replacing them in their appropriate position in his
jaws.   Only one thing was lacking to complete the spectacle.   One
of the Durham schoolboys (who attend officially on this occasion,)
ought to have interjected an irrepressible comment, " Oh, well played,
Sir ! "   But, indeed, I am ashamed of myself for being so amused,
for few octogenarians, certainly not myself, can pretend that such a
calamity is remote from his own experience.   The whole episode
must have been extremely funny, and I laugh whenever I think of it.
Headlam is now in his 85th year, and by that fact is sufficiently excused,
but it is difficult to condone his bad taste, or tactlessness (which comes
to the same thing) in seizing that occasion for a belittling, if not inten-
tionally hostile reference to the local University.   That University
has grave defects, but it has also great merits and performs an indispensable function in the education of Northern England.

Always affectionately your friend,
H. Hensley Henson,
Bishop.

P.S.   The news from India augurs ill for Indian investments, and
I am beginning to bring into my picture of the future the sinister and
salutary feature of Job's dunghill.

180. *A Crucifix.*

Hyntle Place,
November 24th, 1946.

To E. H. Blakeney, Esq.

My dear Blakeney,

Thank you so much for your letter. It gave me much consolation and encouragement. I like your meditation on " the focal
point in history "; and the suggested parallel between the divine
achievement of Redemption perfected on Calvary and the process by
which a great poem is fashioned and made effective. It is a fine
thought and bears reflection. I am grateful for the stimulus which
in it you give to much and helpful thinking. I have increasingly the
conviction that, when St Paul summed up his version of the Gospel
in the declaration that its essential content was "Jesus Christ and Him
crucified ", he got at the root of the matter, and moved far beyond
the entangling envelope of Rabbinic Judaism in which too commonly
his mind was confined. I am one of those, like the great Lord Shaftes-
bury, who find the crucifix the most moving of all spiritual symbols.
Some while ago the late Countess of Limerick, (who was both a great
saint and a great sufferer, as well as the most charming and gifted
person), gave me a very beautiful ivory crucifix of French origin
dating probably from the time of the great controversy of the Jesuits
against the Jansenists in the XVIIth century. I have fixed it up in the
centre of the book case which confronts my study chair, and contains
volumes to which I am accustomed frequently to have recourse. The
top row is filled with the little volumes of the Loeb Classics Library
(nearly 300 of them) the next row contains a number of volumes of
history illustrating the culture of the ancient classical world. Below
that, is the History of the Popes and other volumes (including the
works of Shakespeare), which illustrate Christian civilization. Below
that again, are a whole sheaf of larger volumes including the great
Cambridge series of syndicated history, ancient, medieval and modern,
and then all the volumes of our own National Biography. They form
together a not altogether inadequate illustration of modern civilization
and culture, and there in the middle, I set the crucifix, whereon one
may see both the final judge of human life and the standard of His
judgement. I have in mind to place there, if I can arrange it suitably

the legend from the *Te Deum*—" We believe that thou shalt come to be our judge ".   I have always lamented that at the Reformation we in England did not follow the Lutherans in retaining the crucifix, and though I understand, I do not wholly share Bishop Westcott's preference for the naked cross.   You could not find a more illuminating expression of the anti-Christian mind than Gibbon's description of the crucifix as " the most repulsive object ever offered to the groaning admiration of mankind ".   The Christian view, which was St Paul's, is well stressed in the best lines that Keble ever wrote.   They are also, perhaps, significantly the most familiar.   It is in the poem for Good Friday—

> " Is it not strange the darkest hour
>   That ever dawned on sinful earth,
>   Should touch the heart with softer power
>   For comfort, than an angel's mirth? "

Forgive all this maundering.   It illustrates what I conceive to be the great disadvantage of Dictating letters, viz. the irrelevant discursiveness of their intolerable verbiage !   I am reflecting on the Archbishop's Sermon, which, perhaps, is being most effectively criticized by such letters as those which Slesser wrote to the *Times* and some Cowley Father to the *Guardian*.   It is, surely, apparent that the kind of Anglicanism which such letters disclose, indicates sufficiently where the stumbling block in all essays in reunion with the Non-Episcopal Churches is to be found.   Have you read Ronald Knox's Apologia, which he called *A Spiritual Aeneid*?   I remember reading it when it came out in 1918, and the other day I read it again, not to learn the paths by which that extraordinary youth became a Papist, but to appreciate the revelation of the Anglican situation which his book provides.   I am amazed at the grotesque confusion in which he and his generation were immersed.   Certainly, we need not marvel that we, in our turn, are confronted by the more developed phase of mental and moral anarchy in the C. of E.

Have you seen the little volume which the present Bishop of London published when he was in Australia—*The New Testament Letters*?   It is designed to make the Apostolic Epistles intelligible to the ordinary layman and may be described either as a free translation or as a paraphrase of the English version.   It has merits, but, perhaps, very grave defects, and it is, *me judice*, disfigured by vulgar colloquialisms, which do not really assist an educated reader to take the meaning of the text. The Text itself they seem to desecrate. The Bishop is an advanced Anglo-Catholick, and the fact is disclosed to a discerning eye e.g., in his treatment of the great sacramental passage in I. Cor. 11.

Do you know the Rev. W. J. Brown, who has just come to these parts as Rector of Hadleigh and titular Dean of Bocking? He came here last week with his wife, and I had conversation with him. He said that he writes much for the *Guardian* and expressed himself as largely accordant with my theological position. I don't quite know what to make of the *Guardian*. It is certainly considerably improved, but it hangs on to the Episcopalianism which Willie Temple did so much to stimulate.

Forgive this irrelevant and intolerable letter, and ascribe it to the involuntary infirmity of senectitude and solitude.

Always affectionately your friend,
H. Hensley Henson,
Bishop.

181. *The Archbishop and Reunion.*

Hyntle Place,
December 29th, 1946.

To The Bishop of Chichester.

My dear Bishop,

.   .   .   .

I want also to tell you how much I admire the courage and stedfastness with which you advocate the cause which you have made your own, as well in the matter of the defeated Germans, as in your support of the cause of Reunion. I cannot bring myself to believe that there is any adequate evidence of any genuine repentance in Germany, certainly no sufficient indication that there is any real understanding of the enormous, long continuing wickedness which has been so fearfully disclosed at Nuremberg; and until they are penitent and ashamed, I cannot bring myself to mitigate the severity of their punishment, though I am willing to be as considerate and even generous as is possible within the narrow limits of our power.

I wrote to the Abp of C. a New Year letter, which I hope he will get on Jan. 1st. In it I allowed myself to make some observations on his Cambridge sermon. I told him that he addressed his appeal to the wrong camp; the real hindrance is not with the non-Episcopalians but with ourselves. They may well ask for an answer to the inevitable question—What kind of Episcopacy do you mean that we should add to our systems—Lightfoot's or Gore's? Sir Henry Slesser's or the præ-Tractarian Church of England's?

If he really would take a step forward in Church relations, why doesn't he attend the next session of the General Assembly in Edinburgh, receive Communion in St Giles's with the Ministers and Elders, and then, having openly declared his spiritual fellowship with them, go to the Assembly and make his appeal to non-episcopalians? There would, of course, be an outcry from the Anglo-Catholicks, and possibly a secession, but it would be a small one, and there would be released a great volume of approval within the Anglican Church, save possibly in South Africa. That would be a genuine step forward in Church relations; as it is, he doesn't carry matters an inch beyond the point reached by the abortive Appeal to all Christian People in 1920.

My eyes are now so troublesome, that letter-writing is a burden, as, indeed, the abominable calligraphy of this letter sufficiently shows.

May God bless you, and guide your course in the coming year!

Always affect^{ly} your friend,
H. Hensley Henson,
Bishop.

182.   On the death of Bishop Headlam.

Hyntle Place,
January 18th, 1947.

To The Dean of Durham.

My dearest Dean,

I am greatly shocked by the announcement of Arthur Headlam's death for I think he is my oldest clerical friend. Even before I came into personal contact with him when he was elected in 1885 to the All Souls' Fellowship, a year after my own election, I had, in a

o

queer sort of way, met him, for he was rather conspicuous as an under-
graduate, a big raw-boned North countryman, very fair but not
handsome to look at, very angular.   When we did meet, I felt that
I knew him already, and ever since, through more than 60 years, we
have been correspondents and, in a certain sense, intimates.   I happened
to witness his engagement to his wife and, when she died, he appealed
to me to officiate at her burial as an old friend.   We differed greatly
in many respects, and he dealt me some shrewd knocks from time to
time, but we held together, and only last Monday, I received from
him a long and friendly letter, written with his own (infamous) hand.
It opens thus :

> " Have you seen a book called *Apostolic Ministry*, edited by the
> Bishop of Oxford?   It is a very bad book.   The Bishop writes
> on the ideal of the Episcopal Office, of which he has a very
> narrow conception.   He begins by criticizing you.   He objects
> to your calling a Bishop a " Great National officer."   I should
> like you to amend the wording.   I don't think we are " officers ".
> That reminds me of bureaucrats.   I think we are servants, " great
> national servants ".   And if you say that, I am all with you.
> We are national, just as Christianity concerns the whole of Chris-
> tian life, and the parish priest is the parson of the parish.   We are
> concerned with the whole life of the nation, and I have no sym-
> pathy with the people who want us to retire from the House of
> Lords.   One of the failures in my episcopate is that I had not the
> courage to use my position there.   I had a great deal that I might
> have said there, which in my opinion would have been useful as
> a contribution to the national thought."

I do not think Headlam's opinions would have been other than most
welcome to the majority of the Peers, because, so far as I am able to
appreciate them, they reflected but too faithfully the prejudices of their
Lordships, but I think he would have found that the Lords do not like
episcopal incursions into general politics by members of the episcopal
Bench, and he was not endowed with that very dangerous gift, which
is sometimes called the " orator's temperament ".   I feel that the
world is emptier for Headlam's death, and, of course, it brings home to
me the near advent of my own.   I envy him the ease and " sudden-
ness " of his departure, and I think his record in the *Times* is eminently
creditable.

I have just contributed £50 to the Fund for restoring St Mary's, Oxford, after the unhappy fire which threatened the great disaster of obliterating not the least famous and beautiful of the architectural features of Oxford. Happily, I understand, the damage was less than was at first assumed, but the appeal includes an attempt to add something to the exiguous stipend of the Vicar. Anyhow, as I contemplate the income tax demand, I feel that I cannot add any more to my contributions. Moreover, I am never easily pleased in the matter of war memorials which are in our sacred buildings. There is real danger of the cathedrals and parish churches being crowded in a very short period, so greatly with such memorials as to leave nothing for the coming time, so you must forgive me for sending you nothing in response to the appeal for the work you project in Durham, though I feel a beast in doing so.

My eyes have been uncommonly troublesome during the last few weeks, and I am pledged to see the oculist again in February.

　　　With love to Hester,

I am always affectionately your friend,

H. Hensley Henson,

Bishop.

183.　Bishop Headlam; Neville Chamberlain.

Hyntle Place,
January 26th, 1947.

To E. H. Blakeney, Esq.

My dear Blakeney,

　　　I cannot longer delay writing to you, for you are often in my mind. The truth is that my failure of eyesight has quickened its pace, and I am now seriously impeded, even in such small exertions as writing to a friend. I am very anxious if possible to complete this final volume of the *Retrospect* and I am hoping to do so in time to get it published some time this year, which will complete 60 years since my Ordination, and it will probably be what is picturesquely described as " Swan-song ". It will be rather a mingle-mangle, arranged in five sections, one, introduction, two, autobiography 1939–46, three,

" open Letter " to a Padre on my personal religion, four, list of my publications, five, appendices.

Arthur Headlam's death came as a shock to me. . . . He and I have been closely associated for more than 61 years. He was elected to an All Souls' Fellowship, in 1885, and I in 1884. We have been in touch ever since, and although we have often differed, we have never quarrelled. He was a Durham man and died at Whorlton, where he had been born in his father's house, which he inherited. I first visited Durham as a guest in his father's house, at that time St Oswald's Vicarage in Durham City. He was one of the three Fellows of All Souls who walked out the six miles from Oxford to Cuddesdon to witness my Ordination on Trinity Sunday 1887 in Cuddesdon Parish Church. He had been trained, as was Inge, in a rigid Tractarian household and he never shook off the ecclesiastical and political tendencies under which he grew up. He was proud to affirm, and I have no reason for doubting the affirmation, that he included in his pedigree Peter the Great and Oliver Cromwell. In any case, he might fairly claim to have perpetuated the brutality of their controversial methods. I always liked him, because I felt that he was essentially a true man. He had little sympathy with other points of view than his own, but *au fond* he was loyal to his friendships, as I have said, I think, in the *Retrospect*. His exterior was hard and rough but his heart was sound.

The Dean of Winchester came here for lunch, and I had some pleasant talk with him. He spoke of you, and as soon as he had disappeared, I remembered that I had forgotten to send you an affectionate message, as I had intended, but you will take that for granted. I was interested to hear from him a comparatively favourable account of Canon Roger Lloyd, whose history of the Church of England seemed to me a very preposterous production. I was urged to get it because of his references to myself, but these appeared to me almost grotesque. Is it really the case that he represents the serious judgement of any large number of the English clergy?

Have you read Professor Feiling's Biography of Neville Chamberlain? It was given me as a Christmas present and I have read it with very much interest. As a piece of literary expression and arrangement, it is quite admirable, and although it does not carry conviction when it seeks to explain Munich it certainly does leave one with a very high estimate of Neville Chamberlain's motives and hope and a very deep appreciation of the personal tragedy which his political career illustrates.

I only met him once, when he broke his journey and stayed a night in Auckland Castle, after his return from his South African tour, and was proceeding to join his wife and son at Bamburgh. He came with his daughter, and I had a great talk with him, not about politics but about his African tour. I was delighted with him. His vivid description of what he had seen disclosed a side of him which I had never realized— his keen delight in nature, and his large knowledge of birds and beasts. He told me that the thing which most impressed him on his tour was the flight of the flamingos on Victoria Nyanza. I was so impressed with the book that I wrote to the Professor to congratulate him heartily on his achievement.

The Coventry Cathedral scheme, so brazenly boosted, has collapsed rather ignominiously. I am not surprised, and I think rather relieved for the more I reflect on the project, the more I feel it was ill-advised, and probably mischievous. . . . The inordinate advertisement of the foolish plan indicated the intention of inoculating ecclesiastical procedure with the advertizing adroitness and extravagance which marks modern politics.

I do hope you are well, in spite of this terrible winter. I have found it difficult to endure the cold and have not been too well. After all, one has no right to be well in one's 84th year. . . .

Always, my dear Blakeney,
Affectionately your friend,
H. Hensley Henson,
Bishop.

184. St Barnabas', Oxford.

Hyntle Place,
February 4th, 1947.

To The Rev. Donald Nicholson.

My dear Donald,

This is great news indeed. When I matriculated at Oxford, as long ago as October, 1881, St Barnabas was commonly regarded in the university as the most " advanced " church in the city, and as such it was largely attended by undergraduates who found in its unusual

ceremonial a greater attraction than was presented in other churches.
It was profanely called by some of them " St Barabas ".   So much has
happened during the last 65 years that I should not be surprised to
know that in up-to-date Anglican circles, St Barnabas is now regarded
as a back-number.   It was then surrounded by a very poor neighbourhood, which provided ample opportunities for hard work and pastoral
service.   These, I hope, and believe, you will not fail to give to your
new charge, and I hope you will not wholly forget the things which
you learned in Durham.   I hope and pray that by God's Blessing you
will be happy and serviceable in Oxford.   I hardly ever go there
now, because my failure of eyesight has made travelling difficult and
I hardly leave my house, but then I am in my 84th year, and have not
escaped some of the infirmities of old age.

With all good wishes,

I am affectionately your friend,
H. Hensley Henson,
Bishop.

185. The Coventry Scheme.

Hyntle Place,
February 11th, 1947.

To E. H. Blakeney, Esq.

My dear Blakeney,
        Thank you so much for your letter which I have read twice
with great appreciation, and I wish I could reply to it adequately but
this persistent snow tells badly on my miserable eyes, and I can neither
read nor write, with sufficient facility to make it worth while to attempt
to do either.

I think I quoted to you Headlam's observations on Bishop Kirk's
book in his letter to me.   Headlam, of course, had been living in
Durham during Lightfoot's episcopate and he retained a certain
veneration for that great man, although he himself was on a smaller
scale intellectually and spiritually.   On the subject of the episcopate
he never moved beyond the Dissertation which was published so long
ago as 1868 and did not appreciate sufficiently the far-reaching consequences of Lightfoot's argument.   His interest in the Eastern Churches

did, I think, tend to limit his outlook, and of course, he had an obstinate temperament which made it very difficult for him to overcome the prejudices of his upbringing (Tractarian and Tory). Still, he was fundamentally honest and had succeeded in becoming learned in a measure unusual in these days. His immediate associates all through his career have expressed themselves with loyalty and even affection, and he had wholesome hobbies.

I am sure that there is no real value in the Coventry Cathedral Scheme. Architecturally, it is confessedly an *ad hoc* arrangement, designed to meet the very special conditions of the site. It can provide no precedent for future church building. Religiously, it ignores the central problem which confronts the thoughtful advocate of Christian unity, viz, how to remove from the ecclesiastical arena the persistent delusion which emerged at the first when the Apostle rebuked the man who cast out devils in Christ's name, and yet they protested to Christ, "followed not with US". That delusion that Christ committed the treasures of His redemptive grace to the exclusive charge of a fixed ecclesiastical policy persists to-day in the grotesque exorbitancy of the Papal claim, and less exorbitantly, less grotesquely in the exclusive claim of the episcopate, claiming unbroken succession from the Apostles. It has, of course, from time to time emerged absurdly in the exclusive claims of Protestant sects, but from the Pope to the latest sectary, the claim is contrary to the facts of history and the spirit of Jesus. In the Church of England it is at the present time increasingly insisted upon by the Anglo-Catholicks who perpetuate the least respectable features of the Tractarians, Non-Jurors and Laudians, who were their spiritual ancestors. The Church of England as a whole has never surrendered to that deplorable delusion, although if Canon Roger Lloyd be right, in reading the history of the English Church in the 20th century as disclosing the triumph of Anglo-Catholicism, it would seem that we are within sight of turning our back on the English Reformation. There is only one dénouement to the reactionary process and that is, of course, surrender to the Papal claim, but until the doctrinal standards of the Church of England have been authoritatively repudiated and the weightiest precedents of its history as a Reformed Church have been disallowed, so great an apostasy cannot be proclaimed an accomplished fact. But to return to the Coventry Cathedral Scheme. It enthrones episcopalian exclusiveness as the very ideal to the achievement of which all social fraternizations are properly tributary; it multiplies pulpits and meeting places, for everything but religious teaching and worship. There at the Lord's Table none but an episcopally ordained priest may offer service and none but episcopally confirmed Christians may securely and legally communicate. We have long passed the point at which all Christians, and for the matter of that, non-Christians can co-operate in civic service. The essential scandal which enfeebles the witness of the Christian society is that "all who profess and call themselves Christians" cannot approach together the Lord's Table. I took up my pen more than once to write about the Archbishop's Cambridge sermon but I put it down again partly because I did not wish to adopt the attitude of criticism towards one in his position, who, I think, is really desirous to escape from the impasse, the nature of which I cannot think he really discerns, and partly because I cannot make sense out of his sermon. It seems to me too incoherent, even self-stultifying to be taken as in any true sense "a step forward towards re-union".

I am sorry that Churchill disclaimed "coalition" when Dalton hinted at its possibility last night in the House of Commons, for I hardly see how apart from some form of coalition it will be possible to break up the Socialist supremacy. I fear that he was giving one more evidence of his incapacity to carry over from war the superb qualities which are hardly less needed in the post-war world.

The Archbishop impresses me as a good man, sincere and humble, who is of another spirit than the "Scribes & Pharisees hypocrites" who "make broad their phylacteries" and "compass [sea] and land to make one proselyte".

I wish there were not such distance between Winchester and Hintlesham. It would be much comfort and strength to talk with you. I suspect that the squalid confinement of his lonely Tub told badly on the Cynic philosopher's mind and character! But there is I think, no evidence of his being involuntarily blind, as well as deliberately alone!

May God keep you in this difficult world for the consolation of your friends!

Always affectionately one of them, though like what St Paul called himself in another reference an ἔκτρωμα !!!

H. Hensley Henson,
Bishop.

186.   Grillion's Club ; the Individual and the Community.

Hyntle Place,
February 18th, 1947.

To Dr Elston Grey Turner, M.C.

My dear Elston,

I was so pleased to receive your letter, and hope it will not be the last which you find time and will to address to me.

Your first question is easily answered, for I have a sumptuous volume which records the history of Grillion's Club from its foundation in 1812 to the year 1913.   The volume was published in 1914.   The club has its origin in the minds of two Etonians who met at Constantinople as diplomats.   They discussed together in 1811 " the possibility of founding a club open to members of both contending parties " (Whigs and Tories) and it was agreed that whoever first returned home should do his best to carry out this intention.   The name of the club was adopted more or less accidentally for lack of agreement on any other.   It was the name of the caterer at whose house the club dined in its early years.   Somewhat later in its history its strictly political character was mitigated by the occasional admission to the club of other than political members, besides eminent ecclesiastics.   Lord Houghton's preface to the annals of the Club in 1880 observes that it is " indisputable that all that connects the men of thought with the men of action is at once a rare and appreciated pleasure and a stimulus to the loftier studies."

I have not the least knowledge as to what reason could have induced the club to elect me to its membership, but I have always found the greatest pleasure and profit when I have been able to attend its meetings. It is a dining club and limits its dinners to the parliamentary sessions. It generally meets at the Grosvenor House Hotel, but when I resigned my see and was no longer required to visit London officially I thought it my duty to resign my membership, as the number of members is limited and I might be excluding somebody who could attend more often.   But I never cease to regret the loss of a privilege which I greatly enjoyed.

Your other question is not so easily answered, for it deals with subjects which must not be misunderstood. Roughly it is, perhaps, true to say that " the chief problem which seems to confront the world today is the conflict between the demand of the individual and the demand of the community." But it must not be forgotten that some demands of the individual are valid and must be satisfied and some demands of the community are equally so. In both cases it is important to discriminate between the demands which are valid and those which are not. Moscow and the Vatican both exhibit the same phenomenon viz. the phenomenon of totalitarianism. In both cases external authority claims absolute control of the individual. Of course, neither can succeed completely, because the individual has a sphere within which neither the State nor the Church can effectively exercise control, but both can and do inflict enormous injuries on the individual by their exorbitant procedures.

In the case of the Roman Catholick Church, we must never forget that it is both a Christian Society, part of the Family of Christ, and a monstrous development of the Christian Executive, the last term in the development of clericalism or sacerdotalism, themselves morbid growths on the original Gospel. The man of the world readily accords with the claims of the Vatican i.e. that the Roman Church alone is suffi- ciently strongly organized to beat back the power of organized Com- munism, and if the conflict really lay within the secular sphere it might be not unreasonable to think that the Vatican could make out its case, but the conflict is not so to be limited. Christianity is not so to win its way. No lie is of the truth and Christianity is preeminently in its essence " the Truth ". " My kingdom is not of this world " is the recorded utterance of Jesus to Pilate. The record of the Papacy is sufficient disproof of the Papal claim. It is not insignificant that Papal influence has steadily been cast in the scale against freedom on every plane of human life. It was within my lifetime, that is in 1864, when I was a baby in my cradle, that the Pope issued what was called the *syllabus errorum* in which he set out in a long list the errors which the Roman Church duly pronounced to be accursed. These errors include those very franchises which we now generally agree to be essential to a democracy worthy of the name, freedom of the Press, freedom of religion, freedom of conscience, and so forth. That syllabus has never been withdrawn, still less repudiated, and wherever the Roman Church has freedom of utterance, the syllabus of 1864 finds expression as far as possible. I have written too much, and must make an end, but it must suffice to say that human liberty is bound up with the final discomforture of both forms of totalitarianism, that which has its centre in Moscow, and that which has its centre in the Vatican. Self-respecting men will reject both with the indignant protest, " *non tali auxilio nec defensoribus istis* ".

My eyes are failing so badly that I am glad to avail myself of Miss Booker's generosity and skill to dictate this letter, but dictation has its own drawbacks, and among them an exorbitant verbosity.

H. Hensley Henson,
Bishop.

P.S.   Remember me most kindly to your parents.   I hope they are not suffering too much from the terrible winter, and the untoward aspect of affairs, national and cosmic.   I never felt the cold of winter so hard to endure : but I am in my 84th year, and cannot expect to escape the shadows of old age.

H. H. H.

187.   THE APOSTOLIC MINISTRY; THE RISE OF CHRISTIANITY.

Hyntle Place,
April 5th, 1947.

To The Dean of Winchester.

My dear Dean,

I received this morning your interesting letter and the article. I read both at once.   The article reads very well, and ought to do, I think, some real good in leading serious persons to do some thinking. It was friendly of you to stick my *Bishoprick Papers* in the forefront as a kind of text.   You very properly followed the well-established tradition of the pulpit by not binding your discourse too closely to its text !   I have read a great part of the Bishop of Birmingham's book, and am distressed and dismayed by its contents, and by the light it casts on the Bishop's mind.   You will have seen Raven's review in the *Spectator*.   Its severity is masked, but not mitigated by his compliments.   Under the pretence of complete detachment and impartiality the Bishop has produced a book which might more fitly have been published by the Rationalist Society. It is an eager, energetic, and I feel, highly effective attack on the Christian tradition (in its effect on the half-educated but curious public). As you justly say, it indicates in the writer not only very strong prejudices, but also a really astonishing unacquaintance with the subject on which he dogmatizes so freely. In the little preface he describes himself as "one who worships Jesus the Christ as divine" and as "one who accepts alike the methods of analytical scholarship and the postulate of the large-scale, or finite-scale uniformity of nature, which is fundamental in modern science". It would seem to be claimed that he gives us in the book his own views about the origin of Christianity. I cannot imagine how he could build on such views any intelligible "worship" of such a Person as emerges from his examination of the New Testament.

It is an odd coincidence that almost synchronously there should have appeared two such books as the Bishop of Oxford's *Apostolic Ministry* and the Bishop of Birmingham's *Rise of Christianity*. The first is in my judgement definitely, in tone, in type, temper and tendency not Anglican but Roman, and the last is not even, in any tolerable sense, Christian. Yet the authors are Bishops, holding office as such in the Church of England. How long can that kind of comprehension be maintained, or rightly defended? I do not think it possible that any Church can long cohere when such radical divergence on essentials is acquiesced in. "Can two walk together except they be agreed", asks the Prophet, and he clearly expects an answer which will be decidedly negative. The problem of Anglican policy is how to make sure that the ultimately inevitable disruption follows the right line: the Romeward tending Anglicans to their spiritual home in the Pope's communion, and the Unitarians to their proper fellowship outside the Trinitarian fold. It is not a problem very easy to solve, for the power of self-delusion is amazingly great, and the unrealized influence of interest and "use-and-wont" blinds men to the significance of their own behaviour and the gravity of their own opinions. I am afraid that Barnes' book will serve as a very serviceable weapon in the hands of non-Christians, who will rejoice to discover that their own negations are so powerfully echoed within the Church of England.

You will have seen that Canon Richardson, the Vicar of Harborne, is to succeed Major as the Principal of Ripon Hall. He is, of course, a friend, a disciple, and a champion of his present Bishop, though I think he is a man of a more spiritual type and will express himself less

crudely.   In some respects he would be well suited for guiding young
men *in spiritualibus* but whether he has any power of discipline remains
to be seen.   I never quite understand what the position of Ripon Hall
is in the system of the National Church.   Is it a recognised Training
College for the Clergy, and do the Bishops sanction the training of
candidates there?   I can hardly imagine Bishop Kirk sending young
men for their preparation to it, and yet it would be an unfortunate and
perhaps a dangerous procedure for the Bishops to discriminate against
a theological college on dogmatic grounds.

I hope you have come through this dreadful winter unscathed.   It
imprisoned me in the house for two months and thus deprived me of
my indispensable " constitutional ", and I do feel more than commonly
dilapidated.   Lord Salisbury's death takes away another of my octogenarian acquaintances.   The House of Cecil is a wonderful example
of hereditary ability, disclosing itself surprisingly after a protracted
interval.   No Cecil was of any special importance between the first
Lord Salisbury in James I's reign and the new Lord Salisbury's grandfather.   I suppose the Alderson marriage brought a streak of genius
into the Cecil line, but certainly no family can now exhibit such a
blaze of distinction as the Cecils.   My own career has been so much
affected by contact with that House that I feel almost a personal loss in
the death of the last Marquis.   It is good to know that he will be
succeeded by a man of proved character and intellectual power.

Always, my dear Dean,
Most sincerely yours,
H. Hensley Henson,
Bishop.

188.   Bishop Barnes' book.

Hyntle Place,
May 16th, 1947.

To E. H. Blakeney, Esq.

My dearest Blakeney,

Miss Booker is good enough to act as my amanuensis, and
therein I follow the example of the Blessed Paul, and write to you
through Tertius, I mean Tertia.

My wife read to me your review of Barnes' book, and I heard it with unfeigned and complete satisfaction.   It is certainly rather severe, but not excessively so.   I wish somebody would ask Barnes what public his book is designed to appeal to.   Certainly not to the educated classes, whether scientific or religious, who would have no use for it, and would be mainly impressed by amazement that a man holding his office, and having a reputation for great scientific knowledge could produce a book so inadequate and so insolently dogmatic.   The only public which would welcome, admire and absorb his book will be that provided by the waxing hordes of the intensely ignorant, intensely conceited and intensely greedy of everything which might seem to authenticate their adolescent scepticism which is pouring forth every year from the secondary schools, and in no place are more dogmatic than in Birmingham.   I think it is difficult to understand how any man holding episcopal office in a great industrial centre could write anything so irresponsible, so unworthy, intellectually, and so dangerously suggestive.   It is very difficult to know how Barnes should be treated, but perhaps the wisest course is as far as possible to ignore the un-happy book.   But of course, this may be rendered impossible if some indignant believer should feel himself coerced in conscience to chal-lenge before the courts such teaching as the Bishop publishes.   It has always been an object with me to keep myself as far as I could informed of what Biblical and historical criticism might fairly be said to have established itself.   That was my duty as a preacher, and I was startled to find that Barnes was so hopelessly out of touch with the graver conclusions of Biblical science.   Had I been thirty years younger I could hardly have refrained from challenging him on some details, but now, of course, my powers have largely failed, and my work such as it was, is quite obviously over.   The three reviews which I have read, Raven's in the *Spectator*, that in the *Times Literary Supple-ment*, of which I do not know the author, but which may have been written by Bishop Rawlinson, and yours in the *Guardian* are all justly and effectively severe.

. . . .

Your letters always give me great comfort.   I was more than dis-appointed that Selwyn was again passed over in the appointment to ——.   I do not know the new Bishop, but his record is not impressive. I suppose that he is one of these Christian Socialists, who will multiply rapidly when it is perceived that the fountain of preferment has definitely passed to the Labour Party.

May Heaven keep you, my dear friend, and give you great peace and joy in this last phase of your useful career to the comfort of your friends and the welfare of the Church.

Always affectionately your friend,

H. Hensley Henson,

Bishop.

189.   Discipline and the Establishment.

Hyntle Place,

June 5th, 1947.

To The Dean of Winchester.

My dear Dean,

This is a very short letter to thank you heartily for writing to me, and to beg you to renew your kindness whenever you feel so disposed.

I like your letter to the *Guardian* about Barnes' book very much. I have been turning over in my mind all day the suggestion that the two Archbishops should write to Barnes as you mention might not be improbable, and my conclusion is adverse. Neither of their Graces carries any weight personally in the sphere of Biblical Criticism, and Barnes would make the most of this.   More serious is the rooted objection which Englishmen generally feel to any procedure which deprives a man of his right to defend himself when attacked.   If their Graces say, (as they well may) that Barnes' book is so grave an insult to the Christian religion generally, and to the Church of England in particular, that official procedures ought to be taken against the writer, they are bound to prosecute him in the Courts as a heretic, and give him the full opportunity of making such defence as he can.   If (which I hardly think can be the case) they feel conscientiously unable to make use of the existing legal machinery as being too " Erastian ", then I think they ought to say so plainly, and associate themselves with the policy of Disestablishment.

I am glad, but not surprised, that you liked Jack Clayton.   He is a really good fellow, with an amazing memory and a large heart, save where his Protestant feelings cloud his mind. I wish they had made him Dean of Hereford, a position which he desired, and which he would have adorned.

I think very strongly that Barnes' book should not be left undealt with. It must make things very difficult in the Birmingham diocese, and of course if he gets away with it, a really dreadful scandal, extremely grateful to our Popish adversaries.

Again thanking you for your letter,
I am affectionately yours,
H. Hensley Henson,
Bp.

P.S.   I do not know when I shall get about again.   My failure of eyesight which keeps me from reading, is a terrible aggravation of my present distress.   The Rector here is reading out to me the Report on the Canon Law.   I admire greatly the erudition, skill and literary power which mark it, but of course it also marks the great triumph of the Anglo-Catholick party and leaves open many of the old pitfalls.

190.   The Virgin Birth.

Hyntle Place,
August 1st, 1947.

To The Dean of Winchester.

My dear Dean,

I owe you many apologies for not having answered your very interesting letter long ago, but I was not quite sure where to address myself to you, as you were going away from home, and I wanted to be able to write more about Barnes' melancholy book.

I am glad to hear that the Archbishop plans some action and I cannot suggest anything better than that which you outline, though, of course, it lies open to many formidable objections. I do hope in any case that the " Virgin Birth Issue " will be left out of the argument. You will perhaps remember that my original conflict with Charles Gore arose from his and Bishop Talbot's contention that a ring fence should be placed about the two historical facts affirmed in the Creed.

I have ever contended, and do still contend, that an historical fact is a fact certified to be such by adequate historical testimony, and that neither of these two so-called historical facts, viz. the Virgin Birth and the physical Resurrection is in my opinion, and in that of many historical students, whose belief in the Incarnation cannot be challenged, adequate. This is my own opinion, and I have expressed it frankly. A fact may be none the less a fact, even though not historical, and so these two articles in the Creed may be held as " pious opinions ", or as inferences from the great and essential doctrines of the Incarnation and the Resurrection. I do not myself hold the " pious opinion ", and so far from drawing the inference, I hold with many, and a growing number, of other Christians, that the exemplary character of Christ's Life is jeopardised by the dogma of the " Virgin Birth ". It needs not that I should develop the argument, for it will be familiar to you, whether you agree with it or not. It is worth noting that even so rigidly orthodox a scholar as the late Bishop of Gloucester frankly admitted that there was no necessary connection between the essential truths of the Incarnation and the historic facts of the " Virgin Birth ".

It would be a great pleasure to see you if you can manage to get over from Cambridge to see me. I have got to the stage of being wheeled daily in an invalid chair, and walking a few yards with the aid of an arm and a stick, but the doctor cannot, or will not, commit himself to a period at which I may be able, in any adequate sense, to return to normal activity.

. . . .

I am hoping, perhaps against hope, to finish the Third Volume of my *Retrospect*, but in any case it will be a poor thing, quite other than what I had intended.

Always, my dear Dean,
Affectionately yours,
H. Hensley Henson,
Bishop.

P

191.   The end in sight.

Hyntle Place,
August 5th, 1947.

To The Dean of Durham.

My dearest Dean,

Forgive me for being so long in answering your very kind and welcome letter, but you will understand that my present condition makes correspondence a difficult thing, though my incomparable Fearne acts as my amanuensis, or Tertia.

I am now making my will, and there are a few things about which I want to consult you.

1. I propose to direct that my carcass shall be cremated, and if so, I wonder whether you and the Canons, and of course the Bishop, would think it improper or unseemly if the ashes were deposited in some corner of Durham Cathedral, where they might be comparatively inoffensive.

2. Would you care to have the portraits which I received as a member of Grillions? Some of them, I think, are interesting, as showing how some of our great men looked in earlier life, most of whom you will know. If you would like to have them, I should be pleased to leave, or send them to you.

Davey of the S.P.C.K. sent me a few days ago a small book by one Barrett, a Wesleyan of whom he speaks highly. I cannot read the book for myself, because my eyesight is inadequate, and the Rector, Trotman, is away for a holiday, so I have no one to read to me, at least not that sort of book, though my ladies are most helpful in reading on other subjects.

I am fearfully weary of this tiresome and continuing illness, and I cannot say with any sort of definiteness when I may be restored to any measure of normality, and of course the expense is not inconsiderable for a pensioned ecclesiastic. I reckon that this heart attack has already cost me more than £400. Two nurses in the house complicates the domestic problems, which Fearne solves with amazing skill.

The more I think over Barnes' book, the more it distresses me. I understand that there is some likelihood that the Archbp will make some statement, or perhaps write to him, after the book has been discussed by the Bishops.   Whether this will do any good I am not sure. I wish somebody competent would do for Barnes' book what Bishop Lightfoot did for *Supernatural Religion*, that is, subject it to a detailed criticism, and demonstrate how shallow and arbitrary and indifferent much of it is.

If I were forty years younger, I would have done something of the kind myself, but I am now what Lord Randolph Churchill profanely called the " G.O.M.", " an old man in a hurry."

Give my love to Hester, and

Believe me always,

Affectionately your friend,

H. Hensley Henson,

Bishop.

192.   Mrs Charles Darwin.

Hyntle Place,

August 23rd, 1947.

To Gilbert Darwin, Esq.

My dear Gilbert,

A few days ago I learned that your mother had passed away, and I now send you a few lines of sincere, if somewhat belated, condolence.   She was always very kind to me, and I owe it to her that I made your acquaintance.   You were a boy then, and now you are an important man, carrying worthily the honourable burden of a great name, one of the greatest in our national calendar.

I do not know when I shall be restored to anything like normal activity, but in any case I shall go forward with the Damocles sword hanging over my head.   At any moment I may be called to my account and it is a long one, rather terrifying to think upon.   If I live till November 8th, I shall complete 84 years on this strange planet, and that is more than the normal course.   So many memories crowd in upon me as I lie here, which shame and comfort me by turns.   I often recall Archbishop Trench's lines :

> " Best friends might loathe us, if what things perverse
> We know of our own selves, they also knew :
> Lord, Holy One! if thou who knowest worse
> Shouldst loathe us too ! "

Believe me always to be,
Affectionately your friend,
H. Hensley Henson,
Bishop.

193.   To an octogenarian friend.*

Hyntle Place,
September 7th, 1947.

To Lord Woodbridge.

My dearest Arthur,

I have for the first time dared to come to my study, and make an effort to write a letter with my own hand.   And I must needs write a few lines to you on the occasion of your entering the company of those whom the Psalmist assures us are doomed to " labour and sorrow."   I think he must have been of the melancholy company himself, for he wrote (it was Dean Stanley's favourite text)—" I see that all things come to an end; but Thy commandment is exceeding broad "; and mine is a Christian version of the same, " Jesus Christ is the same yesterday, today, yea and for ever."   And both seem to unite in the words of St John (who was thought to be a very old man when he wrote it), " The world passeth away, and the lust thereof; but he that doeth the will of God abideth for ever."

You have been in my mind all day.   May God, if such be His holy will, extend your life, and make it ever richer in happiness to yourself, and the ever-waxing number of your friends; among whom none loves and values you more than

Your grateful and affectionate
Herbert.

Forgive this miserable handwriting.

* The last letter Hensley Henson wrote with his own hand.

194. *The Archbishops' Commission on Canon Law.*

Hyntle Place,
September 10th, 1947.

To H. A. T. Trehearne, Esq.

Dear Mr Trehearne,

I am greatly obliged to you for sending me your very interesting and important comments on the recently issued report of the Archbishops' Commission and I regret the more that I am unable to give it such adequate attention as it deserves. At the beginning of April I was laid low by a severe heart attack, so severe that my survival was described by my doctor as "miraculous"; but I did survive and have ever since been confined to my bedroom with two nurses in attendance. I am now beginning to show signs of recovery and am able to be wheeled about in an invalid chair and even to walk a few paces with assistance of an arm and a stick. When I shall be, if ever, restored to anything that can be called normal activity appears to be very doubtful. The doctor tells me that I may totter along for a few years, always provided that I avoid any physical shock or emotional strain which might send me into the grave at short notice. Added to this misfortune is the fact that my eyesight has failed badly so that I cannot read for myself but have to depend upon having everything read to me.

I attached sufficient importance to the Archbishops' report to get the Rector here to read it to me *in extenso* and though my legal knowledge is inadequate to following very exactly all your points I find myself in general agreement with all you say. It seems to me that it is very unfortunate that the idea should still be authenticated that the Medieval Canon Law has any continuing authority in England. That law may be said to have received official formulation in the 11th century when, under the ruthless administration of Gregory VIIth the papal power was supreme and was everywhere assumed in the Canon Law. The sacerdotal theory of the Christian Ministry is of course everywhere assumed and the difference between clergy and laity which that theory requires is everywhere insisted upon. Yet the English Reformation proceeded on the assumption that the laity were not so absolutely segregated from the clergy. You will remember that at the very start of her reign Queen Elizabeth had to encounter the protest from the Canterbury Convocation brought to her by Bishop Bonner of London who, in the vacancy of the See of Canterbury, was President of the Convocation. The point of the protest was that the laity had overstepped the limit of their competence. The Queen's reply was sufficiently expressed in the Act of Supremacy and in the Act of Uniformity. But more than this, the Medieval Canon Law is a typical medieval document. Its treatment of Scripture is grotesque and generally it is totally unsuitable for modern use; but so long as it remains there will always be bigoted and irrational or ignorant individuals who will affect to believe that it represents the law of God as against the inferior law of the State and will hold themselves free therefore, nay, bound in conscience to obey it rather than statutes and customs of the realm.

I presume that the object of the Archbishops' Commission was to equip the Church of England for the first time with an adequate intelligible and enforceable code of the law affecting clerical duty.

The Canons of 1604 or as you say 1603 (though I have hitherto preferred to describe them as the Canons of 1604 because somewhere in the Prayer Book they are so described, but I notice that 1603 seems the general usage of lawyers and I suppose there must be a reason for it. I should be glad to know what it is).

No one knows better than the Bishops the humiliating ignorance of the men whom they are in the habit of ordaining. Bishop Lightfoot's great dissertation on the origin of the Christian Ministry demonstrates that the sacerdotal theory is contrary to fundamental Christian principles, and Scripture, was unknown to the Apostolic Age, and only gradually infiltrated into the Christian Church from Judaism (S. Cyprian), and pagan sources. I know of nothing that has been published since 1868 when Lightfoot's great dissertation first appeared, which has in the smallest degree weakened his argument or disallowed his conclusion. But that Dissertation is no longer read by the clergy, and in fact the sacerdotal theory is now dominant in the Theological Colleges and governs the thought and action of an increasing number of the clergy, not excluding the Bishops. It is a great calamity. Personally I think nothing can save the Church of England until disestablishment and disendowment have compelled it to realise its actual character. The parochial system needs to be entirely recast and some reasonable security provided that the clergy shall be adequately employed as well as adequately paid.

There is much more to be said which I should like to say, but I am exhausted and must draw rein. These incessant and almost frenzied appeals for an increase in clerical stipends will lead to nothing until it is made clear that the clergy are adequately employed and under effective discipline.

Again thanking you for your letter,
I am, sincerely yours,
H. Hensley Henson,
Bishop.

195. To a very old friend.

Hyntle Place,
September 11th, 1947.

To The Rev. Preb. A. B. Wynne-Willson.

My dear Prebendary,

I am still *hors de combat*, although now I have got to the stage of being wheeled out in an invalid chair, and even walking a few paces with the aid of an arm and a stick. When, if ever, I shall be restored to anything like normal activity is wholly uncertain. I am happy in the devotion of my wife and Fearne and of a wonderful nurse, whom I inevitably call the Angel, and who is really beyond praise. The night nurse has left me, but will be replaced before long. Meanwhile the valorous and all-competent and devoted Fearne manages somehow to carry on.

I do hope you are not suffering too much, and that your wife is well. I dare not hope that she is free from pain. Of course Nancy's * presence with you must be a great strength and comfort. What a gem she is! She alone is sufficient to counteract the madness of legions of Pankhursts!

. . . .

Meanwhile everything seems going from bad to worse, in the country and in what was once the Empire, and in the world at large. Nothing in any corner of the world gives one cause for hope or comfort. I fear very much that one consequence of the appalling

* Miss Nancy Wynne-Willson.

Jewish tragedy will be the development in England at last of the Anti-Semitic madness which has been indigenous on the Continent for so long. Well, my friend, you and I are at the end of our tether, and we must soon say goodbye to the mad scene.

May God bless you and give you that peace and happiness which you cannot find anywhere else but in Him.

Always most affectionately your friend,

H. Hensley Henson,

Bishop.

196. *Some last reflections.*★

Hyntle Place,

September 27th, 1947.

To The Dean of St Paul's.

My dear Dean,

You will know probably that I have been and am rather seriously ill. As long ago as the beginning of April I was knocked over by a heart attack. For several days I was unconscious of what had happened and then I found a strange doctor, a heart expert, who had been called in and heard him say " I think he will pull through now ". I did pull through after a fashion and have been ever since confined to my bed with two nurses in attendance, and when I shall be restored to anything which could be called normal activity appears to be extremely doubtful. To make my condition worse the failure of my eyesight has made it impossible for me to read books; everything has to be read to me. Much has recently appeared which it is important for me to read. My wife reads to me a good deal of the lighter stuff and she reads very well. The Rector comes in for an hour a day and reads rather heavier material. Miss Booker, who for more than 30 years has been living with us as our " acting daughter " takes down and typewrites letters, but she has been out of action for the last month.

One consequence of my enforced recumbency is that I have become acquainted with the Religious Services of B.B.C. I dislike intensely

---

★ Dictated but not signed by Hensley Henson on the day of his death.

the tone and tendency of B.B.C. religion which I think is thoroughly unwholesome; but there are exceptions. Who are they; the men frequenting the House and presumably employed on work? One of the religious teachers is yourself and for the last few days I have been listening to your voice in " Lift up your hearts " at 7.50 a.m. I found them quite admirable and I wanted to tell you so, and they can do nothing but good and I hope you will give more of such good teaching. They are a welcome change from most of what I hear. The almost total omission of everything theological, the strong and obvious drift towards " Christian " socialism and the pervading colour of what I believe is called " Humanism " revolt me. The " Children's Hour " with its shocking vulgarization of the Bible narratives, its profane familiarity with Jesus Christ and its general picture of the Almighty as a kind of benevolent uncle who visits his people with boxes stuffed with pleasant gifts, is very unwholesome. I cannot think that that kind of stuff could be other than permanently injurious though it accords well with the current religious fashion.

I listened carefully to the report of the Commission on Canon Law, to a pompous and particularly mischievous book edited by the Bishop of Oxford, and worst of all, to a really scandalous production by Barnes of Birmingham. This last book is really so extravagant that I think it ought to be officially repudiated, though what form such repudiation could wisely take is very hard to see. Its effect on those who will be its principal readers—the ignorant, bumptious crowd of elementary and secondary school teachers, must needs be deplorable. It cannot fail to create in their minds most unhappy impressions. First, a mood of " preternatural suspicion " of the worthwhileness of studying the New Testament, since it is plainly an amalgam of anonymous and untrustworthy compositions, unworthy of confidence and of doubtful origin. Next, the suggestion that the clergy taken as a whole are a dishonest crowd who keep the truth from the people for the basest of reasons. There must be many thousands of school teachers who are now preparing themselves more or less for the novel and generally unwelcome task of " teaching " religion in the schools in accordance with the new Education Act. You cannot blame them if they consider that this book of Bishop Barnes, a senior Bishop of the C of E, may safely be regarded as a trustworthy production. They will contrast it eagerly and joyfully with the traditional teaching of the Church and wonderingly contrast it with the pledges at Ordination and Consecration which condition a Bishop's teaching.   Raven in the *Spectator* finds the principal value of the Book in the demonstration it provides that a man holding such opinions as the author's can yet be an English Bishop.   I understand that the Upper House of Convocation will consider the book and that the Archbishop of Canterbury will address a remonstrance of some sort or other to Barnes who will certainly reply and thereby gain even greater publicity and importance for his deplorable volume.   Something more is wanted which he could not so easily twist into the service of his own poisonous interest. I want Sir Frederick Kenyon to address to him an " Open Letter from an Anglican Layman " placing his own name in brackets under that description.   As the late head of the British Museum he will carry weight with the general multitude, and he is disgusted with the book. But then, Kenyon is older than I am, and though I have reason to think that he may attempt something of the kind, I doubt whether he will be able to achieve it.   We want something that is cheap, authoritative, effective, which could be got into the hands of the people and would cause them to think twice before accepting Barnes as an authority on Christian origins.   I think if I were 50 years younger I would have attempted something of the kind myself, but of course I am incapacitated for any such effort.   Neither of their Graces is specially entitled to express an opinion on critical questions, and the Archbishop of York is becoming a public nuisance with his frequent dogmatic and astonishing retrograde pronouncements.

I think better of Fisher, though his pronouncement on the South Indian scheme indicates that he too feels quite unable to stand up to the " Anglo-Catholick socialist " type which is carrying all before it in the Church just now.

I must make an end of this lamentable letter for I am tired and my wits, such as they are, are at their worst.   But I think you should be ready to seize some opportunity of making clear how severely you disapprove of Barnes' pontifical essay. . . . Along the lines on which Barnes would direct the Church I see nothing before it but a complete disintegration of the Christian religion and of Christian morality which that religion has suggested and sustained.   His critical judgements throughout are dictated by such an anti-traditional bias, so strong, persistent, diffused and pervading as to make it almost impossible for a Christian reader to tolerate the spectacle which he presents.   His treatment of St Paul is grotesque and his whole method and outlook are painfully anti-Christian. Yet his tone of triumphant certitude cannot fail to be most impressive on the uninformed, curious and enormously conceited public to which he will mainly appeal.

If I live till November 8th I shall complete 84 years on this miserable planet, and I am warned that though I may totter along for a while I must do so under the "Damocles Sword" of sudden death which may follow immediately any slight physical shock or emotional strain. I am hoping still, rather against hope, to complete the third volume of my *Retrospect*, but it will be far indeed from what I had hoped it might be; if, which is unlikely, I succeed in achieving my purpose.

.   .   .   .

I hope you are well and in better heart than I am.

Always affectionately your friend,

HENSONIANA

Excerpts from Hensley Henson's letters (in chronological order).

13th August, 1909.

I have just had Gore's " Inhibition " framed ! It will hang in my study for the present; when I go to gaol, I shall ask you to make interest for me with the powers that it may adorn the walls of my cell !

27th February, 1913.

I am superstitious : I could not deny that in some respects this Deanery [of Durham] would match my needs : and, as the Psalmist says, " Promotion cometh neither from the East, nor from the West : nor yet from the South ", leaving significantly the North as the predestined quarter. And so I cabled my acceptance.

12th July, 1917.

The Bishop of London makes his contribution to the general confusion by proclaiming his desire to abolish all Deans, and apply their endowments to the provision of more Bishops. Some anonymous correspondent sent me the following lines :

> " Too few are the Bishops ", the Bishop complains,
> " And the Deans many times are too many ".
> But why speaks he thus? There's none so hates brains
> As he who possesses not any.

The intention is better than the poetry.

28th August, 1917.

I have had the large doors between the Galilee and the Cathedral opened. The view from the Galilee up the Church is very splendid; but the effect looking from the Church into the Galilee is not so good.

10th May, 1919.

I am now equipped with what feels like a whole catacomb of dry bones between my jaws !

27th June, 1919.

I never really mind opposition or criticism, and as to a modicum of temperamental excess in the expression of both, it rather interests than exasperates me !

28th September, 1919.

It is a sure sign that Christianity is strong if women are respected; and where there is a low habit with respect to women, you may be sure that Christianity is absent or merely nominal.

9th November, 1919.

Yesterday was my birthday. Do you remember how the cook at the Deanery used to make a cake with my initials, and send it over to the choir-house? There was a sixpence in each slice, and the search for it doubtless improved the quality of the cake! Those were good days in Durham, and must never slip from our minds.

2nd December, 1919.

Last Wednesday I had to go into Shropshire, and there I was taken to see a tiny Norman Church—1,000 feet up in the hills—which was a gem of architecture. The parson told me that last spring when he was ministering at the Altar, when he turned to pronounce the Blessing, he found 3 lambs who had strolled in through the open door, were standing at the Communion rail! They walked in front of him down the church like choirboys in a procession! The churchwarden said his two dogs always came to church with him, and behaved beautifully! So you see that everything was very primitive.

20th January, 1920.

There is something mysteriously impressive about the Gulf Stream, a warm river rushing through the ocean, and bringing fertility and comfort to every coast it washes. One of our great writers compares Christianity to the Gulf Stream, and, if you think it over, it is not unsuitable. All the activities and interests of the world's life are enriched and exalted when they become Christian. There are no such homes as Christian homes; no such friendship as Christian friendship; no such justice as Christian justice, and so on. Even in spite of this dreadful war, which might seem to have plunged Christendom into irrecoverable discredit, I think the comparison holds good.

2nd April, 1920.

On Sunday evening in St George's Chapel, we had " Abide with me ". The Anthem was Mendelssohn's " Hear my prayer ", with the treble solo, " Oh, for the wings of a dove ", which the Westminster boys always chose for the last Sunday in term, when they were given the privilege of choosing the Anthem to be sung in Westminster Abbey.

11th September, 1920.

The service was well-arranged, but my address was interrupted and almost arrested by the persistent coughing of one female, who neither heard anything herself nor permitted anybody else to hear anything! In any complete casuistry there would certainly be included a chapter on the practice of coughing, when where and how it is really consistent with the Christian profession !

18th September, 1920.

The Bishop of Peterborough (who had arrived the night before and makes a great impression on the Swedes by his size and pectoral cross !) became very active and pertinacious.

28th December, 1920.

I judge from all that comes to me that the Bishop of —— is one of those fortunate individuals who can live on the enthusiasms of the hour, making them easily his own, and echoing their shibboleths with the ardour of personal conviction. This is a notable grace, securing perfect intelligibility and unbroken inward tranquillity—two precious conditions of public success.

26th December, 1921.

Modern reviewing is rather disheartening to any serious person, especially an author. There is eulogy, often fulsome and extravagant, from those who approve the man; and there is abuse, always inordinate and sometimes base, from those who don't; but the thesis the poor wretch aspired to maintain is not examined at all.

22nd September, 1922.

As I grow older my dislike of public conferences, congresses, debates, etc., grows ever stronger. The most successful champions are hardly ever the most learned, or reasonable or charitable, or judicious. Men acclaim those who state loudly, forcibly, aggressively, the opinions which they themselves profess : and Error comes off with the prestige of Victory. Among the instruments which have given so large a measure of success to Anglo-Catholics and Socialists I place Church Congresses high in the list !

22nd December, 1922.

Durham School is very dear to me, and I " feel kind " to every Dunelmian.

1st November, 1923.

It is our duty to fit ourselves into the prescribed services : not to make the prescribed services fit into us. I believe you will find, as I certainly found during the 25 years of my career as a parish clergyman, that the system of the Church of England works extremely well as a scheme of pastoral work and regular Teaching.

1st December, 1923.

There are two rules, to which I hold myself so bound that I cannot voluntarily break them. They are these—never to lend to my friends, and never to become security for anybody else.

(N.B.—With this letter I enclose a cheque for £50.)

11th February, 1924.

Rashdall's death removes a notable figure, and makes a large gap in the tenuous rank of learned and independent English clergymen. His critics and traducers will now cant copiously over his coffin in the usual way!

12th June, 1924.

The diocese is in great difficulties but " with the help of my God I will leap over the wall "; and there are some staunch men still.

12th July, 1924.

I was amused at Barking by one of my old club boys, who had shown his affection for me, by having his son christened by my full name " Herbert Hensley Henson Hearne "—so the poor lad has got 4 h's to be dropped!

18th July, 1924.

When Sir Walter Scott was near to die, his son-in-law Lockhart came to the bedside and found him clear and calm. " Lockhart ", he said, " I may have but a minute to speak to you. My dear, be a good man—be virtuous—be religious —be a good man. Nothing else will give you any comfort when you come to lie here ". You know and love Sir Walter as I do, having made friends with him through his books. Take his dying message as spoken to yourself: " BE A GOOD MAN ".

20th December, 1924.

The English language is the only form of human speech which has a good chance of becoming universal; and English literature is the only modern literature which equals the ancient literature of Greece.

5th January, 1925.

I am accustomed always to advise Ordination Candidates to read Burnet's book, and also Baxter's *Gildas Salvianus or the Reformed Pastor*. Dean Swift's *Letter to a Young Gentleman lately entered into Holy Orders* is also full of good counsel conveyed with a sufficient seasoning of mordant wit to make it easily portable in the memory.

15th October, 1925.   .

Personally I find it very difficult to make up my mind on the subject of the large expenditure on the Cathedral services throughout the Kingdom. The circumstances in which the Cathedral Choirs set a standard of worship, and really advanced music, have largely ceased, and certainly, the popular attendance at Cathedral services is deplorably small everywhere.

23rd January, 1926.

Don't scold the people. No good was ever done by scolding; and keep the ideal of service ever before you.

10th March, 1926.

What do you wish from the Bishop of Durham? That he should not concern himself with the interests of the miners? or, that he should become the mere echo of their opinions, true or false?

I hold rather that they can claim from me the faithful use of such intelligence and knowledge as I possess, and such counsel as expresses my genuine convictions. So much I will always try to give them; but flattery of their class prejudice, or an unintelligent echoing of their party-cries, they will never get from me.

17th December, 1926.

Like King James I, I grow pursy and fat, and this condition carries with it a total disinclination to any form of useful activity so you must forgive me.

27th February, 1927.

Every year is a fresh forfeiture of freedom, until at the end, the 6 foot extent of a grave is elbow-room enough for all we can carry there!

10th January, 1928.

Hoadly is rather a repulsive person. Among the many terms of abuse which have been bestowed on me in the course of my life, there is none which I resent more than that which assumes that in character, temperament, and doctrine I am myself *Hoadleius redivivus*.

Bad as I am, I am not so bad as that.

29th January, 1928.

I doubt if the Enabling Act—that *fons malorum*—would ever have been passed, if there had not been a brace of Scots in the Archbishopricks who had dualism in their bones.

14th April, 1928.

Even our long suffering parent *Ecclesia Anglicana*, could hardly have sustained the spectacle of both Arch-bishops advancing with equal strides to an early senility, and ending up with a duet of dodderdum!

10th August, 1928.

I am sorry that you are summoning a " Synod ". We have too many opportunities for irresponsible chatter already.

The life of an Archbishop could have no attractions for me, except the right to stand at the Table when addressing the H. of L. I prefer independence to dignity. I hate societies; and I don't bear gladly with fools. In short I should have been bored stark.

22nd September, 1928.

On the tall spire of N——h a sparrow was sitting.

" Alack, I am lonely " the poor bird cried.

But a hen-bird had heard him and swiftly came flitting.

He sighed, and he fluttered, and was not denied.

20th November, 1928.

The duties of a residentiary canonry are very slight, but the value of leisure for intellectual work might be highly estimated by so eminent a scholar and divine as yourself.

25th November, 1928.

It used to be said that in a large parish you never see your failures, and in a small one you see nothing else. But there is compensation, for while the one consists neither with self-culture nor with pastorate, the other may enable both.

6th January, 1929.

If friendships must perish, one had best give them Christian burial. Only savages mutilate dead bodies.

6th March, 1929.

No one can read the Prayer Book, or the Canons of 1604, or be familiar with the practice of the Church of England since the Reformation, and not know that the intention of the Church is that Morning Prayer should be the regular service on Sunday morning and I am sure that the general edification is well served by that service.

26th March, 1929.

I suspect that your head is a very menagerie of all the crankdoms which, during the last decade, have turned the (Anglican) world upside down—" Life and Liberty ", " Copec ", " The World Call ", etc., etc., etc. Well, well, I have reached an age at which observation of other folk's activities comes more naturally than activities of one's own; and, beyond ejaculating maledictions, I am finding little to do in these days.

22nd April, 1929.

Mosquitoes have plagued us for the last few days, and worked such patterns on our faces, that, if we were entering France, the authorities would not lack *prima facie* evidence for arresting us as plainly suffering from small-pox ! My observations of my fellow-mortals, as they are seen in hotels, leads me to divide men into two classes—those who are waiting on women, and those who are waiting for them. The first are for the most part young and unmarried. The last are almost invariably elderly and married. Neither strike me as wholly contented or quite dignified !

There is nothing like coming abroad to take the conceit out of a Briton. He is compelled to realize that until the New World became commercially and politically considerable, so that Britain held a central position, our island lay outside the main stream of civilized history.

Q

8th September, 1929.

I have an infatuated fool of a parson who has " set the heather on fire " by fatuous twaddle about " High Mass " " Purgatory " etc., and followed it up by making a gross attack on the Council Schools.   For the first time since I was a Bishop Kensit has come on the scene.   A brisk agitation on Protestant lines is in progress, and I wonder where the fire will break out next !

10th September, 1929.

The " Pastoral Letter " of the two Archbishops seemed to me a quite pitiable performance.   Verbose, stilted, and lengthy, it solemnly marched to its panacea for all our ills, and that was—what do you think?—more Bible Classes ! ! !   Nothing but some Providential derangement could have led two such able men to put forth so feeble, even fatuous, a " slogan ".

3rd November, 1929.

———— and ———— are rivals in loquacity, muddleheadedness and—goodness.   I don't think they did much harm except keep off the platform more reasonable folk, but it was trying to listen to them.

4th March, 1930.

Here also is something for you to read.   It has enough dynamite to blow up the Establishment and incidentally to deposit the Palatine Bishop of Durham in a gutter where income tax demands will be an irrelevance !

17th March, 1930.

I have been reflecting on the value of an athletic reputation as a recruiting factor for the ministry.   And I incline to think that, though the Psalmist held that " the Lord delighteth in no man's legs ", it may be the case, that an exception is made in the case of a population so self-dedicated to football as your Northumbrians.

I wish the clergy would not write hymns ; and make their congregations sing them !   My post brings me a hymn of Prayer for Russia from Stephenson which I gather was sung in the parish church yesterday.   S. is a very good man, and I love him ; but he is not a poet.   Few of the saints are.

7th June, 1930.

Certainly, if the Kingdom of Heaven were to be captured by Organising Societies, it would long ago have evicted the god of this world from his disastrous pre-eminence !

10th September, 1930.

What the folly of democratic reformers may do in the future I do not know, but so long as the duty of administering the episcopal patronage remains with the Bishop, I will not delegate it, even to parochial church councils !

12th November, 1930.

I am an " Aunt Sally " again, and everyone from Earl Jellicoe to the Bishop of Ripon is hurling cocoanuts at me. It is, however, not an unfamiliar situation.

17th March, 1931.

I am becoming rather alarmed at the tendency, of which I see many signs, of talking about deceased persons at their funerals, and of preaching funeral sermons. It is a bad tendency, encouraged by the neighbourhood of Scotland, and lends itself to much hypocrisy; so we must discourage it in every way.

6th April, 1931.

The Church would be ill served by the Bishop who, indulging an inevitable reluctance to take a severe course with a man who professed penitence, should allow the return to Ministry of one, respecting whom he could not but feel doubtful.

> " Who is upon the Lord's side? " asked the Count.
> I, who write—
> " On receipt of this command,
> Acquaint Count Guido and his fellows four
> They die to-morrow ".

10th May, 1931.

Join a fakir to a suffragette, and add a considerable dash of the medieval saint—there is Gandhi.

7th July, 1931.

He reminds me in some ways of Fremantle, who also had the power of combining the maximum of spiritual offensiveness with the minimum of practical intelligence.

12th October, 1931.

Parochial Magazines do not, in my opinion, really serve their purpose unless they steer the difficult middle course between the Scylla of didactic pomposity and the Charybdis of pastoral toadyism.

6th November, 1931.

I see that the Nelson tradition is not yet extinct—I mean, act first and ask permission afterwards.

21st February, 1932.

Lord Balfour once said that the real difficulty in the way of Peace lay in the fact that the moral development of the nations was so unequal.

28th February, 1932.

The general objection which I have to S. Stephen's House and to Ripon Hall is that they are situated in Oxford. This applies also to Westcott House (which I like better than the other two) which is placed in Cambridge.

I think that for the immediate preparation for Holy Orders Theological Colleges should be placed in the country away from the hustle of a great University. This would probably be better for the men.

My ideal in Government has always been that of Gordon in the Soudan : " By the help of God I will hold the balance level ". But in these evil days even this pedestrian morality is not easily maintained.

13th March, 1932.

There is, I think, a general tendency, which for obvious reasons is especially strong in the Universities, to over-value the " Movements " which pullulate in the rich soil of " youth " and I cannot but fear that the careful respect and over-tender handling which these receive from age and authority may have the effect of confirming " Youth " in its natural egotism, and blinding it perilously to its own natural defects. School masters and college tutors have ever impressed me as excessively deferential to the opinions of boys and under-graduates.

29th May, 1932.

It is one of the shadows of life as one draws into old age, that one's friends pass away, and one is left to sustain the waxing burden of physical weakness with less and less support from one's friends. Perhaps that is why I value the affection of my younger friends so much.

It has been said that the greatest proof of confidence in a man's character is to lend him your books. So you can see how much I trust you !

15th July, 1932.

I own to having a temperamental dislike of religious emotionalism. My feelings with respect to these ever emerging " Movements " are that of my great predecessor, Bishop Butler, whose speech to John Wesley exactly expresses my mind. " The pretending to extraordinary revelations of the Holy Spirit is a horrid thing, a very horrid thing."

31st July, 1932.

Modern Democracy lives in an atmosphere of adulation and cannot understand how anybody can think it other than perfect !

4th September, 1932.

I have a sneaking sympathy with the Sanhedrin which, even when it deferred to the sage Fabianism of Gamaliel, indulged the luxury of " beating " the Apostles before they let them go.

3rd October, 1932.

It is related of the famous French Preacher, Bishop Dupanloup, that when he returned to his lodgings after preaching the wonderful sermons which thrilled Paris, he used to go on all fours round his room licking the floor, in order to take down his vanity ! That seems rather a violent procedure, but he was a

Frenchman, and stood in the ascetic tradition of the Middle Ages. His object was right, whatever we may think of his method.

3rd October, 1932.

You might do well to read *Woodstock* and *Old Mortality* now, while you are seriously at work on the XVIIth century. I have re-read them recently, and think them astonishingly true to the facts of history. Scott was a rare diviner, and he did not misunderstand men and motives.

3rd October, 1932.

I was admitted as a Fellow of the Royal Society of Antiquaries last Thursday. The collection of antiquities which witnessed that modest function was impressive indeed!

8th November, 1932.

There's a dreadful disease which comes upon folks who leave the decent obscurity of the sixties for the sinister prominence of the seventies, which is called Senility and in its worser developments Second Childhood! I begin to scent its oncoming!

23rd April, 1933.

The two most important happenings in my life-time are the revolt of women against their natural and traditional subordination, and the repudiation of Christianity, " lock, stock and barrel " in Soviet Russia. I find it extremely difficult to imagine any harmonizing of these with Christianity : for the one destroys the family and the other banishes God; and both these are integral to Christ's Revelation of Faith and Duty.

29th July, 1933.

Don't fret over your disappointment. I am sure you have worked well, and gained much in the process. Classes are at best a very rough test, and always the main thing is, not what class you got, but whether your career at Oxford has really educated you.

18th August, 1933.

We spend our time mainly in fighting matutinal wasps, and in visiting perpendicular churches. Our delight in the last goes some way towards counterbalancing our fury with the first! There are ominous warnings of a water-famine; and there are suggestions that the Rectory pump may give out. If that should happen, we shall be driven into that rigour of asceticism which magnified the spiritual worth of—DIRT! May Heaven (is not cleanliness next to godliness? and is it not, as they say in the schools, a good Second?) avert so grievous a contingency!

30th September, 1933.

The worst thing I know about the Mothers' Union is the monotonous tale of its triumphs! It is hardly decent for a really sound spiritual work to march forward with such continuity of advance! This is a clear case of carping at one's blessings!!

21st November, 1933.

I don't really (publish it not in Gath) feel much drawn to that eminent Saint [Cuthbert] for his type of sanctity doesn't please me. I like to trace my official pedigree rather from St Aidan than from St Cuthbert.

22nd December, 1933.

It is not wholly insignificant that the *Times*, in reporting yesterday's Ordination, places Winchester (that is the miserable rump of the historic diocese which arrogates its name) above Durham, in spite of the fact that the immemorial order of precedence gives priority to the Palatine See. Durham, like a penniless Hidalgo, who has nothing but his pedigree to sustain his self-respect, clings to its trifling survivals of vanished power.

25th December, 1933.

The sermon was charming, though, perhaps open to the charge once advanced against a sermon of Magee, that " it hadn't Gospel enough to save a tom-tit ".

19th June, 1934.

My sermon on Sunday morning in S. Paul's drew a large congregation, and was remunerated by a cheque for £2.11.8 and a small bottle of sherry! That was no doubt a reminiscence of a time when Christians had not wholly abandoned the cultus of Dionysus!

12th August, 1934.

Valedictories are very difficult compositions, and the writer may be congratulated if he succeed in steering his course between an offensive egotism and a mawkish sentimentalism.

12th August, 1934.

Give a wide berth to the Pressmen; and avoid " topical " sermons as you would the plague!

15th August, 1934.

I begin to look with an evil eye on cars, and to give entrance to the suspicion that they are snares of the devil. They take parsons from their parishes; and parishioners from their parish churches!

14th August, 1935.

One use of a holiday is that it lifts off the normal burden of multiplying distractions, and makes us enter into communion with our own hearts and with One Whom too easily we forget. It is certainly true that solitude is the tonic of the spirit, not the barren loneliness of being in a crowd, where the babel of many voices makes it impossible to hear any one Voice clearly and continuously, but the rich fellowship with the Master, when we are alone with Him.

25th December, 1935.

I fear it must be owned—" The dreadful truth stares me in the face " as Alington's Pedagogue confessed when he read the unflattering description of him which the Boys of Shrewsbury School had written on the black-board— that the Bishop of Durham is a horrible creature and as a Bishop unspeakable, but he does love his colleagues, and rejoices when they are good enough to love him.

21st May, 1936.

The longer I live, the more convinced I grow of the ethical value of children, alike to their parents and to society. They provide the greatest force of moral development in the first, and the strongest barricade against moral degeneration in the last. Childless husbands and wives fall easily apart : and a predomin- antly middle-aged and aged society is inevitably valetudinarian, selfish, and cynical.

14th June, 1936.

Children are acquiring a rather pathetic interest in a society which is be- coming in ever increasing measure childless. I do not think our social students attach sufficient importance to the moral aspect of this new phenomenon. The absence of children involves the failure of standards and types of self- sacrifice, which are among the most precious possessions of civilized humanity.

23rd August, 1936.

Nearly 50 years ago I had tea with Thomas Hardy. I was staying with my friend Davis, afterwards the Regius Professor of Modern History in Oxford, who then lived with his mother at Weymouth, and he took me to see the novelist. I recall him as a curiously shy little man with a big head! His novels are extremely interesting and beautifully written; but they are inspired by a deep and a half-cynical pessimism, which is not morally or mentally wholesome.

5th March, 1937.

I am so glad that you have taken to Dr Johnson. He was a horible old savage, and his table manners were indescribable : but his genuine goodness made amends for everything, and his habit of detecting a humbug at sight and felling him with a brutal dictum must needs make him morally stimulating to all who, in whatever measure, have an honest spirit in them.

4th April, 1937.

This is an ill-world! The people one loves are inaccessible, and those whom one loathes are like the poor always with us !

There are at least 100 rooks' nests in the trees about the Castle, and the Black company keep up an unceasing commentary of their own on the silly pageant of human life below them !

24th August, 1937.

The estimate for the dilapidations at the [Auckland] Castle amounts to £1,485 which is unpleasant. It would seem that the Apostolic Grace of poverty is not withheld from English Bishops in these latter days.

4th September, 1937.

I have been rash enough to buy a small Elizabethan house in Suffolk with about 2 acres of ground. It will, perhaps, provide a final " earth " for that old fox, the Bishop of Durham, when he also makes the last run of his season!

15th December, 1937.

I hope that you will find yourself able to accept the Hon. Canonry. This distinction, carrying no material advantage, is, like charity, something which honours both the giver and the receiver.

20th December, 1937.

I often ask myself how I should carry myself in such circumstances as those which confront the German clergy. Should I preach faithfully if I knew that my doing so would carry me into one of Hitler's " Concentration camps "? I don't feel at all sure.

9th January, 1938.

You were right about the new Dean. But I have not yet recovered from my astonishment. He is amiable and well-liked, a gentle Evangelical whom one inevitably associates with adoring old maids and pietistic buttered toast: but I cannot discover any of the special qualifications for that great Chair.

23rd January, 1938.

Do you know the story of the Shah of Persia who, whilst on a state visit to England, was entertained to a classical concert at Queen's Hall? When the music was over, equerries enquired whether his Highness had enjoyed himself, to which the reply was understood to be that he had failed to enjoy anything except the first item, viz., the tuning up of the instruments!

27th January, 1938.

Petrarch asked my learned predecessor, Richard de Bury, where *ultima Thule* was situated. My predecessor couldn't tell him, but I can: it is now called " Auckland Castle ".

9th August, 1938.

What with the longevity of duffers, and the breaking down of good men, we are being brought into deep waters.

30th October, 1938.

The Church of England has suffered much from the incipient senility of so many of its Archbishops and Bishops, and not always incipient, though never acknowledged!

At Auckland Castle, 1932.

[Facing p. 232

3rd January, 1939.

It is like rifling a cemetery to tear up letters, which carried freights of affection —and now some of the writers are dead and some—worse—are alienated.

24th January, 1939.

I am sitting like Marius amid the ruins of Carthage, surrounded with a *melange* of superfluous books and unwanted furniture! and I dislike immensely the thought that I have no longer (after Sunday) any *pied à terre* in the *patrimonium S. Cuthberti*.

2nd February, 1939.

The outburst of personal affection, which my retirement has occasioned, has reduced me to a condition of emotional instability, in which I am capable of making an ass of myself at short notice!

3rd March, 1939.

I have often thought that of Dr Frederick Temple far more suitably than Lord Salisbury, to whom the *mot* was originally aimed, it might be said " that he was a lath painted to look like iron ", for under a brusque and rather alarming exterior, he was really " as sentimental as a maiden of seventeen "!

12th March, 1939.

I often find myself echoing Selden's caustic monition Chain up the clergy!

20th March, 1939.

I am trying to settle into this little house, and to the narrow accommodation of the shelf to which Resignation introduces a Bishop.   My soul will no doubt in time shrink to the dimensions of my Diogenes-Tub, until I move to a still narrower tenement in the churchyard.

26th March, 1939.

For more than a week past I have been shut in with a villainous and persistent cough.   My wife sympathetically calls it a " Judgment cough ", because I have always resented the exasperating clamour of the coughing ladies who frequent the sanctuary to the discomforture of preachers and the discomfort of the congregation!   Well did the Psalmist pray " Let not their precious balms break my head ".   Probably Michal (or was it Bathsheba?) had been giving the tuneful monarch a " curtain lecture "!

2nd April, 1939.

It is odd to be, as the common phrase runs " on the shelf " and it will take me long to " find myself " in an obscurity and unimportance which I have never experienced since my Ordination.   It is probably wholesome for the " higher self " to discover how very little one really counts for in the world, but the " lower self " now and again kicks and prances.

28th April, 1939.

The appointment to London is excellent. How the Headmasters are romping in!

4th May, 1939.

I was the " guest of honour " (!) at the lunch of the Press and Publications Board of the Church Assembly, an institution for which I have an extreme dislike. It had been agreed beforehand, that I should be free to " talk large ", so I spoke with brutal divisiveness on some aspects of the Board's activities. *Inter alia* . . . I said sweetly that the general body of lay opinion desired the ending of the Dual system, and the decent sepulture of the National Society. My hearers " looked down their noses ", applauded with disciplined decorum, and went away greatly wondering.

14th May, 1939.

My journal, extending from the eighties of the XIXth century almost to the forties of the XXth is crowded with the petty details of a busy but unimportant career and the opinions of an eccentric and unrepresentative individual. Probably I should do most wisely if I treated it as the Ephesians, in an access of penitence, treated their far more valuable books! I feel acutely the absence of my friends, and when I received a letter signed " Dunelm " I felt an instinctive resentment, as violent as it was intrinsically absurd!

20th June, 1939.

People do not seem to understand that a sermon is like an iceberg, not only in its chilling effect, but also in the fact, that it has small relation to its real mass. To preach for 20 minutes involves an expenditure of time which may run to as many hours. Popular preachers, who need no preparation will think this ridiculous, but a pedestrian orator like myself cannot preach *ex tempore*.

2nd August, 1939.

The late Dean Church once comforted my old chief, Festing, who was mortally dull in the pulpit, by confessing that he himself (though eminent as a sacred orator) was often so destitute of ideas that, when he sat at his desk with the purpose of composing a sermon, he felt " like a hen contemplating a chalk egg ". Something like that is my mental condition this morning.

8th October, 1939.

When I was a young clergyman, nothing tried my faith so much as the moral impotence of Sacraments, and now as I consider everything in the cold but clear light of old age, I am disposed to hold with the late Lord Morley, that the contrast between the theory and the effect of Christianity is " the unconquerable problem for the Christian believer, the keystone of the grim arch of religious doubt and despair."

More and more I am convinced that the mechanical externalism of these Anglo-Catholics is a perilous caricature of Christian truth: and as S. Paul says of the arbitrary regulations of the Colossian gnostics " is of no value against the indulgence of the flesh ".

18*th January*, 1940.

When a man keeps the lamp of reason under the bushel of emotion, he is in danger of illustrating a cryptic saying of Christ, " If the light that is in thee be darkness, how great is the darkness " !

25*th January*, 1940.

Our pipes have been frozen : our water supply cut off : our electric pump out of action, and we ourselves driven back into a prae-human squalor of unbathed filth ! I meditate on adopting the godly discipline of the Ancient People, which required the Leper, when he went about the streets, to be adorned with the minatory and humiliating legend—UNCLEAN.

My mind is as the Sahara !

1*st March*, 1940.

By all means, let questions be asked, if you think that would be desirable ; though my experience of questions after lectures does not lead me to think highly of the process. It serves rather as a hobbey-horse for crank-riding than as a serviceable lamp-post for illumination.

3*rd March*, 1940.

To-morrow I am pledged to go to Norwich and lecture in the Cathedral on a windy-preposterous subject—" The parish Church as the centre around which the life of the parishioners was gathered between the Reformation and the Reform Act 1832 ". I can assure you, from inside knowledge, that my lecture will be entirely worthy of its appointed theme ! I could sum the argument up pithily in the Latin dictum—" *E nihilo nihil fit* ".

2*nd May*, 1940.

Why must these people go out of their way to disobey the rubricks for disobedience sake ? If the Rubrick tells the priest to face the people : he will turn his back on them. If he is bidden say " Here endeth the Epistle ", he will say " Here endeth the appointed lesson ", if the Prayer Book speaks of St Peter, he must say " the blessed St Peter " : and so on *ad infinitum*. It indicates their normal habit. Their minds are saturated with Papist phrases. They have their reward. The Churches are at their disposal, but the Churches are empty.

10*th November*, 1940.

My health is good : my gluttony unlessened, and my sloth deepening daily ! There you have the picture of my episcopal degeneration, not I trust, often presented by senior bishops.

25th May, 1941.

I have heard of men much immersed in affairs, who have got through unusually heavy correspondence by the simple device of never answering any letters but " letting them answer themselves ".

1st June, 1941.

This morning a little withered " guinea-pig " from —— was brought in to officiate.   As I listened to the discourse, I reflected that a Franciscan friar in the 13th century would not have found it necessary to alter a word in order to make it express his own conception of the " Catholick Faith " !

8th June, 1941.

I wander, like a dubious ghost, in the shadowed areas which abut on the theological domain, both affecting it, and being affected by it : and there I stop always in half lights and never quite at home.   S. Paul never seems quite to have cleared up his own doctrine about the Holy Spirit : and I suspect that he would not have been wholly pleased with the orthodox mathematics of the *Quicunque Vult*.

27th July, 1941.

I find my experience of Anglo-Catholicism as a parishioner distinctly trying. What tries me most is the plusquam-prophetic assumption of Authority with which the banal platitudes and half truths are poured out on the very small collection of rustics who attend the Church.

27th July, 1941.

As I go through my old journals and letters, I find myself increasingly impressed by the power which Gore wielded.   He had Abp Davidson " in the hollow of his hand " and in Bishop Talbot of Winchester, he found one of the astutest party-leaders of the century : and, of course, the pitiable imbecility of the Evangelicals played into his hands.

I am wondering what is to happen to my garden when my gardener is " called up ".   " I cannot dig : to beg I am ashamed."

14th September, 1941.

Have you ever had experience of moles?   They are the very Nazis of the animal world—cryptic, rapid, ruinous.   A young farmer was good enough to set a mole-trap ; but the little velvet-coats were far too clever to go into it ; and showed their scorn by throwing up no less than four new molehills on the lawn !

14th September, 1941.

The very violence of Hitler's methods makes it almost impossible for him to admit defeat.   Unfortunately, assassination appears to be a lost art on the Continent of Europe : and just now it is both more morally respectable, and more politically desirable than ever !   Imagine that a respectable Christian

Bishop should have been brought to the pass of giving bed and board in his ethical scheme to ASSASSINATION !

29th November, 1941.

This awful Autobiography hangs about my neck with the fell and persistent tenacity of the slaughtered albatross round the Ancient Mariner's.

24th December, 1941.

How I wish you could come, and talk with me " heart to heart " ! Among your good resolutions for 1942, be sure and include one for coming to see me as soon as you can. We will divide a crust together, and drink to our mutual prosperity in the best of cold water !

2nd August, 1942.

I wish it could be pointed out to Lord Lang of Lambeth, that he has no right to sign himself " Archbishop ". He is a Bishop until he dies or is formally " degraded "; but he ceased to be Archbishop when he resigned office. If he must supplement his legal description, he should call himself " Ex-Archbishop ".

11th September, 1942.

If we could capture Hitler himself; bring him to trial before an international court, and after his conviction in due form, have him publicly shot with all imaginable parade in the presence of the representatives of the peoples he has crushed, the tonic effect on public morality could not but be profound and permanent. Anyway if I had the chance, I would like to preach the sermon at the execution !

11th November, 1942.

My little household is again dislocated by the withdrawal of our (temporary) cook, and I await with anxiety the fate of my gardener, who is just fifty. Fearne has risen to her waxing responsibilities very wonderfully, and, indeed has become Eyes to the Blind (that's me) and Ears to the Deaf (that's the missus) and domestically a kind of Feminine Pooh-Bah !

The pot of marmalade has kept me reasonably civil for a whole week ! Thank you.

12th December, 1942.

Canon Clayton is charging himself with enough preaching and lecturing for a whole Synod of ordinary clerics ! I warn him solemnly that so much preaching may lead him finally into the woeful company of WINDBAGS, but I might as well expostulate with Niagara !

20th December, 1942.

Don't repeat the error which worked such havock after the last War, and has not ceased even now to cloud our vision. I mean, the error of seeing pastoral duty in its bearing on " Youth ". The majority of Christ's sheep will not come under that description : and their problems and difficulties are certainly not less serious than those which disturb adolescent minds. And a too exclusive surrender to the claims and moods of adolescence may diminish the pastor's competence to help those, the majority of his charge, who have left adolescence with its paradoxes and quick changes behind them in their life's journey.

22nd March, 1943.

My wife's deafness and my own blindness in combination impose a veto on so much which we would not willingly abandon. We cannot visit our friends, for though their kindness may invite, our own infirmities forbid acceptance of their invitations. We are (to compare small things with great) coming to be as were Bishop Talbot of Winchester and Mrs Talbot. Our appearance as guests is anticipated with apprehension, endured with anxiety, and remembered with relief that it has concluded !

18th April, 1943.

I don't know the new Dean of ——, and I don't envy his position. Gaiters apart, it has little to commend it : but then to some men Gaiters are irresistible ! It is an odd taste.

18th April, 1943.

There is coming into existence what can only be described as a " Black market " in domestic servants. The wages demanded, even by untrained and incompetent women are fantastic, quite beyond the power of episcopal pensioners !

9th May, 1943.

The congregations in the parish church are proofs of the soundness of the old proverb now generally ignored in Anglican circles—" A house-going parson means a church-going people ". The war provides an excuse for acquiescing in all measures, which are not actually scandalous, of pastoral neglect. Certainly, the treasured citadel of pastoral independence known as the Freehold of the benefice is more serviceable to the idleness than to the efficiency of the incumbents : and now the brisk agitation for the Ordination of Women brings a new element of dubiety into the practical problem. Well, one thing is assured : that problem will not be solved in my time.

22nd May, 1943.

My preaching days are definitely ended since I can no longer read my sermons with sufficient facility, but occasionally I allow myself to be carried into a local pulpit in order there to exhibit my incapacity for " extemporane-ous " homiletics ! But I don't like that kind of preaching, and it conflicts with the habit of a fairly long ministry.

28th May, 1943.

I am sorry to hear from the Dean that the Bishop of Durham has again been indisposed. I suspect that he is one of those good men who fail to do justice to that " patient ass " the body. It may be heroic, but it is not reasonable or right. The Body is an indispensable instrument of service : and if it fail, we may no longer serve. Therefore, my son, take warning and do not put more on your body than it can bear.

24th June, 1943.

The other day, the Bishop of Gloucester pleasantly criticized Abp Temple's exposition of the secular Paradise which he has exalted to the dignity of a Christian Ideal—" Your Grace, I find that in St John the Divine's description of the New Jerusalem, there was no TEMPLE therein ! "

5th August, 1943.

I am coming to the conclusion that his Grace is, like Pharaoh, King of Egypt, a staff which will pierce the hand of the man who is foolish enough to lean on it for support. He is like a circus-rider, committed to the startling and precarious venture of riding two horses at once, and that is a venture which cannot be long maintained, and is pretty sure to end in a fall.

27th September, 1943.

I dislike intensely the multiplication of special services. I think that they encourage the notion which is too well-established already in the general mind, that public worship is really only obligatory on Christian folks when it is ordered and " topical " ! Moreover the sermons usually take the form of self-glorification, and are (like the extempore prayers of Dissenters) directed rather to the entertainment of the audience than to any more spiritual purpose.

27th September, 1943.

The enormous multiplication of flatteries, and veiled briberies, and a thousand other pseudo-ethical histrionics threatens to confuse beyond repair the boundary lines of truth and falsehood and immerse us all in a quagmire of co-operative humbug.

28th September, 1943.

Inge expresses himself as a gnostic, rather than a Christian, and, indeed, the more I think over what he has said, the more deeply I feel that he is wrong, in spirit and attitude. His use of the Scriptures appears to me arbitrary, and almost whimsical, and, indeed, I think it cannot commend itself to serious thinkers. He seems to ignore altogether the redemptive purpose of the Incarnation, and to regard the Redeemer as no more than the greatest of the Prophets, and properly to be classed with other religious Founders. But, as I read the New Testament, the Redemptive significance of the Incarnation disclosed completely on Calvary, and the Uniqueness of the Redeemer as vindicated in the Resurrection, are dominating features of the Christian message to men, as it is variously but consistently expressed by the inspired writers.

4th October, 1943.

I think, perhaps, as I am plainly degenerating into a hybrid species of home metic, I had better bring my epistle to a close.

4th October, 1943.

I think the two principal regrets of my life are that I never went to a great Public School, and that I am childless. But (who knows?) had it been otherwise I might have been a Prophet of " the Old School Tie " nonsense, and as money-hunting as the rest !

20th October, 1943.

I am in considerable perplexity as to the true estimate of William Temple. I admire and like him, but I thoroughly distrust his judgment, and I think that he is (but who is not?) in perpetual contradiction between his personal religion and his public procedure. He is trying to maintain the liberal attitude in theological and ecclesiastical matters, which is congruous with his temperament, his tradition, and his deliberate mind, but he is deeply affected by the compromising habit of Lambeth, and by the political fashions of his present environment. Thus, he ever seems to be " running with the hare and hunting with the hounds " an ultimately impossible procedure; his sympathies are I imagine with the hare, but his influence is with the hounds.

16th November, 1943.

Thanks no doubt to the announcement of the date in the Sunday newspapers, I received an unusually dropsical budget of letters on that rather melancholy anniversary.

16th November, 1943.

If the Bishop of Durham can put a stopper on the length and discursiveness of Mrs ——'s orations there can be few diocesan problems which he is unable to solve.

29th November, 1943.

I indulge the habit of shouting (I will not say singing) in my morning bath, and this private liturgy generally includes my favourite psalms—the 11th, the 103rd, the 130th and the 139th. The older I grow, the more I value, and the more often I repeat the psalms and the collects. They are better buttresses of Anglicanism than the vain dream of what is called apostolic succession.

29th November, 1943.

You will be sorry to hear that Oliver Quick has been forced by ill-health to resign the Divinity Professorship in Oxford. It is strange and suggestive that so many gifted and spiritually influential persons should be hindered and even driven out of the fighting line by bodily infirmities. Inge, Bishop Barry, and Cunningham—deaf. Vernon Storr, always breaking down; and many others, illustrate the same paradox. Is it designed to teach us the difficult truth that Christ's power is made perfect in weakness?

4th December, 1943.

It is a melancholy reflection that I am now included in that dolorous company, pleasantly described, as Alington has reminded us, by Dean Hole's gardener, (not without a touch of professional sympathy) as OCTOGERANIUMS!

4th December, 1943.

Christianity, as presented by the B.B.C. is no longer a Religion of Redemption, but rather a Christianised humanism which patronises GOD and advertises Man. I don't like it, and I wish that it did not receive such substantial and continuing assistance from Lambeth and Lambeth's attendant tail of busy and thoughtless agitators.

5th January, 1944.

You refer with touching modesty to what you are pleased to call my English. Let me give you one word of advice, which I think my own experience, in some sense sanctions : if you want to form yourself on any English writer, I think Dean Swift would be your wisest choice.

4th February, 1944.

I hope the Germans won't destroy Rome, for if they do a vast number of the Protestant underworld will have to be " certified "!

15th February, 1944.

There are few efforts of didactic virtue more futile and exasperating than urging obligations which no one disputes, and denouncing faults which everybody condemns.

4th March, 1944.

The clergyman's home must surely be the Christian home *in excelsis.* St Chrisostom somewhere says that the Christian home is " a little church ". Churches may be neglected, disordered, and profane, but the clergyman's home finds its *raison d'etre* and its spiritual power in its order, affection and piety.

6th March, 1944.

I wonder whether the Archbishop of York realized the hollowness of the osculations and compliments which flowed so freely from ecclesiastical lips when he was in Moscow. It would be interesting to know what Sergius reported to Stalin, and also to his holy Brethren, after his pleasant English visitor had taken leave.

R

8th March, 1944.

I have often reflected on the mischievous influence of what I call " Rump-Churches " e.g., the Popish Church in England, the Protestant Church in Ireland, the Episcopal Church in Scotland, and, perhaps, also in U.S.A., and a lot of little similar survivals on the Continent. They have all got historic justification, more or less respectable, and they all preserve elements, more or less worth preserving but they steadily shrivel in outlook and temper, and finally become so many embarrassments and obstacles in the march of healthy ecclesiastical development.

8th April, 1944.

Every morning I disturb my wondering household by audible recitation in my bath of some favourite Psalm, which I have by heart, and among them the most constant is that which begins " In the Lord put I my trust : how say ye then to my soul that she should flee as a bird unto the hill ? ". Why is the matutinal bath the chosen music room of the unmusical ! The best men of my acquaintance have ever been vocal in their baths. There must be some subtle connexion between cleanliness and praise, or is it only the irrepressible delight in being for the moment really clean? Anyway, the water shortage famine with which we are threatened, endangers even this fountain of melody.

11th June, 1944.

Reformers and restorers are ever a hasty, even reckless class ; and their achievements are more often lamented than treasured by the men that come after ! !

1st July, 1944.

I think the Deans and Chapters do not sufficiently take account of the preferences and natural prejudices of the lay folk. Being, I think probably strengthened in this error by the deceptive complaisance of those excellent people, the " Friends " of the Cathedral, who have no real title to speak for the civil community as a whole, and are very likely seriously to misrepresent its mind. Nor must it be forgotten that the aesthetic handling of our great churches is closely, perhaps unavoidably, associated with the astonishing development among the clergy, not generally among the laity, of a curious resuscitation of medievalist sentiments and fashions.

1st August, 1944.

I cannot understand why the Germans continue to accumulate gratuitous crimes, when they must see that the writing is on the wall, and that they must soon face the worst. As Sydney Smith said somewhere "We want a lunatic asylum for nations ".

21st September, 1944.

Lord Roche was a splendid ally in the great business of saving the Castle, and I am glad to have him among my friends : and David Rolt and his brothers are charming. If you see him, tell him that I said so.

21st September, 1944.

If there be any fitness in your generous approval of my prose, the credit largely belongs to the two sustaining pillars of Anglican Christianity—the English Bible and the Prayer Book.

15th January, 1945.

I find a general condemnation of the project for smothering Durham in cooling towers and kindred abominations. The Dean, Bishop and Warden would have been universally condemned if, being as they are the official guardians and representatives of the imperilled spiritual influence embodied in the great buildings of Durham, they had not exerted themselves to avert so great a disaster as NESCO'S proposals foreshadowed.

15th January, 1945.

The majority of the country clergy are no doubt underpaid, but they are also very generally inadequately employed. They loiter through life in discomfort and discontent, steadily degenerating as age strengthens their prejudices, diminishes their natural powers, and destroys the effect of such efforts as they make. But I am in this matter a "*vox clamantis in eremo*", and if I have the consolation of knowing that I am speaking truly, I cannot avoid the uncomfortable knowledge that I am also speaking vainly.

15th January, 1945.

I think on the whole that Fisher's appointment to the Primacy is good. He is certainly a man of considerable ability, and has made good so far in every position which he has held; and incidentally he has the personal recommendation of being married and the father of six most promising sons. He can speak with recognized authority on those questions of domestic morality which steadily become more important as the general moral anarchy of the civilized world develops.

17th February, 1945.

This letter will serve you for something of Lenten discipline. My discipline is provided by the Hintlesham villagers, who have disclosed with commendable frankness their estimate of the late Bishop of Durham's capacity as a preacher by resolutely absenting themselves when he ascends the pulpit!

17th February, 1945.

Of him, as formerly of Masterman, John Burns' description might not unfitly be spoken, "'eart of gold; 'ead full of feathers!'".

18th February, 1945.

I celebrated the Holy Communion (10 communicants) and preached the sermon which I had prepared, to a congregation which was slightly more numerous than heretofore, but, even so, lamentably small. I had the humiliation of receiving the Lay Reader's thanks in the Vestry!

18th February, 1945.

I have seen so many clerical careers arrested, and (to all outward seeming) definitely marred, by the clergyman's marriage, that I never hear of a clergyman's becoming "engaged" without a shiver of anxiety.

18th February, 1945.

It is just five months since I began preaching on Sunday mornings and I think there has been only one occasion on which I have not "filled the pulpit". It is rather a burden and incidentally something of a disciplinary exercise: for the congregations are significantly meagre. Of course the weather has been generally abominable: "there is a war on" and there is much sickness. Still, when all allowance has been made, it cannot be doubted that the late Bishop of D. has been "put in his place" by the villagers, and must dutifully "kiss the rod".

20th February, 1945.

I wrote a letter of condolence to Mrs —— whose husband died a few days ago at the age of 88. He was a considerable antiquary, and exhibited 2 traits which are distinctive of antiquaries, viz., longevity and incapacity for agreeing with other antiquaries! He was certainly an extraordinarily gifted man, intellectually acute, alert, and uncertain, extremely positive and loquacious and immensely industrious. In many respects, he exhibited the type under modern conditions of the Laird of Monkbarns. I liked him, but he bored me horribly!

26th February, 1945.

In this Christian nation, it would appear to be the case, that the former monopoly of education by the clergy has been exchanged for a definite disqualification! Need it be matter for astonishment that the prospect of Ordination is becoming increasingly unattractive to our young men?

27th February, 1945.

I hate confusion, obscurity, slovenliness, vulgarity, topicality, and personal anecdotes.

2nd March, 1945.

The witty Frenchman who said that the 2 Sacraments of British Christianity were the Bible and the Sabbath, was not far wrong. If so, it may be fairly held that as means of grace, if the test be sound morality, they do not appear to fall behind more orthodox Sacraments.

8th March, 1945.

The Death of Dr Garvie, the Congregationalist leader and scholar, is announced at the age of 83. He was a dull stockish man, reputed to be vastly learned, and belonged to the cohort of domesticated sectaries whom I was wont to describe profanely as the "Lambeth tame cats". Their names could be counted upon as appendages to the multiplying Archiepiscopal letters which affected to express the mind of " the Churches ".

11th March, 1945.

If Hugh Cecil could have escaped ecclesiasticism he would have been one of the immortals.

11th March, 1945.

I am much cast down by the passing of so many of my contemporaries. Lord Scarbrough I held in special affection. He combined the " great gentleman, the great citizen, and the great Christian " more completely than any man of his type whom I have chanced to meet.   I hope the new Earl will live at Lumley Castle.

19th March, 1945.

I have now (with a single exception) preached in Hintlesham Church for nearly 6 months; and am getting rather " fed up ", especially as the rustics disclose no very keen appetite for the wholesome doctrine which I deliver! They yearn for a more Boanergic type of preaching than I can provide!

25th March, 1945.

Dr Johnson's disproof of determinism is quite satisfying to my pedestrian intellect!

30th March, 1945.

The failure of the attempt to revise the Prayer Book led to my decision to abandon the championship of the Establishment, and that definitely ended my public career.   I became only a curiosity!

3rd April, 1945.

Richard Baxter disliked being interrupted by visitors when at work in his study :

> " When some visitors to Mr Baxter, after having sat a while with him, said, ' We are afraid, sir, that we break in upon your time? ', his answer was ' To be sure you do ' ".   (*v*. Orme's Life of Baxter, p. 772).

It is refreshing to be assured that so eminent a saint could emulate the curt candour of Abp Frederick Temple.

4th April, 1945.

I pleasantly assured him that, in my belief, based on the experience of a long ministry, it would be roughly true to say of the married clergy of the Church of England that probably fifty per cent were ruined by their wives, and fifty per cent were saved.

15th April, 1945.

The Snaky Papist, von Papen, infamous in both the World Wars, and a spectacular diplomatic blunderer, has been captured among the 115,000 prisoners taken in the Ruhr. He should be requested to address the Conference at Sn Francisco on " Ethical Conditions of Civilized Diplomacy ", and " Diplomatic Method—how not to do it, by an Old hand ". The lectures should be broadcast to the world, and furnished with a Preface by Adolf Hitler.

22nd April, 1945.

We attended Mattins; I read the service, and preached the sermon which I had prepared with rather special care, to a very small congregation. I donned my pectoral cross of St Cuthbert, and the eight-pointed star of St John's Order, which, as a sub-prelate, I am entitled to wear. For some reason or other, I was so moved by my preaching as to find difficulty in avoiding an outbreak of weeping! Is this a case of that grace of tears, which medieval ascetics (but I am not an ascetic) and Puritan preachers (but I am not a Puritan) held in such high regard? Moreover, and perhaps this comes nearer to a reasonable explanation, I was afflicted with an acute attack of lumbago!

27th April, 1945.

Yes, I will come and talk about the Church of England, and offer myself as an " Aunt Sally " to the " cocoa-nuts " which my hearers may be disposed to hurl at me in the form of questions and criticisms.

16th May, 1945.

Not to have been at one of the great public schools was to pass through life as a suspected person—an alien and, perhaps, in some sense a pariah, always an object of pity or contempt, or dislike. And, of course, it makes one unintelligible to the young.

18th May, 1945.

I once spent much of a Long Vacation in Oxford trying to form an estimate of the intrinsic quality of the " Sacred Books of the East " published in translations by the Clarendon Press, being moved thereto by Max Muller's enthusiasm, but I found that most of them didn't rise above the level of inferior ritual rules, like Leviticus, and the rare ethical treasures were as needles in a hay-stack! Most of us only know the Old Testament in a translation. I decided that the much boosted literature which would seem to be its spiritual rival, simply didn't justify the labour of study from a religious point of view.

24th May, 1945.

It is ever the nearer public of their own supporters rather than the larger public of considering men which deflects the policy of prelates and politicians.

24th May, 1945.

The incessant expansion of obsolete pomposities in our ecclesiastical functions creates a repugnance in our more thoughtful lay-folks which is none the less deep and just because it is compassionately unexpressed.

3rd June, 1945.

Did you chance to see my letter on the Coventry Cathedral which appeared in the *Times* a short while ago? In the official booklet that pretentious scheme is modestly described as having by publication "made history not only in Coventry but in the C. of E. and throughout the world". There must be a vast amount of history making in the w.p.b.!

3rd June, 1945.

Nothing has caused me more regret than the fact that I never was at a good public school, but it is not so much the intellectual penury which the fact may or may not have involved; as the isolation which it entails, and which deepens as old age draws on. For old men live mostly in their boyhood memories, and these are rooted and sustained by their school friendships. My contemporaries are rejoicing in sons and grandsons—and these keep school memories vivid and strong. I have no links with these younger folk, and move among them as a tolerated Enigma, not altogether repugnant, but always rather suspected!

14th August, 1945.

I think you are well-advised in avoiding the late Bishop of Durham as illustrating Bishop Walcher. I never thought I should come so near to the crowning profanation of a stained glass window!

14th September, 1945.

Perhaps octogenarians, from Petain upwards ought to recognize that the hour has struck for their definite and final exclusion from the arena of public conflict. They must be more or less as deaf mentally and morally as they are (more or less completely) physically!

14th October, 1945.

If only I could obtain really good goose-quills, I should still be able to write tolerably. These hateful steel nibs reduce one to the level of an elementary school-boy. Lucidity is purchased at the cost of a revolting scribal scrupulosity! But reading is another matter.

10th November, 1945.

Insensibly and inevitably I am becoming a *laudator temporis acti* saying of those distant days of Youth what epicures say of wine : "The Old is good". At least we had not been subjected to motor cars, B.B.C., trowsered feminists, and (as a crowning gift of Science) Atomic Bombs!

1st April, 1946.

One privilege of all who are members of the O.O. (Order of the Octogenarians) is a certain disinterestedness in the matter of threatening disaster. *Après nous le deluge*!

6th April, 1946.

I am very glad that Selwyn has produced this work, and I hope that it will be brought to the notice of the Prime Minister who has just now unusual opportunities of showing how far he is able to appreciate the importance of enriching the episcopal bench with some measure of intellectual quality to counterbalance the waxing number of episcopal Philistines, " The business men of the Churches " who are steadily dragging down the Church of England to the low-toned level of American " realism ".

22nd April, 1946.

The lilac bushes in my little garden have, with a pretty exception " nothing but leaves ". Their appearance had seemed to promise an abundance of flower, but they have " let me down " and I feel like the ruthless gardener felt towards the Barren Fig tree.

Good Friday, 1946.

I often recall the story of Bishop Butler's melancholy observation when his chaplain ventured to interrupt his silence as he walked in his garden at Auckland Castle, by inquiring what he was thinking about—

He stopped suddenly to ask, " What security is there against the insanity of individuals? The physicians know of none." And then after a pause, " then may not whole communities and public bodies be seized with fits of insanity as well as individuals? Nothing but this principle can account for the major part of those transactions of which we read in history ".

Against one great Bishop of Durham—Butler—I will set the dictum of another in whose chair I am sitting as I write—Bishop Lightfoot. He said " The best cordial for drooping spirits is history ". I think this is true, and if it is true, it implies the old conviction of the Psalmist's " The Lord is King, be the earth never so unquiet ".

Good Friday, 1946.

Your hand-writing pleases me greatly. It is both lucid and characteristic—two excellences not often combined.

4th June, 1946.

I agree with you in thinking that Don's appointment to Westminster Deanery is a good one. There is only one serious objection to it, and that is equally irremovable and impersonal. He is a Scot, and the Abbey is the very symbol and centre of Englishry! I think that the normal oaths taken by the Dean at his installation ought in this case to include one pledging the Dean neither *per se* nor *per alios* to cause the Stone of Scone to be transferred to Scotland, from which that admirable Englishman, the late King Edward I so properly transferred it to Westminster.

1st July, 1946.

I am glad to know that the Bishop of Norwich means to inhabit his Palace. As an Establishment we ought to die game!

5th July, 1946.

Our letters must have crossed.   We are like two Oriental monarchs exchanging presents and accompanying them with the usual competitive flowers!

6th August, 1946.

I read Inge's speech on the Birthday Celebrations of Bernard Shaw, and it displeased and distressed me.   It offended me that an eminent Christian Teacher should be prominent among the mingled host of non-Christian and anti-Christian toadies of the Voltaire of our generation.   For such, in temperament, effort and influence I must needs think Bernard Shaw to be.

16th August, 1946.

The Americans speak well and wisely when they say " To err is Truman ".

4th October, 1946.

I sympathize with you deeply in having again to put shoulder to the task of raising money, all the more repulsive for being required in connection with the attempt to keep in some degree of life the " dual system ", which has long been ripe for decent sepulture, and is only kept in being by frequent in-pumping of fanaticism.

6th November, 1946.

Avoid the error of the sage, who, absorbed in contemplating the heavens, fell into the ditch.

4th December, 1946.

It is assuredly true that no part of my episcopal duty weighed more heavily on my heart and conscience than that which attaches to the Ordinations.

18th December, 1946.

Still, even in this winter of our discontent, there are some things which remain to us, and hold us back from the Egyptian night of cynicism, and amongst them, certainly, is affectionate contact with such friends as yourself.

18th December, 1946.

I have acquired the inconvenient attribute of antiquity, " Shortness of breath ", so that I have to stop and puff, like the expiring patriarch " leaning on the top of my staff " every hundred yards or so.
And, the crowning humiliation!   I have been brought to wearing " mittens " which I have ever looked upon as the sure badge of senility!

24th December, 1946.

Inge tells me that he is planning two new books now, in his 86th year. Has his friendship with Bernard Shaw really kindled in his mind the desire to go " back to Methuselah " ?

24th December, 1946.

The sooner the Anglo-Catholick faction betakes itself to its true " spiritual home " in the Church of Rome the better for the Church of England. So long as that faction remains, the Church of England is reduced to helplessness. " Can two walk together except they be agreed? " asks the Prophet. The *Ecclesia Anglicana* exhibits a painful effort to answer the Prophet's question in the affirmative : nevertheless, it can't be done permanently.

31st January, 1947.

I have compared him [Headlam] to a Brazil nut, repulsively hard in the shell, and admirable in the kernel.

9th February, 1947.

I have had a long innings, and now, as I recall the past, I have much to thank the goodness of God for, and amongst my blessings I count my friendship and fellowship in work with you and some other of my Durham friends.

16th September, 1947.

Jack Clayton wore himself out by an almost insane over-straining of his physical powers, and constant preaching became something like an obsession with him. In vain I implored him to remember the dictum of Ecclesiasticus that " God hath given no man a licence to sin " and the well known dictum of Bishop Andrewes " if I preach twice on the Lord's Day I prate once ".

INDEX

Bishops are entered under their personal surnames. An asterisk precedes the names of recipients of letters printed in the text.